CSS Hacks and Filters

Making Cascading Style Sheets Work

CSS Hacks and Filters

Making Cascading Style Sheets Work

Joseph Lowery

WILEY

Wiley Publishing, Inc.

CSS Hacks and Filters: Making Cascading Style Sheets Work

Published by
Wiley Publishing, Inc.
10475 Crosspoint Boulevard
Indianapolis, IN 46256
www.wiley.com

Published by Wiley Publishing, Inc., Indianapolis, Indiana

Published simultaneously in Canada

ISBN 13: 978-0-7645-7985-1
ISBN 10: 0-7645-7985-1

Manufactured in the United States of America

10 9 8 7 6 5 4 3 2 1

1B/ST/QV/QV/IN

For general information on our other products and services, please contact our Customer Care Department within the U.S. at 800-762-2974, outside the U.S. at 317-572-3993, or fax 317-572-4002.

For technical support, please visit www.wiley.com/techsupport.

Wiley also publishes its books in a variety of electronic formats. Some content that appears in print may not be available in electronic books.

Library of Congress Cataloging-in-Publication Data

Lowery, Joseph (Joseph W.)
  CSS hacks and filters / Joseph Lowery.
       p. cm.
  Includes bibliographical references and index.
  ISBN 0-7645-7985-1 (paper/website)
1.   Web sites--Design. 2.   Computer graphics. 3.   Cascading style sheets. I.   Title.
  TK5105.888.L693 2005
  006.7--dc22

                                        2005007456

About the Author

Joseph Lowery is the author of the *Dreamweaver MX 2004 Bible* (Indianapolis, IN, Wiley Publishing, 2004) and the *Fireworks MX Bible* (Indianapolis, IN: Wiley Publishing, 2002), as well as *Design and Deploy* (San Francisco: Macromedia Press, 2004) and *Joseph Lowery's Beyond Dreamweaver* (Berkeley, CA: New Riders Press, 2002). In recent years, he co-authored *Dreamweaver MX 2004 Web Application Recipes* (Berkeley, CA: New Riders Press, 2003) with Eric Ott and the *Dreamweaver MX Killer Tips* book (Berkeley, CA: New Riders Press, 2003) with Angela Buraglia. His books are international bestsellers, having sold more than 400,000 copies worldwide in nine different languages. As a programmer, he has developed numerous extensions for the Dreamweaver community, both free and commercial, including FlashBang! and Deva Tools for Dreamweaver. He also has presented at MacDesign in Chicago, Seybold in both Boston and San Francisco, and Macromedia MAX conferences in the U.S. and Europe.

Credits

Executive Editor
Chris Webb

Development Editor
Kevin Shafer

Technical Editor
Mark Fletcher

Production Editor
Gabrielle Nabi

Copy Editor
Kim Cofer

Editorial Manager
Mary Beth Wakefield

Vice President & Executive Group Publisher
Richard Swadley

Vice President and Publisher
Joseph B. Wikert

Project Coordinator
Erin Smith

Graphic and Layout Technicians
Lauren Goddard
Jennifer Heleine
Melanee Prendergast
Amanda Spagnuolo
Julie Trippetti

Quality Control Technicians
Laura Albert
John Greenough
Joe Niesen

Proofreading and Indexing
TECHBOOKS Production Services

To the hundreds of CSS explorers who
have charted this rough new terrain
with unflinching vigilance
and unwavering selflessness.

Contents at a Glance

Contents

Acknowledgments

I'd like to thank Wiley's Chris Webb for first opening the door to this book and then encouraging the idea and execution. I also owe Chris for bringing in Kevin Shafer as editor. Kevin has been a terrific guide and has helped focus the work time and again. My greatest debt of gratitude goes out to Mark Fletcher, who, as Technical Editor, has shared his enthusiasm, encyclopedic knowledge, and real-world experience since the project's inception. Throughout the writing process, Mark has generously pointed out resources, breaking trends, and hard-earned insights. I feel honored to have Mark by my side and look forward to working together with him in the near future.

Introduction

I'll be upfront about it: I wrote this book for myself. I was working on one too many sites with impossible browser-spanning specs while trying to harness the demanding CSS requirements, both self- and client-driven. While I found a wealth of information about CSS hacks and filters on the Web, it was overwhelming. I wanted a central resource that I could rely on to quickly give me the solutions I needed with the deeper understanding I craved. I couldn't find it in any one place—so I wrote it.

My hope, and fervent belief, is that there are a lot of designers in the same boat. CSS has come on in a whirlwind and the reality of the browser situation demands that you deal with it on its own terms or get blown away. There are, of course, numerous ways to handle CSS display issues. Rather than try to force one method to the exclusion of others, this book offers the full gamut of techniques. For example, if you don't feel comfortable applying multiple hacks to adapt a single style sheet, you can use any of the JavaScript or server-side methods for serving the right CSS file to the right browser. I did, however, attempt to ensure that whatever suggestions I made validated; where there was no recourse, the invalid technique is noted as such.

CSS Hacks and Filters follows, roughly, an old-to-new, simple-to-complex structure. The oldest browsers CSS designers are still struggling with are covered first, followed by more up-to-date, standards-based browsers. Internet Explorer's proprietary conditional comment technology is important enough (given Internet Explorer's continued prevalence and CSS bugs) to deserve a chapter by itself. In all these early chapters, I tackled real-world CSS problems and explained how the hacks covered can solve them. Later chapters explore the intersection of CSS with other Web technologies such as JavaScript, the Document Object Model (DOM), and application servers. Graphics and other visual media weigh heavily in the modern Web, and manipulating them properly with CSS is the subject of Chapter 7. Accessibility is a well-deserved hot button and techniques for applying CSS in a responsible fashion are explored in Chapter 8.

The latter portion of the book is intended to offer practical examples for designers trying to put it all together—and keep it there. You'll find separate chapters on CSS layouts, navigations systems, and debugging. My ongoing work with Dreamweaver persuaded me to present a couple of additional real-world chapters to address the use of CSS in Macromedia's world-class and widely used authoring tool: one chapter is on core CSS use in Dreamweaver and the other concerns Dreamweaver templates and CSS. This "getting-it-done" attitude is carried over into the two appendixes. The resources listed in Appendix A should give you a full spectrum of jumping-off places, and the tables in Appendix B are intended to help you find a safe place to land.

Knowing the passionate nature of the CSS community, I fully expect to get an earful or two. If you'd like to get in touch with me to share an opinion or ask a question, please feel free to write me at jlowery@idest.com. You'll find more book-related information on my site at www.idest.com/csshacks/.

Why Hack CSS?

The theory of Cascading Style Sheets (CSS) is a means to an end: better, more efficient Web site design. In the real world, however, CSS does not provide a perfect, clear-cut path to that goal. To achieve the promise of CSS, working designers have employed a series of workarounds known collectively as *hacks*. At the most basic level, a CSS hack is a modification to the standard CSS code. Like any deviation from the norm, the use of CSS hacks has both its supporters and detractors: Some designers feel CSS hacks are an absolute necessity and others are fervently opposed to them.

To figure out why the Web design community is divided over CSS hacks—and which camp you should be in—you'll need a little background on the emergence of CSS.

The Cascading Style Sheets Promise

When work was begun in 1995 on the first CSS specification, the Web was one giant kludge. Hypertext Markup Language (HTML) tags were being pressed into service to handle chores they were never intended for. Tables, for example, meant to contain structured data were largely used for layout. But missapplied tags were the least of the designer's woes when it came to working with HTML.

HTML is perfectly suited for its original design: to represent scientific papers and other documents that adhered to a highly structured format. A structured document is formatted with headings and, where necessary, subheadings, for all titles along with standard paragraphs for all body text. HTML hit a major stumbling block when the Internet was eclipsed by the World Wide Web—and graphic design came to the Web.

Designers used every trick in the book, and invented quite a few along the way, to reproduce their designs with HTML. Presentation tags, such as font, were inextricably entwined into the content—which meant sitewide style changes required a Herculean effort. To alter the typeface for all of a Web site's
primary headings, you had to either modify every single tag instance by hand or cross your fingers and perform an all-encompassing (and terrifying) search-and-replace operation. If you wanted to repurpose Web content for print or any other media, you had one choice and one choice only: redesign the site, page-by-page. Pages were top-heavy with dense mark-up code: a

real structural jungle that designers had to hack through to make the smallest change. Moreover, any hope of HTML working with assistive technologies such as screen readers was completely off the table.

The original drafters of the CSS specification hoped to cut away all the clutter brought by styling Web pages with HTML. CSS was conceived with numerous key advantages in mind:

- Separate presentation from content
- Flexible design model
- Faster loading times
- Easy, instant maintenance
- Portability
- Advanced design possibilities
- Enhanced user control
- Accessibility

The following sections examine each of these in detail so you grasp completely what CSS can do.

Separate Presentation from Content

The first and foremost mission was to disconnect the tight stranglehold that HTML style tags brought to a Web page. By isolating the control of a page's look-and-feel from the content, a clear pathway to building structured pages opens up where you can still get the design you want. Additionally, both content and design benefit in terms of accessibility. Search engines can get at the content easier for indexing, while designers have hands-on control of their presentation. The core concept of separating presentation from content leads to many other benefits of the CSS model.

Flexible Design Model

Even with the most basic implementation of text styling, CSS runs rings around HTML. Whereas font tags are limited to seven browser-dependent sizes, CSS offers both absolute, number-based systems in the measurement unit of your choice (points, pixels, ems, percentages, and many others) and relative keyword-based systems (that is, small, medium, large, smaller, larger, and so on). Design considerations common in print publishing (such as line spacing) are impossible in HTML but a snap in CSS.

Aside from the specific properties available, the CSS methodology of assigning those properties is wonderfully robust. With CSS, you can re-style existing HTML tags or create custom styles in a variety of ways with classes, IDs, and through selectors. Selectors (whether as common as a descendent selector or as rare as adjacent-sibling selectors) encourage structural Web coding while delivering enhanced design control.

Faster Loading Times

To the casual Internet user, a Web page is completely virtual with no real substance or weight. Web designers, however, are very aware of the weight of their pages; the more code that's in a page, the heavier it is and the longer it takes to load. For example, here's the minimum code it takes to place a sentence on the page in the common HTML container, a font tag:

```
<table>
  <tr>
    <td>
      Welcome to my world.
    </td>
  </tr>
</table>
```

Now, here's the same content in the standard CSS container, a div tag:

```
<div>
  Welcome to my world.
</div>
```

Multiply that doubled-difference many, many times for a single page—and then again for an entire Web site—and you have some idea of CSS's edge in speed.

Easy, Instant Maintenance

As noted earlier, it's a nightmare to change an HTML style across a site because styles are all applied at the lowest level, the tag. Not only must all pages with all the styles be altered one at a time, each page must be re-saved and then re-put to the server. With well-structured CSS, on the other hand, your styles are kept in a separate file where they can be modified in any text editor. Once published, a style change is immediately seen by anyone who views an affected page within the site.

Portability

Although the Internet may at times seem pervasive, it's just one of many media. For example, many sites strive to have their Web pages available for print as well. With HTML-styled pages, the only viable route is to redesign the page with print in mind—a terrible chore to do it once and a never-ending time-suck if the site is updated frequently. CSS turns the HTML model on its head and allows you to simply specify a different style sheet for print—and, if desired, one for speech synthesizers, projectors, and hand-held devices, among others—and you're done.

Advanced Design Possibilities

As defined, CSS is highly interactive and throws open the door to a multitude of design options. Just a few of the advanced text options were mentioned earlier; in addition to advanced sizing and line spacing, CSS also provides more robust alignment and far more specific margin and padding options. Text is not the only element to gain a power surge under CSS. The capability to control the position and tiling of background images (see Figure 1-1) is reason enough to use CSS in and of itself.

FIGURE 1-1: With CSS image control, you can place a single, non-tiling image like this control panel in the background, precisely positioned.

Another key element in the CSS toolchest is the div tag, commonly referred to in Web authoring programs like Macromedia Dreamweaver as *layers*. Content within a div tag can be placed anywhere on a page or made to flow in the context of a document. A div tag, like span, is a non-semantic tag that is used as a generic container; div tags are nothing more than block elements that enable you to mark up broad sections of a document. From a dynamic point of view, div tags can be programmatically hidden, revealed, change style, and even move across (or off) the page.

Enhanced User Control

While CSS provides a great deal of design-time flexibility, it also opens up the run-time options for Web page visitors. The entire notion of the cascade in Cascading Style Sheets stems from the originators' desire to blend the designer's style sheet with the user's. The end result is a cascade of several style sheets all coming together to render the page optimally. Some CSS-savvy designers have taken this a step further and designed their sites with multiple CSS styles attached to each page. Modern browsers include a style switching command that lists available style sheets.

One of the most commonly adjusted user settings is font size. The smallish text that looks good on the design spec may be too tiny to be read by a particular visitor—and that's okay, if the page is styled properly with CSS and the text can expand to a readable size, as shown in Figure 1-2. When designed correctly, the text grows and the layout flows: site designer, site visitor, and site owner are all happy.

Accessibility

Adjustable text size is just one aspect of a vital trend in Web design: accessibility. Fueled by the Federal Rehabilitation Act, a U.S. law mandating that all government-run Web sites follow the guidelines established in Section 508 of that act, accessibility is on every designer's watch list. The very core of Cascading Style Sheets—separating presentation from content—makes the content within the pages more available.

This openness, or accessibility, is immediately noticeable when you listen to software screen readers. Screen readers are a crucial assistive technology. If you ever want to demonstrate the benefit of CSS, just point a screen reader–enabled browser to a page in a CSS-based layout— and then visit the same page in a table-based layout, especially those with deeply nested tables. You won't believe your ears when you hear what a difference CSS makes.

FIGURE 1-2: Define your font sizes correctly with CSS, and text is easily rescaled with no sacrifice of design integrity.

One CSS 2.1 specification goes to the next level in aiding the visually impaired to browse the Web by carving out a new media type: *speech*. Speech is a separate media type (just like print or hand-held devices) that allows designers to control how CSS classes and other selectors sound, just like the screen media type controls how CSS selectors look. Support for the speech media type is pretty much nonexistent at this time, but a much fuller implementation already on the table for CSS 3 bodes well for this much-needed functionality.

Why CSS Is Broken

Cascading Style Sheets certainly were intended to be the Web designer's promised land. Unfortunately, the first time you attempt to implement a CSS solution for a site, you'll quickly realize that the promise has not been kept.

How bad can it be? Take a look at a typical CSS problem shown in Figures 1-3 and 1-4. Figure 1-3 displays the page as designed in Macromedia Dreamweaver MX 2004, whereas Figure 1-4 renders the same page in Internet Explorer 6. Look carefully at the model's head in both figures and you'll see that in Internet Explorer, the top of her head has come off and is shifted to the left by a number of pixels. What's happening is that the design requires that the head image be sliced and placed in two CSS-styled `div` tags and Internet Explorer is adding several pixels to the bottom `div`. It's enough to make CSS designers lose their minds—if not their heads.

FIGURE 1-3: Dreamweaver gets it right, and the model's head looks as it should.

FIGURE 1-4: Internet Explorer 6 is flawed when rendering floated div tags—and the top of the model's head is noticeably off.

Cross-Reference You can find two different approaches to fixing the Internet Explorer pixel shift in Chapter 3, "Hiding CSS from Newer Browsers," and Chapter 4, "Applying Conditional Comments."

So, what went wrong with CSS? Although some errors have appeared in the CSS recommendations themselves, the major problem has been spotty, inconsistent, or downright wrong browser implementation. The reasons for the browser inconsistencies are as varied as the browsers themselves. For example, one of the biggest ongoing CSS headaches has been working with Netscape 4.x browsers. The primary problem with this version was one of timing: the CSS recommendations were finalized while Netscape 4 was in the final stages of its development cycle. Consequently, only a fraction of CSS specifications were enabled—and not all of them well.

Even the same browser version from the same company can differ wildly. Take, for example, Internet Explorer 5. On the PC, Internet Explorer 5 supported much larger portions of the CSS specification than ever before. When Internet Explorer 5 was released for the Macintosh, the design community was stunned to see that CSS support was even better—not just from Netscape's latest release, but also from the PC version of the same browser. This development further complicated life for the Web designer, who often developed sites on a Macintosh, only to see them break on the PC.

The fact that CSS works as well as it does is pretty amazing. Think of it: You're working with a standard developed over a long period of time by many large groups of independent thinkers, which is then implemented by another assortment of organizations (of varying resources and expertise) who are expected to create identical results from within their own. It's like handing the blueprints of the Taj Mahal to 10 architects in 10 different countries with 10 different cultures and the full spectrum of economic standing and material and saying, "Go for it."

Naturally, there are going to be differences in design, as well as omissions and unrequested and market-confusing enhancements.

In recent years, the latest generation of browsers have been focused squarely on getting CSS right. Browsers from Mozilla.org (including Firefox and Mozilla) along with the latest releases of Apple's Safari browser have made tremendous strides in correctly interpreting the recommendations of the World Wide Web Consortium (W3C). And yet, they are all still rife with inconsistencies and contradictory behavior. To some, the details of their differences are fairly minor, but to designers with a perfectionist eye and a mandate to build universally accessible Web sites, details matter.

To Hack or Not to Hack

So, the situation, in brief, is this: Web designers have in their hands a wonderful technology with loads of benefits across the board, but it doesn't work as well as it should. Or rather, CSS doesn't work as well as it *could*—with a little help. And help is available, an amazing amount of help, in fact, in the form of CSS hacks and filters uncovered by a legion of working Web designers.

What exactly is a CSS hack? Typically, a CSS hack is a slight modification to the CSS or HTML code developed to work around a particular CSS problem on a specific browser. Many CSS hacks act as filters, hiding one or more styles from a problematic browser. For example, suppose you have a style sheet that includes an absolutely positioned `div` area on the right edge of the screen. Unfortunately, Internet Explorer 5.x on the Mac doesn't render this properly and, as shown in Figure 1-5, an unnecessary and unwanted scroll bar appears at the bottom of the browser window. You can fix this problem in Internet Explorer Mac by declaring a negative right margin for the `div` style—which, of course, breaks the page in all other browsers. To ensure the design of the page looks the way you want it to when viewed with this browser version and all others, you must first set the style rule so that it works in Internet Explorer 5 Mac, as shown here:

```
div#rightEdge {
  position:absolute;
  top: 20px; right: 10px;
  margin: 0 -10px 0 0;
}
```

Next, you need to reset to properties so the area renders correctly for all browsers, but is hidden from the problem browser, as shown here:

```
/* hide from IE mac \*/
div#rightEdge {
right: 0;
margin: 0
} /* reveal to IE Mac */
```

The hack is contained within the two comments surrounding the style declaration. The key is escaping the end of the first comment with a backslash, */, which makes Internet Explorer Macintosh disregard the rest of the style until the second closing comment delimiter, */, is encountered. In this case, two CSS-style comment tags (one slightly altered) comprise the hack.

FIGURE 1-5: When a certain type of style is defined, the unnecessary
scroll bar at the bottom of the browser window appears in
Internet Explorer 5 on the Macintosh, but no other browser.

A school of CSS usage experts has just been outraged. According to them, the change just
made to this code is, on all levels, wrong. Coding a CSS hack goes against the very nature of
a W3C-recommended standard and should be considered an affront to Web designers every-
where. The faithful application of standards (whether they govern XHTML, CSS, or any
other) is absolute. To code in any other way diminishes the standard and concedes a victory to
the chaotic nature of the Web standards that they are created to battle.

I regard myself as a practical Web designer and, to me, this argument against CSS hacks is
purely academic. A good friend of mine, Massimo Foti (known in Dreamweaver circles as a
"developer's developer") once said, "Web standards are suggestions, not religion." I think he's
right.

Other arguments against the user of CSS hacks are more meaningful. Some coders point out that
such hacks may not be forward-compatible and may break in the next round of browser releases. I
agree that such an event is a possibility, but I'm not at all sure it's a certainty. Moreover, the very
nature of external style sheets means that correcting any such issues in the future is a relatively
centralized action: You're not updating hundreds of pages in a site, you're modifying one or two
style sheets.

Consider this real-world story. A designer friend asked me to consult on a Web site redesign for a major metropolitan public library. She's an excellent designer, but new to CSS, especially when it comes to layout (a client requirement for this job). The mandate was to use CSS layout techniques coupled with full compliance with Section 508.

"Not a problem," I said. "What are the target browsers?"

The answer was, as you might expect, "Everything."

It seems that although the vast majority of people outside of the library system used Internet Explorer 6, all the computers inside the library branches throughout the city used Netscape 4. Budget cut after budget cut had prevented an administrative rollout of a more modern browser. To satisfy all of the client's bottom-line goals (CSS layout and full cross-browser compatibility), the only recourse was to employ CSS hacks.

Designers are often perfectionists and, given that someone else is paying for their work, often need to be. The client isn't (and shouldn't be) concerned with the ins and outs of CSS. That's not the client's responsibility; that's why the client hired you, the designer. Clients want a Web site designer. They don't want a Web site design that charges according to who is looking at it on what browser or operating system.

Learning and implementing CSS is no trivial task. It takes a great deal of practice, study, and application. After struggling up the learning curve and designing their first CSS-based site, many designers rightfully say, "You mean to tell me that after all that work, it still isn't right?"

Complications in applying CSS are, in essence, a fact of life. Software engineers often shorten the phrase "fact of life" to FOL when referring to an unchangeable condition. Some bugs can be fixed, while others are FOL. The implication is, of course, that when some aspect of a technology is FOL, you're SOL.

Whether or not you're incorporating CSS hacks is a choice every Web designer must make. For me, CSS hacks are a FOL—and they get the job done. To hack or not to hack: in a perfect world, no; in the real world, yes.

Filtering CSS for Older Browsers

In the spring of 2001, just after the introduction of Internet Explorer 6 and with the Mozilla project well under way, I made a complete fool of myself—in public, no less. I was giving a Dreamweaver seminar at a conference before a large group of developers and came to the subject of browser compatibility. Based on the stats I had garnered from a global Web site (thecounter.com), I announced that, with less than 7% market share, Netscape 4 was dead and developers didn't need to design for it anymore.

A member of the audience raised his hand and said, "That's just not true." He explained that his clientele was based in the medical industry and "... doctors never upgrade their browsers." His stats showed that more than 20 percent of his visitors were using some version of Netscape 4. For his sites, this browser was—and may still be—very much a present-day requirement.

Although certain browsers may be long gone from the mainstream, if visitors to your client's site are using them, you must account for those browser versions in your design. For most clients, however, this does not mean that your sites have to appear pixel-perfect across all browsers. If that is the case, and you are supporting the oldest browsers, you'd be better off throwing out Cascading Style Sheets altogether.

The majority of clients understand the rapid pace of technology and value the benefits that CSS brings to the table. Your primary goal should be to degrade your design gracefully; if a visitor browses the site with an older browser, no errors should occur and the content should all be accessible.

Of the browsers covered in this chapter, you're far more likely to run into Netscape 4. For whatever reason, that browser remains much more prevalent than either Internet Explorer 3 or 4. Should you design with any or all of these browsers in mind? The deciding factor, of course, is what your client needs.

Hacking Netscape 4

Ever heard the saying, "The road to hell is paved with good intentions"? Netscape engineers were filled with good intentions when they tried to incorporate the then recently sanctioned CSS 1 functionality into version 4 of their browser. Without enough time to fully implement the specification,

Netscape 4 is a hodgepodge of fully supported, partially functioning, and totally broken CSS rules. What initially appeared to be a designer's godsend turned out to be an ongoing nightmare.

Only a few CSS properties are fully supported in Netscape 4. Careful use of the color property as well as margins, `background-color`, and `background-image` on the `body` tag leads to good results in this browser. Certain font properties (`font-families`, non-proportional `font-sizes`, `font-weight`) applied to selectors are properly rendered. Likewise `text-indent` and `text-align` are handled well.

CSS properties not supported at all are numerous and all over the map:

- `background-attachment`
- `background-position`
- `background-repeat`
- `border-top`
- `border-left`
- `border-bottom`
- `border-right`
- `display` (except `display:none`)
- `font-variant`
- `letter-spacing`
- `list-style-image`
- `list-style-position`
- `vertical-align`
- `word-spacing`
- `white-space:nowrap`
- `!important`
- `@import`
- `a:hover`
- `:first-line`
- `:first-letter`

You'll also find that the vast majority of CSS selectors do not work in Netscape 4. Only class selectors work as expected; ID selectors function correctly only when formatted like #yourID, but not when combined with a class or tag (that is, `div#yourID`).

How bad can it be? Take a look at Figure 2-1 to see a page that renders fine in every modern browser except Netscape 4. The jumbled text is caused by misaligned `div` tags, while the overlay of text and image comes from Netscape's non-support of the `background-position` property.

The focus of this section is on areas where CSS causes problems in Netscape 4 and can be fixed or worked around. The primary trouble spots include the following:

- *Fonts*—Font properties are not inherited; headings with adjacent `font-size` grow incorrectly; `font-weight` interferes with `<bold>` and `<strong>` tags; improper application of `color` displays text in a vivid green.

- *Margins and Borders*—Block elements on top and bottom margins work incorrectly; `line-height` use causes page feeds and hides parts of images; proper `border` syntax required; borders applied to inline elements result in browser crash.

- *Background*—Background color not completed between element and border; positioned backgrounds mislocated; color set for background not visible behind anchor tags; background image and color disappears on positioned elements.

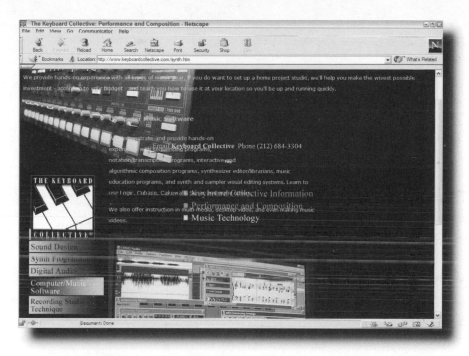

FIGURE 2-1: This nightmare of a page is the result of viewing a standards-compliant page in Netscape 4.

- *Lists*—Styles only affect bullet and not the text; `list-style-type` shows wrong character; applying margins or padding shows bullet intentionally hidden.

- *Table*—Neither `table` nor `tr` tags are supported; margin, padding, and border don't work correctly on any table element.

There are two solutions for handling Netscape 4 issues. The first method is to use two style sheets: one for Netscape 4 and another for all the other more modern browsers. You'll need to attach your style sheets in a particular manner to take advantage of this technique. The other strategy is to use a single style sheet, but selectively hide problematic CSS style rules from Netscape 4.

Linking vs. Importing Style Sheets

Believe it or not, there is a silver lining waiting in Netscape 4's lack of support of key CSS concepts. Unlike the rest of modern browsers (including Internet Explorer 4 and above, Netscape 6 and higher, all Mozilla-based browsers, Opera 3.6 and higher, and Safari), Netscape 4 does not recognize the `@import` method for attaching an external style sheet. To include an external style sheet so that it is readable by Netscape 4 (and all other browsers), use the `link` syntax:

```
<link href="mainstyleNS.css" rel="stylesheet" type="text/css">
```

The other approach (readable by all other browsers except Netscape 4) is to attach a style sheet using @import:

```
<style type="text/css">
<!--
@import url("mainstyle.css");
-->
</style>
```

To assign the proper styles to the right browser, these two techniques are used together to refer to two different style sheets:

```
<link href="mainstyleNS.css" rel="stylesheet" type="text/css">
<style type="text/css">
<!--
@import url("mainstyle.css");
-->
</style>
```

The link first, @import second sequence is vital. If you mistakenly define the @import rule first and then follow it with the link tag, the styles intended for just Netscape will be applied to all browsers—definitely not the way to go.

Tip

There's one more key benefit to taking advantage of the lack of support for @import—the equally problematic Internet Explorer 3 also only supports the link method of attaching a style sheet.

It's important to realize that for the multiple-sheet method to be successful, you must include the same selectors and properties in both sheets. The properties may have different values, but if you want the imported sheet to override the styles established in the linked sheet, both selectors and properties must be identical.

Note

There's another reason to make sure that your sequence is link first, @import second. Reversing the sequence can cause your page to appear unstyled in later versions of Internet Explorer for a brief second; this phenomenon is called Flash of Unstyled Content and is covered in depth in Chapter 11, "Troubleshooting CSS."

Hiding Individual Rules from Netscape 4

Some designers prefer not to maintain multiple style sheets, but find it more manageable to merge Netscape and non-Netscape styles in a single sheet. Once again, Netscape omissions come to the struggling designer's rescue. A slew of methods exist for hiding individual rules from this older browser version; there's even one that conceals the CSS from every browser but Netscape 4. The four techniques covered in this section work equally well and have the added advantage of being valid for a CSS.

Netscape 4 Comment Hack

The first CSS hack covered is good for hiding multiple style rules from Netscape 4. It's known as the *Netscape 4 comment hack*. To use it, you'll need to be familiar with how a comment is coded in CSS. The following code in a style sheet or within a style tag is ignored by browsers:

```
/* CSS comments go here... */
```

Theoretically, you could put as much (or as little) text as you like between the opening /* and the closing */ and the enclosed characters will be skipped over by the browser. Netscape 4, however, has a problem with the following comment:

```
/*/*/
```

All other browsers recognize that code as a CSS comment containing a single slash mark, but Netscape 4 sees the internal slash as an escape character and, thus, does not recognize the closing of the comment tag. You need simply to add a second CSS comment to end the comment as far as Netscape 4 is concerned. Consider the following CSS rules:

```
p {font-size: 18px; }
/* Start hiding from NS4 */
/*/*/
.para1 { font-weight: bold }
.para2 { font-weight: bold }
/* Resume showing to NS4 */
.para3 { font-weight: bold }
```

This produces the result shown in Figure 2-2. Both browsers pick up the p style rule that sets the text to 18 pixels. Netscape 4, however (the top browser in the figure), does not bold the first two paragraphs but only the third one where the para3 class is applied to the tag. Internet Explorer 6, on the other hand, correctly interprets the /*/*/ code as a complete CSS comment and picks up the bold declarations for all three classes defined. The key thing to remember here is that you always have to add another comment to the CSS styles to stop hiding the code from Netscape 4.

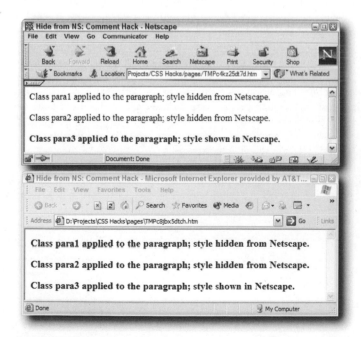

FIGURE 2-2: The Netscape 4 comment hack is an effective way to hide multiple CSS style rules.

Note   To my knowledge, only one modern browser has an adverse reaction to the Netscape 4 comment hack: Opera 5. Unlike all other browsers, Opera 5 ignores the rule right after /*/*/ code. Thus, in the code example, Opera 5 would not make `para1` bold. To get around this, simply add an empty style rule (one with no declaration) right after the opening section of the comment hack, like this: /*/*/p{}. Be sure to check your logs for Opera 5 users before you start to worry about this: Opera users tend to upgrade their browsers when new versions appear.

Netscape 4 Element ID Hack

Although the Netscape 4 comment hack is a good way to obscure multiple rules from Netscape, there are simpler ways to hide a single CSS declaration. As noted earlier, Netscape 4 doesn't recognize descendent selectors that specify an element as the ancestor to an ID selector. For example, this rule is recognized by Netscape 4:

```
#header p {
    font-family: Verdana, Arial, Helvetica, sans-serif;
}
```

This one is not:

```
div#header p {
    font-family: Verdana, Arial, Helvetica, sans-serif;
}
```

Typically, you would use the two declarations as a pair: one to declare a rule that Netscape 4 understands, immediately followed by a more specific rule intended for the other browsers that Netscape 4 doesn't understand. Here's an example:

```
#content h1 { margin-bottom: -18px }
div#content h1 { margin-bottom: 0px }

#content p { margin-top: -18px }
div#content p { margin-top: 0px }
```

The first pair eliminates the bottom margin from the h1 tag for both Netscape and all other browsers, and the second pair performs the same chore for the top margin of the p tag, previously sized to 18px. Figure 2-3 shows the matching output in Netscape 4 and Mozilla. In this example, if the `margin-bottom` was not reset to 0 for other browsers, the heading and paragraph text would overlap (this effect is shown later in Figure 2-7).

Note   To a lesser extent, Netscape has the same problem with class selectors used in combination with an ancestor selector. For example, you won't get any stylings from this declaration in a Netscape 4.8 browser:

```
body.heads {
    color: blue;
}
```

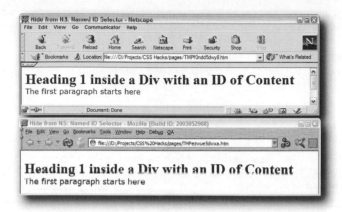

FIGURE 2-3: Effective use of the Netscape 4 Element ID hack gives the desired result cross-browser.

Netscape 4 !important Hack

If you want to hide CSS from Netscape even more selectively than demonstrated with the previous hack, try the Netscape 4 !important hack. Modern browsers give any property marked as !important a higher weight. Not only does Netscape 4 not recognize !important as a useful keyword, it also disregards the property (but not the entire rule) it is attached to. For example, consider this declaration:

```
.legalPhrase {
  font-family: "Courier New", Courier, mono;
  font-weight: bold;
  border: 1px solid red !important;
}
.legalPhrase {
  border: 1px solid green;
}
```

Note Be cautious when applying !important—any such declared style prevents site visitors from overriding styles via their user style sheet, a helpful step for accessibility purposes.

Here, only the border property in the first declaration is not applied in Netscape. The font will still be monofaced and bold, but the border around the text will be green instead of red. All other browsers would honor the !important keyword and present the border as red.

Excluding All Browsers Except Netscape 4

Sometimes you must travel the opposite route when hacking CSS. Rather than applying a technique that hides a rule or property from Netscape 4, occasionally it's better to hide the CSS from all browsers *except* Netscape 4. A comment-based hack discovered by Fabrice Pascal does the job—almost. The hack is applied by Netscape 4 as well as the relatively obscure Opera 4 and 5 on Windows and Opera 5 on Mac.

The basic syntax is exemplified by this code:

```
body { color: black; }
#footer {
  /*/*//*/ color:green; /* */
}
```

Amazingly enough, it still is acceptable by a CSS validator.

Assuming there's no other CSS rule that targets the `color` property in the `#footer` ID, all browsers (with the exception of Netscape 4 and the Opera versions listed previously) will color the text in any element with the ID of `#footer` black. Netscape 4, however, paints it green.

Dealing with Fonts Properly

Working with fonts in Netscape 4 is like wielding a real double-edged sword. On one hand, font properties are among the most widely supported in the browser; on the other, a number of fundamental concepts typically used in conjunction with fonts are sorely lacking. If you're not aware of the problems, sooner or later you're going to get cut.

Inheritance Concerns

Arguably the biggest overall issue with Netscape 4 concerns a key concept of Cascading Style Sheets: *inheritance*. All CSS-savvy browsers provide inheritance support except Netscape 4. A common technique practiced by CSS designers is to set the `font-family` property using the `body` tag selector. With the expected inheritance quality, the font family chosen for the `body` tag would be automatically applied to paragraphs, headings, and content in tables. Netscape always ignores the property values that should be inherited when rendering content in tables and, quirkily, sometimes when applied to other elements such as `p`, `h1-h6`, `ol`, `ul`, `li`, and `blockquote` tags, among others.

One of the most common practices when it comes to designing with Netscape 4 in mind is to explicitly define styles for selectors that rightfully should be covered by inheritance, but aren't. This technique is often used in conjunction with the multiple style sheets approach described earlier in this chapter. For example, the style sheet intended for all browsers except Netscape 4 might have this declaration:

```
body {
    font-family: Verdana, Arial, Helvetica, sans-serif;
    color: #666666;
}
```

You can see for yourself in Figure 2-4 the kind of effect (or rather, non-effect) inheritance has in Netscape 4. To achieve the desired result, the Netscape 4 style sheet would need a rule like this:

```
body, div, p, blockquote, ol, ul, dl, li, dt, dd, td {
    font-family: Verdana, Arial, Helvetica, sans-serif;
    color: #666666;
}
```

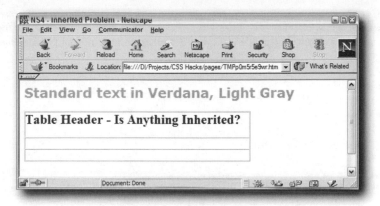

Figure 2-4: You'll need to compensate for Netscape 4's inability to properly apply inheritance rules.

A related problem is found with the `inherit` value. When you apply the `inherit` value to any property, the selector picks up the value of the same property applied to the parent element. For example, suppose you have two rules:

```
#content { color: #999999; }
p { color: inherit; }
```

Normally (that is, in all browsers except Netscape 4), any paragraph tag within a `div` with an ID of `content` will be the same color as its parent: a dark gray. With Netscape 4, however, text in this position is colored a vibrant green (#00c000). The solution in this case is again to be specific. For Netscape 4, you'll need to include a rule like this:

```
#content p { color: #999999; }
```

According to the CSS specifications, the `inherit` value is available to any property. To avoid unpredicatable results in Netscape 4, you'll need to specify an expected value in your Netscape style sheet wherever it is used in your standard style sheet.

Interfering font-weight

By default, the `font-weight` property for a browser page is `normal`—you'll need to set it to `bold`, `lighter` or a number value from `100` to `900` to see a difference. Some designers, however, see the need to specify the `font-weight` with a value of `normal` for the body tag or other specific elements. This shouldn't cause a problem and it doesn't—in any browser but Netscape 4, of course.

Suppose you have the following CSS declaration:

```
body { font-weight: normal; }
```

And suppose you have this HTML code:

```
<p>That is <strong>not</strong> the way of the world.</p>
```

Every other browser properly bolds the text marked with the `strong` tag; Netscape 4, however, resets both `strong` and `bold` tags to a normal `font-weight`, effectively neutralizing the tags. This aberration is clearly noticeable in Figure 2-5 when comparing the Netscape 4 output to that of Firefox.

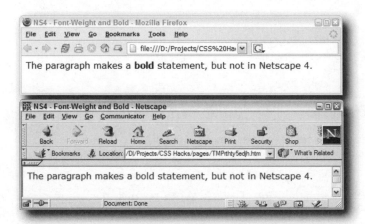

FIGURE 2-5: The top browser, Firefox, shows the expected result, whereas Netscape 4 improperly removes the bold formatting.

To restore the effects of your `bold` or `strong` tags when a parent element has expressly set `font-weight` to `normal`, you must actively define the affected tags' `font-weight` to either `bold` or `900`, like this:

```
bold, strong { font-weight: bold; }
```

Expanding Heading Tags

You can experience one of Netscape 4's more spectacularly bizarre rendering effects by combining `font-size` and adjacent heading tags. What would you expect if you defined style rules for three heading tags in this manner?

```
h1    { font-size: 2.00em; }
h2    { font-size: 1.75em; }
h3    { font-size: 1.50em; }
```

The headings should decrease in size—and do, even in Netscape 4, as long as you don't place the tags directly next to one another. As shown in Figure 2-6, the following HTML has some very strange results, but again, only in Netscape 4:

```
<h1>Header 1</h1><h2>Header 2</h2><h3>Header 3</h3>
```

The way to avoid the problem has nothing to do with CSS—you have to adjust the HTML to achieve the desired effect. Separate each header with a bit of white space, either a space or line return.

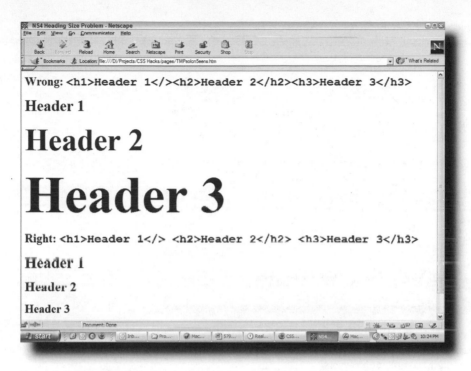

FIGURE 2-6: Even the lack of a single space can cause bizarre sizes to appear in Netscape 4.

Adjusting Margins and Borders

When designers first move from formatting with HTML to styling with CSS, they tend to be a little giddy over the complete control you gain over margins and borders. The ability to banish the automatic space between two headings or a heading and the first paragraph is greatly relished. Unfortunately, what works for the rest of the world's modern browsers doesn't affect Netscape 4—and what works in Netscape 4 is detrimental to all other browsers.

Normally, your style sheet includes two rules like these when you want to remove the space between a heading and a sub-heading:

```
h1 { margin-bottom: 0; }
h2 { margin-top; 0; }
```

Zero margins for block elements are ignored in Netscape 4. To achieve the same effect, you must use negative values:

```
h1 { margin-bottom: -20; }
h2 { margin-top; -20; }
```

Such negative values in CSS rules would cause other browsers to overlap the text in the two headings, as shown in Figure 2-7, where Netscape 4 is on top and Firefox is on the bottom.

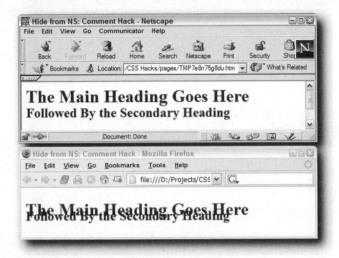

FIGURE 2-7: When correcting CSS margin styles for Netscape 4, you must also reapply the proper CSS to avoid impacting standards-compliant browsers.

The solution here is to have it both ways. You may remember a similar example when the Netscape 4 Element ID hack was discussed. In this case, the CSS style rules used are these:

```
#content h1 { margin-bottom: -20px }
div#content h1 { margin-bottom: 0px }

#content h2 { margin-top: -20px }
div#content h2 { margin-top: 0px }
```

Again, the sequence is vital here—you want to make sure that you set the value for the problem browser (Netscape 4) before you reset it for every other browser.

Another striking problem emerges when you mix the body tag, the line-height property, images, and Netscape 4. Declaring a line-height of any value for the body tag has the potential to truncate images in Netscape 4 (see Figure 2-8). To avoid this problem you have to refrain from applying line-height to the body tag; for this issue, it's best to use a separate style sheet for Netscape 4 and set line-height on p tags and other block elements.

Netscape 4's CSS border implementation is a case of all or none. To display any borders in this older browser, you'll need to define your CSS rule to show all four sides. Other browsers have the luxury of showing just the top and bottom border, or any other combination, but with Netscape 4, it's everything or nothing.

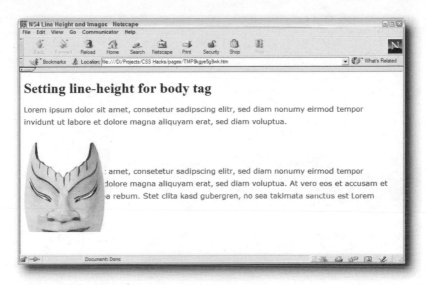

FIGURE 2-8: In a Netscape 4 style sheet, defining line-height declarations in the body property has a disastrous effect on images.

Avoid the long-hand syntax when declaring borders with Netscape 4 in mind. Rather than this syntax,

```
.boxedIn {
  border-top: 1px solid #FF0000;
  border-right: 1px solid #FF0000;
  border-bottom: 1px solid #FF0000;
  border-left: 1px solid #FF0000;
}
```

use the CSS shorthand method for Netscape 4:

```
.boxedIn { border:2px solid #000000; }
```

Unfortunately, this means that your border-creation techniques are severely limited in Netscape 4.

Tip   Although I have not been able to replicate it, some designers have reported browser crashes when Netscape 4 tries to render a border around an inline element.

Working Through Background Problems

Through CSS, designers have control over two aspects of a page's background: color and image. I'm sorry—but not surprised—to report that Netscape 4 has problems in both areas. In general, color is handled better than image, although a fairly glaring error is present when you attempt to combine a background color, border, and an absolutely positioned div tag. If you look at Figure 2-9, you'll find two `div` tags. The top `div` uses standard syntax to create a background color:

```
background-color: #000099;
```

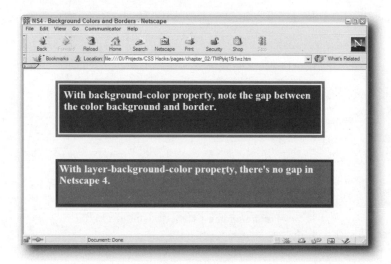

FIGURE 2-9: You'll need to rely on a proprietary tag—layer-background-color—to banish the gap between background color and border in Netscape 4.

The white background of the page is clearly visible between the `div` tag's background color and the surrounding border when viewed in Netscape 4. To remove that gap, you'll need to adopt the following proprietary syntax:

```
layer-background-color: #FF0000;
```

The `layer-background-color` property is useful only when applied to an absolutely positioned `div` tag. If you're a Dreamweaver user, you'll recognize the term "layer" as applied to a `div` tag; this was originally a Netscape 4 conceit. Interestingly enough, although `layer-background-color` is not a standard CSS property, it is supported in the majority of modern browsers, including Internet Explorer 6, and Mozilla-based browsers; it will, however, not validate.

With background images, the major failing of Netscape 4 is in its lack of support of `background-position` properties. Without these key properties, designers are limited to single images placed in the upper-left corner of the browser window—a major setback. Say, for example, you have a logo image that you want to center in a page like a watermark. The way to handle this in CSS is to declare a style rule like the following:

```
body {
    background-image: url(../../images/jay-ell_logo.jpg);
    background-repeat: no-repeat;
    background-position: center center;
}
```

Apply this same rule in both a more recent browser like Firefox and in Netscape 4 and you get two wildly different results (see Figure 2-10). Firefox honors both the positioning and the repeat values, whereas Netscape 4 manages to not repeat the graphic. It places the image squarely in the upper-left corner.

FIGURE 2-10: Unless you provide an alternative image for Netscape 4, a CSS-centered image will not be depicted as expected.

To emulate the background prowess enjoyed by more modern browsers, you'll need to use a single image and a lot of white space. One suggested technique is to create an alternative background image the dimensions of your expected browser window that centers the logo in the background color. Any of the Netscape 4 hiding methods can be used to apply an alternative image, but the catch here is the phrase "dimensions of your expected browser window." Very often, designers try to create fluid page layouts that adjust themselves according to the user's browser size. Locked layouts that demand a fixed window width and height are not very user-friendly—but that's, unfortuantely, what the alternative image technique demands.

Correcting List Issues

Ordered and unordered lists (more commonly referred to as "numbered" and "bulleted" lists) are impossible to style in Netscape 4. Any style applied to the list item tag, `li`, only affects the bullet and not the accompanying text, as is plainly visible in Figure 2-11.

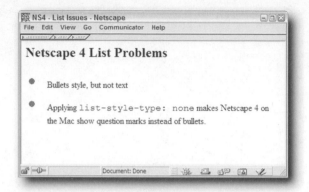

FIGURE 2-11: Styles defined for a li tag are misapplied to the bullet, but not the text of the list item.

Unfortunately, there's not a straight-up CSS solution for this problem. The way to get style lists cross-browser is to first create a class with the same characteristics as your li tag. Then wrap the list text with a span tag and assign the list-emulating class to the span. Admittedly, this is far more trouble than you ever bargained for, but it will solve the Netscape list problem.

Note   Another list-related property to look out for with Netscape is list-style-position; it's unsupported in Netscape 4.x.

Netscape 4 on the Macintosh has an even weirder issue: bullets are replaced with question marks if your list includes a list-style or list-style-type: none declaration, coupled with margin or padding values. Although Netscape 4 Macintosh is fairly rare, if you have to work around it, you'll need to do without either the bullet-less, unordered list look, or the margin/padding—one of them has to go to get rid of the mysterious question marks.

Handling Table Discrepancies

As noted earlier, Netscape 4 has a real problem with inheritance, especially when it comes to the various table tags. Unfortunately, those aren't the only problems with this aging browser in these frequently used HTML elements. Neither the table nor tr tags handle CSS properties appropriately; support is so spotty, it's best to apply styles directly to td tags only.

Moreover, three key properties—margin, padding, and border—don't work as expected in Netscape 4. Unfortunately, the work-around is only partially CSS-based whereas with newer browsers, your td cells can be styled directly or with classes:

```
<td class="tableBody">Southeast Regional Sales</td>
```

To achieve the same result in Netscape 4, you must insert a div tag within the td cell itself, like this:

```
<td><div class="tableBody">Southeast Regional Sales</div></td>
```

Even with this technique, your table designs won't be flawless in Netscape 4. As shown in Figure 2-12, gaps like those in the upper-left cell are a fact of life.

FIGURE 2-12: Even the savviest of CSS hacks can't fix rendering issues like the misdrawn upper-left table cell border.

Fixing Internet Explorer 3 and 4

Designers recently entering the market may find it hard to believe, but in the early days of the Web, Microsoft's Internet Explorer was an also-ran. Yet, even though Netscape was king of the browsers, it was Internet Explorer 3 that first included Cascading Style Sheets support when it was released in August 1996. True, support was spotty at best, but it did start the CSS ball rolling. By the time Internet Explorer 4 was introduced a little more than a year later, Microsoft held the lead in CSS development—and was tipping the balance in the browser war.

In my experience, these older versions of Internet Explorer are far less prevelant than Netscape 4. One of the main benefits that Microsoft enjoys as the manufacturer of the leading operating systems is that new computers come with the latest version of its browser. As Windows computers were upgraded, so were the versions of Internet Explorer.

However, all the statistics in the world demonstrating that Internet Explorer 4 has a very small marketshare globally are moot if your client's CEO still uses it.

Hiding Style Sheets from Internet Explorer 3 and 4

As noted earlier in this chapter, some of the same techniques used to divert CSS for Netscape 4 also work for Internet Explorer 3 and 4. Again, you have an option to either use separate style sheets—one for the older browsers and one or more for the modern browsers—or hide styles individually.

Neither Netscape 4 nor Internet Explorer 3 recognize the `@import` method for attaching style sheets. The easiest approach to designing for both, therefore, is to use the `link` tag to attach the style sheet for the older browsers and `@import` for all the others, like this:

```
<link href="mainstyleNS4IE3.css" rel="stylesheet" type="text/css">
<style type="text/css">
<!--
@import url("mainstyle.css");
-->
</style>
```

Internet Explorer 4 does, to some extent, recognize the @import construct. However, it only acknowledges it under a specific syntax. The CSS2 specifications offer two ways to apply the @import rule:

```
@import "mystyle.css";
@import url("mystyle.css");
```

Although the latter approach is more prevantly used by designers, the initial version is primarily interesting because it is not recognized by Internet Explorer 4. If you had one style sheet intended for Internet Explorer 3 and 4 (and Netscape 4) and another for more standards-compliant browsers, you could rely on this Internet Explorer 4 failing and use code like this:

```
<link href="mainstyleIE3IE4NS4.css" rel="stylesheet"
type="text/css">
<style type="text/css">
<!--
@import "mainstyle.css";
-->
</style>
```

Concealing Individual Rules

As the earliest entry into the CSS realm, Internet Explorer 3 implements numerous key concepts incorrectly. Chief among these problem areas is the cascade. Normally, in CSS, if you declare the same element and property, the last occuring in the page determines the style. For example, you could use these CSS rules:

```
p { color: red; }
p { color: blue; }
```

The more standards-compliant browsers would color the p tags blue. Internet Explorer 3, however, only recognizes the first rule—all others are ignored. This behavior provides an easy pathway to controlling what Internet Explorer 3 sees and what it doesn't.

To hide a single rule from Internet Explorer 4, you can wrap the rule with another at-sign tag, @media. The complete syntax is as follows:

```
@media all {
  tr { margin: 3px; }
}
```

Internet Explorer 4 doesn't recognize @media as a selector and so it ignores the definition of the property.

Adjusting for Table Properties

While Internet Explorer 3 just flat out doesn't support a lot of CSS, most of the problems with Internet Explorer 4 are centered on badly implemented CSS properties rather than missing ones. A primary area that suffers from this mistreatment concerns table tags.

Any style rules using the `margin`, `padding`, or `border` properties do not work on the range of table tags: `table`, `tr`, `td`, and `td`. The work-around here, as it was with Netscape 4, is to insert a `div` tag within a `td` (or around the `table` tag) and style the `div`:

```
<td><div class="tableBody">Southeast Sales Region</div></td>
<td><div class="tableBody">$23,000.00</div></td>
```

As you can see from Figure 2-13, Internet Explorer 4 handles this work-around far better.

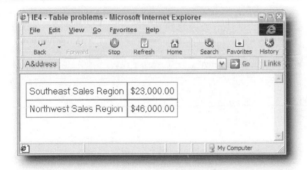

FIGURE 2-13: Table cell borders in Internet Explorer 4 are good to go, once a CSS work-around is put in place.

Note Inheritance is also a problem for Internet Explorer 4 with regard to tables. When working with font properties, the only one that is inherited by the `table` or any table-related tag is `font-family`; any other style must be applied directly to the `td` or `tr` tags.

Font Problems to Avoid

Both HTML and CSS allow for the declaring of font families: a comma-separated list of fonts applied to a tag or selector. If the first font listed does not exist on the user's machine, the browser tries to render with the second one, and proceeds down the list. Internet Explorer 3 has a real problem with the `font-family` property in CSS: should the first listed font be unavailable, the rest are ignored.

The work-around for this odd issue—font families are recognized perfectly when applied through HTML—is equally odd. Your style rule may look like this:

```
p {
  font-family: Verdana, Arial, Helvetica, sans-serif;
}
```

To get it work properly in Internet Explorer 3, you'll need to use this syntax:

```
p {
  font-family: sans-serif;
  font-family: Helvetica;
  font-family: Arial;
  font-family: Verdana;
}
```

Internet Explorer 3 ignores the multiple font options if presented in a string, so each option must be presented separately. The order is reversed to make sure the best font possible is chosen. With this CSS sequence, Internet Explorer 3 starts out with sans-serif and then changes to Helvetica if it finds it. Next, it changes the style to Arial if available and, finally, to Verdana if that font is present.

Another problem (common to both Internet Explorer 3 and 4) is related to the font-family property. Both browsers stumble when trying to render style declarations within a selector that come after font-family declarations. The simple cure is to move font-family declarations so that they are the last in the style rule.

Another, somewhat more bizarre fix is to add a named color after the font-family declaration, like this:

```
p {
  font-family:sans-serif;
  color: red;
}
```

Making Margins and Padding Useful

Here's one that could keep you scratching your head for days. Say you've got two div tags, one inside the other. For the inner div, you set the left and right padding to be a percentage, like this:

```
#outer {
    height: 200px;
    width: 500px;
    border: 1px solid #FF0000;
}
#inner {
    border: 1px solid #0000FF;
    padding-right: 5%;
    padding-left: 5%;
    text-align: justify;
}
```

The correct way for the browser to interpret this setting would be to calculate the percentage of the width of the outer div and (assuming that the outer div was a set width) would always be the same. In this example the padding on the left and right should equal 25 pixels (5 percent of 500 = 25). Yet, if you look at the page through Internet Explorer 4, you'll find that the padding expands or contracts—depending on the size of the browser window (see Figure 2-14).

Internet Explorer 4 is calculating the percentage according to the size of the viewport. To adjust your CSS style sheet for this problem, you'll need to substitute a style rule for your inner `div` where the padding is set with a measurement unit other than percentage.

Another poser emerges if you apply CSS margin values to images that previously have used the HTML attributes `vspace` or `hspace`. CSS-compliant browsers disregard the older HTML attribute values and apply the CSS margins instead. Internet Explorer 4, on the other hand, actually adds the CSS values on top of the HTML values. This is a very tricky scenario to avoid because there is no way to adjust your CSS if the HTML attributes are present. A better solution would be to use a good search-and-replace engine and strip the no-longer-needed `vspace` and `hspace` attributes.

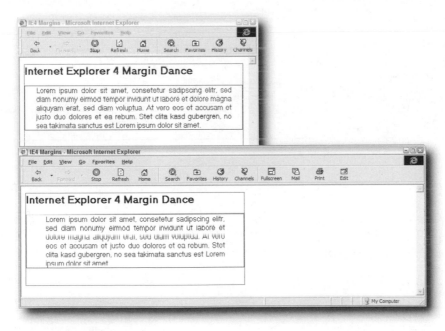

FIGURE 2-14: A margin issue in Internet Explorer 4 causes the padding to incorrectly expand along with the browser window.

Hiding CSS from Newer Browsers

With the release of Internet Explorer 5, Microsoft's browser began to establish dominance and appeared to be on the right track to becoming the *de facto* standard. Although that version of Internet Explorer still had a significant number of bugs and unsupported features, subsequent releases have improved on its increasingly solid base of CSS compliance. Unfortunately, browser development largely halted with the release of Internet Explorer 6, Service Pack 1 in September 2002. Microsoft has said that there will no further updates to the standalone browser, and the next major revision will not be available until the latest operating system (code-named Longhorn) is available. Even more unfortunately, the cracks in Internet Explorer 6's CSS support are becoming quite apparent.

From the Netscape side of the browser war, a stunning defeat appears to have been turned into a victory for designers. Mozilla 1 and the initial release of Firefox boast a high degree of standards compliance for Gecko-based browsers, especially where CSS is concerned. Apple's Safari, based on the Linux program Konqueror, definitely took advantage of previous advances and released a highly reliable browser with excellent CSS capabilities. Opera has been up and down in the CSS world, but has bounced back with a solid implementation in its latest version; Opera 7 supports almost all of CSS 1 and the majority of CSS 2.

No matter how close the latest round of browsers are to the CSS standard, none is perfect—and a hack or filter may be the only way to achieve your client-driven goals. In this chapter, you'll find ways to correct problems stemming from the majority of the browsers in use today, starting with the somewhat special case of Internet Explorer 5 for Mac. The Internet Explorer discussion continues with a focus on the recent versions of the browser for Windows: Internet Explorer 5, 5.5, and 6.

In many ways, Internet Explorer was a great example of how not to make a browser. Although these competitive browsers (including Gecko-based browsers like Mozilla and Firefox, as well as Safari and Opera) learned from observing Internet Explorer's mistakes, they're not perfect. The balance of the chapter dives into some of their problems and possible hacks.

chapter 3

in this chapter

☑ Controlling Internet Explorer 5 and Above

☑ Taming Gecko-Based Browsers

☑ Filtering Out Safari

☑ Handling Opera Problems

Controlling Internet Explorer 5 and Above

The pivotal moment in the browser wars came with the release of Internet Explorer 5 when Microsoft's new free browser was demonstrably more powerful (and more CSS-rich) than Netscape's current commercial offering. Internet Explorer cemented its position with the next series of releases on various platforms, with widely different capabilities on the Macintosh and Windows. The latest versions of Internet Explorer made CSS more available to Web visitors, while simultaneously making it more complicated for Web developers to support.

To properly target the full range of modern Internet Explorer browsers, you'll need a variety of techniques under your belt. In addition to being able to handle problems in specific browser versions, for the greatest degree of efficiency, you'll also want to master CSS hacks that address a range of versions. For example, there's a bug that causes text within multiple `div` tags to move increasingly to the left—but only in Internet Explorer 5.5 and Internet Explorer 6, and not Internet Explorer 5. You must know which hack resolves the problem in both of the later browser versions, while leaving the earlier browser release unaffected. (Massive hint: This particular issue is solved by the Holly Hack, covered later in this chapter.)

Managing CSS in Internet Explorer 5.x for Mac

Although the Windows version of Internet Explorer 5 was a serviceable improvement over the previous release on that platform, Microsoft Internet Explorer 5 for Mac was a whole other animal. Designed from the ground up to be more Mac-centric than any of Microsoft's previous browsers, Internet Explorer 5 for Mac implemented many new features including the best support for the DOM and CSS to date. Although Safari has made significant inroads as the dominant browser in the market, Internet Explorer 5 definitely remains a player.

Unfortunately, as cool a browser as Internet Explorer 5 for Mac was when introduced, it also included a fair number of CSS-related bugs. Following are some of the key issues:

- Content within absolutely positioned elements unnecessarily triggers scrollbars if placed too close to a window's edge.

- Images with align attributes pop in front of `div` tags with a higher z-index.

- Text does not wrap correctly around floated elements without a width defined.

- Checkbox boxes and radio buttons incorrectly inherit the background color of another form element in the same container (only in Internet Explorer 5.1, the OS X version).

- Background images do not display when the defining rule uses single quotation marks rather than double quotation marks.

- The browser crashes when the `vertical-align` (with any value) and `background: inherit` properties are defined together in any selector.

It's important to realize that Internet Explorer 5 for Mac and the one for Windows are completely different browsers, developed by independent teams. CSS hacks that work for one version won't necessarily work for the other.

Note A number of great online resources list CSS bugs you might encounter in Internet Explorer 5 for Mac, including Peter-Paul Koch's QuirksMode (www.quirksmode.org/index.html?/browsers/explorer5mac.html); MacEdition's CodeBitch (www.macedition.com/cb/ie5macbugs/); and some from Philippe Wittenbergh (www.l-c-n.com/IE5tests/).

The next sections look at the top four hacks for Internet Explorer 5 for Mac: the @media, the Mac Band Pass, the Commented Backslash, and the Mac-modified Tan Hacks.

@media Hack

The @media rule is useful for embedding CSS styles in a document, targeted to specific media types (such as print, screen, or projection). For a more general approach, you can use this type of selector: @media all. Any such @media selector-based rule is not recognized by Internet Explorer 5 for Mac and can be effectively used to hide any style rules from it. For example, in the following code, the p tag would be underlined in Internet Explorer 5 for Mac, but not elsewhere, as shown in Figure 3-1.

FIGURE 3-1: The @media hack hides styles from Internet Explorer 5 for Mac, as well as most other fourth-generation browsers.

```
/* read by IE5 Mac and all browsers */
#mainHeading { text-decoration: underline; }

/* hide from Internet Explorer 5 for Mac */
@media all {
  #mainHeading { text-decoration: none; }
}
```

The @media hack also hides style rules from Netscape 4, and Internet Explorer 4 on both Mac and Windows platforms.

Mac Band Pass Filter

While the @media all hack is good for filtering out rules for Internet Explorer 5 for Mac and a number of other legacy browsers, if you've developed a separate style sheet just for Internet Explorer 5 for Mac, there's a better way. The Mac Band Pass filter, developed by Tantek Çelik, is perfect for targeting a style sheet to this browser.

The Mac Band Pass filter relies on Internet Explorer 5 for Mac's particular method of interpreting escaped characters within CSS comment tags. Let's jump in and take a look at a completed example:

```
/*\*//*/
  @import "../styles/default.css";
/**/
```

If it looks complex, don't worry—it is. But it's also highly functional: only Internet Explorer 5 for Mac sees the @import declaration; all other browsers treat it as text within a comment.

All browsers, including Internet Explorer 5 for Mac, look at the example code and see two comments. The difference is that Internet Explorer 5 for Mac sees a comment on the top line and on the bottom line. I've bolded the start and end of each of the two comments, as seen by the Mac browser:

```
/*\*//*/
  @import "../styles/default.css";
/**/
```

By contrast, for all other browsers, the first comment starts and ends in the opening line and the second comment wraps around the declaration. To make this clear, I've added a little white space between the two comments, as well as bolding them:

```
/*\*/   /*/
  @import "../styles/default.css";
/**/
```

All browsers except Internet Explorer 5 for Mac will, therefore, ignore external style sheets linked in this way—which makes this filter perfect for Internet Explorer 5 for Mac–only use.

Commented Backslash Hack

If you find the Mac Band Pass filter a bit too difficult to remember, there's a simpler variation called the Commented Backslash Hack. I first saw this hack on Sam Foster's Sam-I-Am.com site (http://www.sam-i-am.com/work/css/).

There are two ways to apply the Commented Backslash Hack—one is good for hiding single rules and the other is useful for concealing multiple style rules from Internet Explorer 5 for Mac. Both are based on this browser's particular problem with parsing backslashes within a comment. If you place a backslash anywhere within a CSS comment except before the closing asterisk-forward slash), Internet Explorer 5 for Mac skips over the rule defined next. For example, in this code, Internet Explorer 5 for Mac would apply the –15 pixel margin-bottom and ignore the 0 value for the pullQuote ID selector:

```
#pullQuote { margin-bottom: -15px; }
/* Use backslash within comment \ to ignore next rule in IE5 Mac
*/
#pullQuote { margin-bottom: 0px; }
```

Any subsequent rules defined will be interpreted by Internet Explorer 5 for Mac.

Simply moving the backslash to just before the closing delimiters allows the Commented Backslash Hack to hide multiple style declarations from Internet Explorer 5 for Mac. When you want to reveal styles to the browser again, simply add another complete comment. Here's an example:

```
#pullQuote { margin-bottom: -15px; }
.raiseUp {vertical-align: 50%; background: transparent;}

/* commented backslash hack - multiple styles \*/
#pullQuote { margin-bottom: 0px; }
.raiseUp {vertical-align: 50%; background: inherit;}
/* end commented backslash hack */
```

For the multiple-rule variation of the Commented Backslash Hack to work, it's important that there are no characters or white space between the backslash and the closing delimiters.

Mac-Modified Tan Hack

Here's another method to pass a declaration just to Internet Explorer 5 for Mac. The Mac-modified Tan Hack excludes all other browsers through a combination of methods. Most browsers ignore the following style rule:

```
*>html .endSection {height: auto;}
```

The particular opening syntax, `*>html`, is seen only by Internet Explorer 5 on both Macintosh and Windows systems. To further limit the declaration to just the Macintosh platform, you'll need to exclude Internet Explorer 5 for Windows by including an escape character in the property, like this:

```
*>html .endSection {he\ight: auto;}
```

You'll want to make sure that the backslash character is placed within the property correctly. CSS interprets the characters \a through \f as hexadecimal values; inserting the backslash before any letter following "f" in the alphabet does the trick and completes the Internet Explorer 5 for Mac hack.

Balancing Internet Explorer 5, 5.5, and 6

Check any global stats on browser usage and there's no doubt: Internet Explorer is king. While the latest version (Internet Explorer 6) definitely has the lion's share of the market, Internet Explorer 5 and 5.5 still are used by a significant number of users. Although this widespread use of a limited number of browsers does bring a degree of stability to the Web, numerous serious CSS issues in these browsers directly affect virtually every design.

Understanding Internet Explorer's Box Model Problem

Perhaps the most notorious (and most significant) Internet Explorer bug centers on the CSS Box Model. The Box Model is a true cornerstone of the Cascading Style Sheets specifications and affects every single block element: `div`, `p`, `h1-h6`, `table`, `blockquote`, `ul`, `ol`, and `form` tags, among others. Before you can grasp how Internet Explorer gets the Box Model wrong, you must understand how it is intended to work—and does in all other modern browsers.

In the CSS specifications, any block element consists of four primary elements, nested inside of each other: content, padding, border, and margins. The content is surrounded by the padding, which, in turn, is enclosed by the border—all of which is within the margins. Figure 3-2 shows a representation of a Box Model where the content area is 200 pixels wide by 100 pixels high, and there is a 10-pixel padding, 5-pixel border, and 10-pixel margin.

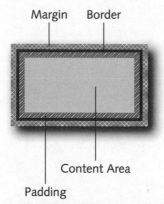

Margin   Border

Content Area

Padding

FIGURE 3-2: Under CSS specifications, an applied style rule with a 200-pixel width actually takes up 250 pixels of space on the page.

When you set a width in CSS for a style rule intended for a block element, the specification intends for that width to apply only to the content area. The rendering of all other portions of the Box Model are based on that assumption. In this example, the entire Box Model is 250 pixels wide by 150 pixels high. Here's how the width is figured:

```
200 pixel content area width
 10 pixel padding-left
 10 pixel padding-right
  5 pixel border-left
  5 pixel border-right
 10 pixel margin-left
 10 pixel margin-right
250 pixel width total
```

A similar process is used to calculate the height:

```
100 pixel content area height
 10 pixel padding-top
 10 pixel padding-bottom
  5 pixel border-top
  5 pixel border-bottom
 10 pixel margin-top
 10 pixel margin-bottom
250 pixel height total
```

This seems pretty straightforward, right? The width specified in any CSS rule refers to the content area of a block element—or at least it does for Mozilla, Firefox, Safari, and other CSS-compliant browsers.

Internet Explorer 5, 5.5, and 6 (under certain circumstances explained a bit later), however, see it differently. For these browsers, the width defined in a CSS rule encompasses the content area as well as the padding and borders; only the margins are outside of the width (see Figure 3-3).

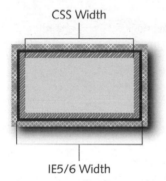

CSS Width

IE5/6 Width

FIGURE 3-3: **When calculating how to render a block element's width and height, Internet Explorer uses a different baseline than CSS specifications.**

This means that, in Internet Explorer 5 and above, the CSS rule previously described with a width of 200 pixels and a height of 100 pixels would be rendered in an area significantly smaller than in other browsers, as shown in Figure 3-4. Instead of taking up 250 pixels by 150 pixels, the Internet Explorer Box Model would be shown at 220 pixels by 120 pixels.

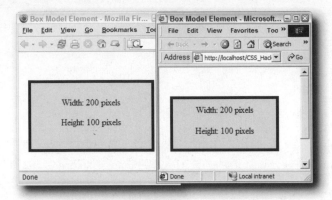

FIGURE 3-4: The same file is shown in a browser that gets the CSS Box Model right, Firefox on the left, and one that gets it wrong, Internet Explorer 5.5 on the right.

As if this were not bad enough, there are additional complications that vary according to the design. Not all CSS rules involving the Box Model include padding, border, or margin values and, therefore, depending on the design, the Box Models could be the same. For example, say you have a `div` tag with a width of 400 and a height of 200, but no padding or border is specified. In this situation the `div` tag would render the same in both Internet Explorer and standards-compliant browsers (see Figure 3-5). What this means is that there is no global solution and that each block element must be addressed separately.

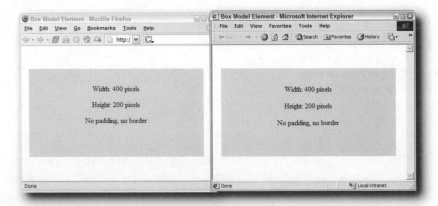

FIGURE 3-5: When padding and borders properties are both set to 0, the Box Model appears uniform across modern browsers.

You'll also have to keep straight which browsers represent the Box Model wrong and which ones get it right. All versions of Internet Explorer 5 on Windows (including 5.5) interpret the Box Model incorrectly. The Macintosh version of Internet Explorer 5, on the other hand, presents the Box Model properly. Internet Explorer 6, however, gets it right—but only when in the so-called *standards* mode. As you may or may not be aware, to handle backward-compatibility issues, Internet Explorer 5 for the Mac introduced the concept of DOCTYPE switching. When a proper DOCTYPE is included on the page before the opening html tag, Internet Explorer 6 renders the page according to the latest standards. When no DOCTYPE or an improperly formed DOCTYPE is employed (typically caused by omitting the URL reference), the browser enters what is known as *quirks* mode. Quirks mode uses the incorrect Box Model calculations, emulating Internet Explorer 5 browsers, while standards mode uses the correct Box Model according to CSS specifications.

Fixing the Box Model with the Tan Hack

For numerous designers, the need to fix a Box Model–related issue brings their first exposure to a CSS hack. Because this problem is so significant and the solution requirements so precise, a number of steps must be followed to achieve a complete resolution.

Perhaps the most famous hack, developed by Tantek Çelik, was created to solve the problem. Although still workable, his original technique is moderately difficult to apply and causes some unwanted effects with other browsers. A more appropriate solution was created by Edwardson Tan and is known as the Tan Hack. To understand how the Tan Hack is used, here's a look at a problematic style rule:

```
.boxModel {
  width: 200px;
  height: 100px;
  padding: 10px;
  border: 5px solid #000000;
  margin: 10px;
  background-color: #FFFF00;
}
```

To adjust this class so that Internet Explorer 5.x on Windows displays it properly, you'll need to add this rule:

```
* html .boxModel {
  width: 230px;
  height: 230px;
}
```

The results of including the Tan Hack are shown in Figure 3-6.

 Note It's important to realize that the height property is used here purely to demonstrate Box Model issues. Most designers only apply height properties in the rarest of circumstances, preferring to let the content determine the tallness of the box.

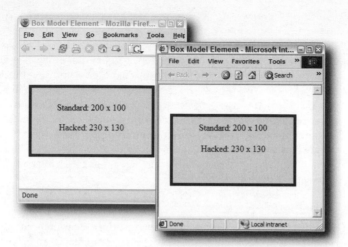

FIGURE 3-6: With the Tan Hack in place, both Firefox (the standards-compliant browser on the left) and Internet Explorer 5.5 (on the right) display the div element at the same width and height.

The selector used is applied to any element with a class attribute of boxModel, which is a descendant of the html element that, in turn, is the descendant of any other element. The key here, of course, is the universal selector, the asterisk, used in combination with the html tag. Only Internet Explorer browsers accept the * html selector as a viable condition; for some reason, the Microsoft engineers have structured their browsers to regard the html tag as within some other element that wraps around it. All other browsers see html as the outermost element on the page, and see no opportunity to apply this rule.

The new values within the Tan Hack are calculated using this formula:

```
Hack Width = originalWidth + originalPadding-Left + originalPadding-Right +
originalBorder-Left + originalBorder-Right

Hack Height = originalWidth + originalPadding-Top + originalPadding-Bottom +
originalBorder-Top + originalBorder-Bottom
```

Note The Tan Hack can be applied to a block element, ID, or class selector. In this example, the class .boxModel would be substituted for another selector.

You may have noticed the sentence, "Only Internet Explorer browsers accept the * html selector as a viable condition." Unfortunately, this condition applies to all Internet Explorer browsers version 5 and higher—even browsers such as Internet Explorer 5 for Mac and Internet Explorer 6 in standards mode that get the Box Model right. The implications of this are that another hack must be employed to ensure that all browsers are handled correctly. Which hack you use depends on the mode with which Internet Explorer renders the page. For standards mode, you'll need to adapt the Tan Hack like this:

```
* html .boxModel {
  width: 230px;
  height: 130px;
  w\idth: 200px;
  he\ight: 100px;
}
```

The backslash within the property names width and height is not readable by Internet Explorer 5.x on Windows, but does come through for Internet Explorer 5 for Mac and Internet Explorer 6. The values used here correspond to the original width and height. This combination of the Tan Hack and backslash is also known as the Modified Simple Box Model Hack.

Note As noted previously, the placement of the backslash within the property name is important to get right. Don't place the backslash in front of any character in the a–f range. If you do, the combination (that is, \d) is seen as representing a hexadecimal value. It is safest to always place the backslash before the "i" character.

For pages viewed in quirks mode, a different hack is required to ensure that the style renders properly cross-browser. You'll remember that when Internet Explorer 6 is in quirks mode, it behaves like Internet Explorer 5.x. Therefore, no readjustment is needed for that browser. Internet Explorer 5 for Mac, however, still needs to include the resetting rule. Luckily, the Commented Backslash Hack, covered earlier in this chapter, provides the perfect solution:

```
/* Start Commented Backslash Hack \*/
* html .boxModel {
  width: 230px;
  height: 230px;
}
/* Close Commented Backslash Hack */
```

Given the market prominence that Internet Explorer 5 and especially 6 have for the foreseeable future, you'll be well served by learning how to apply the various hacks needed to solve the Box Model problem.

Cross-Reference If you need to solve Internet Explorer–related problems, but are skittish about employing traditional CSS hacks, take a look at Chapter 4, "Applying Conditional Comments," for a valid, manufacturer-sanctioned method of hiding code from and revealing code to Internet Explorer browsers.

Owen Hack

If you're looking for a way to hide CSS styles from all Internet Explorer browsers on Windows, but not Gecko-based browsers, Safari, or the Internet Explorer 5 for Mac, consider the Owen Hack. The Owen Hack was created by John Albin Wilkins and centers on a CSS construct called a *pseudo-element*. A pseudo-element is a selector that is dynamically created. Two prime examples are :first-letter and :first-line—both are CSS selectors that are applied to text in a particular position (that is, either the first letter of a sentence or the first line in a paragraph, respectively).

Although most modern browsers recognize `:first-letter` and `:first-line`, no version of Internet Explorer recognizes another pseudo-element, `:first-child`—and the rules of CSS insist that any unrecognized selector be ignored. To ensure that other browsers do apply the rule, however, you must establish the rule so that the `:first-child` pseudo-element is always present. The following code does the trick:

```
head:first-child+body #navSection {
  background-image: url("navbar.gif");
}
```

Translated into English, this selector addresses the ID named `navSection` (for which you can substitute any other selector) within the `body` tag as long as the `body` tag is the tag adjacent to a `head` tag, which, in turn, is the first child of its parent. The initial section of the selector—`head:first-child+body`—is always true; the `head` tag is always the first child of its parent, `html`, and the `body` tag is always adjacent to the `head` tag.

Note   You may be curious about the decidedly non-technical name of the Owen Hack. Creator John Albin Williams named this hack after his own first child, Owen.

Aside from styles defined in this way being ignored by Internet Explorer browsers on Windows, they are also not recognized by Opera, version 6 and earlier.

Comment After Selector Hack

When you must define rules hidden from Internet Explorer 5 (on either Windows or Macintosh, but not version 5.5 or higher), the Comment After Selector Hack is good to know about. The hack, which passes as valid CSS, is very straightforward to implement. All that's necessary is a CSS comment placed between the selector and the opening curly brace that starts the declaration block, like this:

```
#header/* */ { text-align: left; }
```

Any property/value pairs set within these curly braces are ignored by Internet Explorer 5, but available to Internet Explorer 6, as well as other modern browsers.

Resolving Internet Explorer Issues

Now that you have a few strategies for working with CSS hacks and Internet Explorer in hand, you can put them to work. In this section, you'll encounter several of the most vexing CSS bugs in Internet Explorer—and their solutions.

Cross-Reference   The problems covered in this section are just the tip of a very large iceberg. You'll find a number of great online resources listed in Appendix A, "Resources."

Revealing the Peekaboo Bug

Here's a completely startling bug. Imagine you've created a `div` tag that includes a floating element along with some text, links, or other content. Below the floated `div` is another `div` that is used to clear the float—a common CSS layout. If you preview your page in Firefox, Safari, or any other modern browser, everything looks as expected. However, when you test the page in Internet Explorer 6, none of the content next to the floated element is visible (see Figure 3-7). Even weirder, if you switch to another program or minimize and then restore the browser, the content suddenly appears. Is there any wonder why this is known as the Peekaboo bug?

Enabling Internet Explorer 7 Functionality

One of the more interesting approaches to solving the myriad problems with Internet Explorer has been undertaken by Dean Edwards: IE7. Through a JavaScript library, Dean manages to get Internet Explorer to behave in the CSS standards-compliant manner everyone wishes it would. Once the IE7 JavaScript library is included in a page, CSS designers can take advantage of numerous key CSS2 and CSS3 implementations, including a great number of additional selectors such as multiple classes, adjacent sibling, attributes, and pseudo-elements like `:first-child` and `:last-child`.

The IE7 project also addresses major Internet Explorer problems like the Box Model bug (in both standard and quirks mode) and the double-margin float issue. It also corrects significant omissions in Internet Explorer, like the ability to handle `min-width` and `background-position` properties.

You can find out more about Dean's IE7 project—and download the current version—at `http://dean.edwards.name/IE7/`.

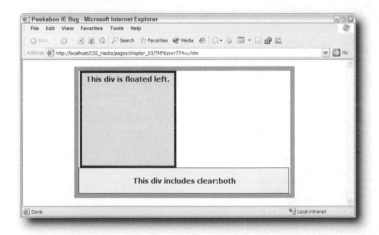

FIGURE 3-7: It's what you don't see here that's important. The Internet Explorer 6 Peekaboo bug is keeping content to the right of the floated div from appearing.

Cross-Reference If you look closely at the layout in the Internet Explorer 6 browser in Figure 3-7, you'll notice a slight gap between the left side of the container `div` and the floated `div`. This gap is the result of another Internet Explorer 6 bug, appropriately called the Three Pixel Gap; this bug, and its solution, is discussed in Chapter 4.

The bug appears to be caused when the floated `div` is physically touching the clearer `div`. If the content within the container `div` is substantial enough to push the clearer `div` away from the floated div, the bug will not be triggered. This, however, is not a guaranteed universal solution and not a viable approach for the designer. A better method is to selectively apply a small height to the containing element. This forces Internet Explorer 6 to correctly render the content within it. A minimal height declaration does the trick:

```
#container {height: 1%;}
```

This fix is known as the Holly Hack and was discovered and documented at the Position Is Everything (PIE) site (http://www.positioniseverything.net/articles/hollyhack.html).

In many situations, designers would rather not specify a height for a containing div, but prefer to allow the container to expand automatically. Standards-compliant browsers restrict a div to a specified height, whereas Windows versions of Internet Explorer improperly expand it to hold the excess content. For this reason, you only want to apply the fix for the Peekaboo bug to Internet Explorer on Windows, and specifically avoid affecting Internet Explorer on the Mac and other standards-compliant browsers. The combination Tan Hack and Commented Backslash Hack discussed earlier is just the ticket:

```
/* Start Commented Backslash Hack \*/
* html #container {height: 1%;}
/* Close Commented Backslash Hack */
```

Once applied, all the content is visible all the time—regardless of the browser used (see Figure 3-8).

Why does the Holly Hack work? Evidently, when the Internet Explorer engine evaluates a float for rendering, it looks to see if the property hasLayout is true. If so, the float is displayed according to standards. If not, you'll get the Peekaboo bug, as well as a host of others. According to Microsoft's only documentation on this mysterious function (http://msdn.microsoft.com/workshop/browser/mshtml/reference/ifaces/currentstyle2/haslayout.asp), hasLayout is set to true if any of the following conditions are met:

- display is set to inline-block
- height is set to any value
- float is set to either left or right
- position is set to absolute
- width is set to any value
- writing-mode is set to tb-rl
- zoom is set to any value

The Holly Hack uses height set to 1%, which makes hasLayout true, which, in turn, causes Internet Explorer to render the float correctly.

Although most of the other properties are easily recognized, you probably are not as familiar with either writing-mode or zoom. The writing-mode property is a proposed addition to

CSS that determines how the text should be written; the tb-rl value stands for "top to bottom, right to left," a typography style used in East Asia. By contrast, Western typography is depicted left to right, top to bottom or, as a value for writing-mode, lr-tb.

The zoom property sets the magnification or scaling of an element. For example, if you set the zoom for an image to 200%, it would appear to be magnified to twice its normal size, but keep the same dimensions. When used to trigger the hasLayout function, the property is typically set to its 100% state, like this:

```
#container { zoom: 1; }
```

Both the writing-mode and zoom properties are proprietary to Internet Explorer 5.5 and up, and neither will validate. To use these and maintain validation, you'd need to wrap them with Internet Explorer conditional comments, as discussed in Chapter 4, "Applying Conditional Comments."

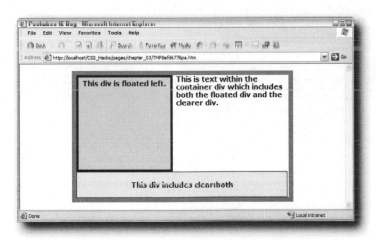

FIGURE 3-8: With the Holly Hack in place, your content's peek-a-boo playing days are over.

Solving the Doubled Float-Margin Problem

The float property is fast becoming a designer's favorite. Not only does it allow content outside of the float to flow around it on either the left or right side of a containing element, but it also provides methods for more precise placement. If the design calls for an image floated to the left, but not touching the outer edge, setting a margin-left property to the appropriate value does the trick. Unfortunately, Internet Explorer on Windows doubles the specified margin, thus obliterating the designer's fine-tuning. You can clearly see the effect in Figure 3-9.

FIGURE 3-9: Firefox and other standards-compliant browsers render the margin on a floated div as expected, whereas Internet Explorer doubles the specified amount.

To resolve this problem (and get your floats back to where they should be in Internet Explorer), you simply add a single declaration to your style that controls the float: `display: inline`. Here's one fix that, at least for the time being, doesn't need to be hidden from other browsers. All other standards-compliant browsers correctly ignore the `display: inline` declaration when applied to a floating element. However, if you are concerned about future compatibility, you can always use the Tan Hack or a conditional comment (discussed in Chapter 4) to limit the modification to Internet Explorer browsers. Here's an example of how it would look with the Tan Hack:

```
* html #mainFloat {display: inline;}
```

There's no need to hide it from Internet Explorer 5 for Mac because that browser properly ignores the display property when set to `inline` within a floating element—and there's very little chance that Microsoft will be developing a new version of that browser anytime soon.

Taming Gecko-Based Browsers

If you ever need to make an argument for the Open Source method of software development, just tell folks to compare the bug lists for Internet Explorer and Mozilla. The number of CSS problems with Gecko-based browsers (including Mozilla, Firefox, and Camino) is tiny—and, best of all, shrinking. A large number of volunteers have made it their collective life-mission to stamp out bugs in Mozilla as quickly as they can be identified.

Does this mean that there are no issues facing CSS-oriented designers when working with Mozilla? No, there probably always will be some imperfections—but the problems currently plaguing designers are few and far between. Nonetheless, it's important to understand what your options are when it comes to providing CSS hacks for Gecko-based browsers. Although you may not need the support right now, you may need it in the future.

CSS Hack Strategies

Many CSS hacks rely on browsers not properly recognizing and processing legitimate CSS rules. Here's a bit of good news and bad news all rolled into one: Gecko-based browsers adhere to CSS standards so closely that there are very few possibilities for CSS hacks to be developed. In fact, most of the CSS hack possibilities stem from aspects that Gecko-based browsers got right that every other browser got wrong.

One such application has been previously discussed in this chapter: the Tan Hack. CSS rules wrapped within the Tan Hack are only applied by Internet Explorer browsers, leaving Mozilla and Firefox untouched. The Tan Hack, therefore, is an effective tool for hiding CSS rules from Gecko-based browsers. For example, many float bugs in Internet Explorer are solved by adding a minor height to the containing div tags, which causes Internet Explorer to render the area properly. Often, such containing div tags are styled to expand as needed and declaring any height is counterproductive. In these cases, you would use the Tan Hack to hide the fix, known as the Holly Hack, from Gecko-based browsers:

```
* html #container {height: 1%;}
```

Another way to distinguish rules for Mozilla-related browsers is to apply the !important property. Under CSS guidelines, the use of !important within any declaration increases the specificity of a particular property/value pair, overriding any value assigned to the same property not designated as !important. For example, in the following style rule, the resulting color would be blue in Mozilla and Firefox, but red in Internet Explorer, which incorrectly ignores the !important designation:

```
#footer {
  color: blue !important;
  color: red;
}
```

 Note   All bets with !important are off the table if the visitor has opted to override the designer. Browsers typically provide a method for the user's styles to be rendered, if so chosen. You can find the option for doing this in the browser Preferences.

Other browsers that apply this rule correctly (and, thus, will behave like Gecko-based browsers) are Internet Explorer 5 for Mac, Opera, and Safari.

Float Clearing with the :after Pseudo-Element

It seems only fitting that the problem caused by a farsighted CSS specification should be fixed by another advanced CSS feature. Take a look at Figure 3-10. The content within the floated element has caused the float to extend beyond the boundaries of the containing div. Although this, in most cases, is not desirable behavior (typically, the expectation would be that the container expand to include the larger float), it is, according to CSS specifications, rendered correctly.

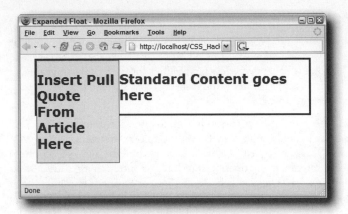

FIGURE 3-10: It may look funky, but the expanded float dropping outside of the container is actually the way CSS specifications intended it.

Oddly enough, Internet Explorer errs on the side of the designer on this issue. If you preview the same page in a recent version of Internet Explorer, you'll see the container automatically expand to contain the float. To achieve the same effect in Gecko-based browsers, the standard approach is to add an element below the float where the `clear:both` style rule has been applied, like this:

```
div.clearer { clear: both; }
```

While this is effective in Mozilla, Firefox, and other similarly CSS-compliant browsers, it also adds additional markup to a page that is not strictly necessary for the page's structure. Luckily, these browsers also support an advanced CSS2 feature that can be used to solve the expanded float issue through styles alone: the `:after` pseudo-element. The `:after` pseudo-element is intended to be used to insert content after a specified selector. For example, say you wanted to make sure that after every instance of a copyrighted name, the proper symbol (©) appeared. Rather than insert each of these symbols by hand, you could create this style:

```
.regTrademark:after { content: "\A9"; vertical-align: super; font-
size: smaller; }
```

This style inserts the letters "TM" after every element marked with a `.regTrademark` class and then styles them to be smaller and raised up.

Note Although it would be ideal to use a character entity like `&copy;` as the `content` value in the `:after` pseudo-element, CSS does not recognize character entities.

Tony Aslett from csscreator.com suggested another use for the `:after` pseudo-element. What if, rather than adding visible content, hidden content was inserted—which included the `clear: both` style declaration? Such a style rule might look like this:

```
.addClear:after {
    content: ".";
    display: block;
    height: 0;
    clear: both;
    visibility: hidden;
}
```

The display: block declaration is included so that clear: both might be used; to achieve minimum layout intrusion, both the height: 0 and visibility: hidden declarations are inserted. Now, your Gecko-based browsers will represent the expanded float within the container (see Figure 3-11) when the container is set to the .addClear class.

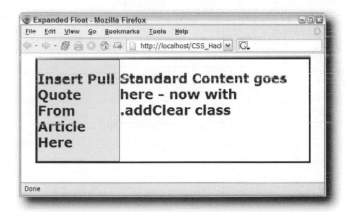

FIGURE 3-11: Without actually adding another element to the page, the :after pseudo-element adds an invisible space with a clear: both declaration.

Internet Explorer (which doesn't need this correction) ignores the :after pseudo-element completely. However, to make sure Internet Explorer doesn't trip you up with its own particular way of handling floats, you'll need to include the Holly Hack to your page as well:

```
* html .addClear {height: 1%;}
```

Filtering Out Safari

When Safari was previewed in January 2003, midway between Macintosh's OS X Jaguar and Panther releases, it was an instant hit. Based on the Unix-developed Konqueror libraries, Safari was a stylish, nimble browser with a small footprint. Much to the developer's relief, the CSS support in Safari was quite robust and a welcome antidote to the then-standard browser on the Macintosh, Internet Explorer 5 for Mac. Most major CSS bugs or omissions were corrected by the 1.2 update of Safari.

You can find a good resource for Safari issues at `http://www.macedition.com/cb/ resources/safari/safari_surprises.html`.

Note As of this writing, the major omission in Safari is the minimal amount of support for styling form elements; only `font-size` and `font-family` are supported—and then, only when applied to a text field. Other styling such as `background-color` on form fields is also missing. Unfortunately, there is no current work-around for this discrepancy.

The Lang Pseudo-Class Hack

As with Gecko-based browsers, Safari's substantial CSS support limits the number of hacks needed or available. One property supported by current versions of Gecko-based browsers that is not available to Safari 1.0 or 1.1 (used on Mac OS systems earlier than 10.3, Panther) is the `:lang` pseudo-class selector. Should a style incorporate the `:lang` selector, the rule is applied only when the specified element is targeted to a specific language. For example, suppose you have a p tag with a `lang` attribute set to `fr` (French), like this:

```
<p lang="fr">Regardez, s'il vous plait!</>
```

To make this paragraph red, you would create a style like this:

```
p:lang(fr) { color: red; }
```

This type of selector is ignored in Safari, and so it could potentially be used to pass style rules to other browsers. Admittedly, when this construct is used as a hack, it requires additional steps including setting the `html` tag to use a `lang` attribute.

The Lang Pseudo-Class Hack also hides styles from Internet Explorer on Windows and Netscape 4.

Note Safari 1.2 now supports the :lang pseudo-class selector and so this hack can only be used to correct problems in Safari 1.0 – 1.1.x.

The Exclamation Mark Hack

Another technique for hiding CSS from Safari—both versions 1.0 and 1.2—has emerged. Placing an exclamation mark after the property/value pair of one declaration prevents any rules that follow from being recognized by Safari. For example, in the following code, the h2 declaration will not be viewed by Safari:

```
h2 { color: red; }
.nothingBelowForSafari {color: red; ! }
h2 { color: blue; }
```

Any h2 headings on associated pages would appear blue in every browser but Safari 1.0–1.2. Keep in mind that no style declaration appearing after the Exclamation Mark Hack will be processed by Safari, so place the hack with care.

Handling Opera Problems

As you might suspect for a browser company that includes the acknowledged father of Cascading Style Sheets, Håkon Wium Lie, as their Chief Technology Officer, Opera has far-reaching CSS support. However, a variety of issues have emerged in various releases—typically fixed in the next version. The current version (7.54 as of this writing) is quite robust, with most major bugs squashed.

Several Opera-related hacks, however, are still useful. The following section covers the three main ones: the Be Nice to Opera, Media Query, and Owen Hacks.

Be Nice to Opera Hack

The primary challenge when building pages to be viewed in Opera is targeting the various versions. One of the most famous examples of this is a part of the Tantek Hack, the Be Nice to Opera 5 rule. The opening section of the Tantek Hack—used to correct the Internet Explorer Box Model—looks like this:

```
.boxModel {
  width:230px;
  voice-family: "\"}\"";
  voice-family:inherit;
  width:200px;
}
```

The primary target for this hack, Internet Explorer 5, cannot properly handle escaped quotes, so it only sees the initial declaration, throwing away the voice-family property because it has no declared value:

```
.boxModel {
  width:230px;
}
```

Browsers that do render the Box Model according to specification are also capable of getting past the escaped quotes and, thus, the quoted curly brace. These browsers (including all Mozilla, Firefox, and Safari) all see the second width rule, width:200px. When developing this hack, it was thought that the current version of Opera at the time (5) was also unable to parse the escaped quotes correctly, and so the Be Nice to Opera 5 rule was developed to restate the width in a manner that would be readable by Opera, but not by Internet Explorer 5:

```
html>body .boxModel { width:200px }
```

Altogether, the code looks like this:

```
.boxModel {
  width:230px;
  voice-family: "\"}\"";
  voice-family:inherit;
  width:200px;
}
html>body .boxModel { width:200px }
```

It now appears that most versions of Opera (from version 3.5 and up) can handle the escaped quotes correctly, and so there is no real need for the Be Nice to Opera 5 rule in this case. However, that doesn't mean it cannot be used as its own hack to pass a rule to Opera (as well as Mozilla, Firefox, and Safari) while hiding it from Internet Explorer on Windows.

Media Queries Hack

With each new version, Opera often paves new ground in implementing a cutting-edge CSS specification well before any other browser. Currently, Opera 7.x is the only browser that comprehends a fascinating proposed CSS3 feature called Media Queries. A Media Query allows the designer to specify a style rule for one or more particular media types (such as screen, handheld, and so on) exhibiting a particular characteristic. With Media Queries, you could, for example, craft a style that would only be visible on a screen if the screen were in color. Such a selector would look like this:

```
@media screen and (color) { ... }
```

Arve Bersvendsen (`http://www.virtuelvis.com/archives/145.html`) realized that since Opera 7 was the only browser currently supporting Media Queries, they could be used to pass styles exclusively to that browser. Media Queries are, at their heart, a logical statement. Only if the statement evaluates to true are the declared styles rendered. To ensure that all Opera 7 browsers can see a style, use a Media Query that always is true:

```
@media all and (min-width: 0px){ ... }
```

This selector is valid for all media in which a minimum width of 0 pixels is available—a universally true statement for all visual-based browsers.

To see the Media Queries Hack in action, here's a look at an Opera 7–only bug. If you have a fixed position `div` that contains an absolutely positioned child `div`, the child improperly inherits the parent's left and top positioning. In the example displayed in Figure 3-12, you can see the parent `div` peeking out from behind the child `div` in Opera 7, even though the child `div` should completely cover the parent.

By applying the Media Queries Hack and adjusting the position of the parent `div`, you can ensure that you'll get the desired effect cross-browser (see Figure 3-13). The code for the hack adjusting the parent `div` values looks like this:

```
@media all and (min-width: 0px){
  div {
    left: 0px;
    top: 0px;
  }
}
```

Hacks that depend on cutting-edge features should be regarded as having a built-in (albeit unknown) expiration date. Although Opera 7 is the only browser now supporting Media Queries, you can be sure others are not far behind.

FIGURE 3-12: In all modern browsers except Opera 7, you only see the child div.

FIGURE 3-13: The Media Queries Hack ensures that only Opera 7 is affected.

Applying the Owen Hack

As seen earlier, the Owen Hack is effective for hiding styles from Internet Explorer browsers on Windows, but it's better known for performing the same chore for Opera, version 6 and earlier. You'll remember that the Owen Hack, created by John Albin Wilkins, is based on the :first-child pseudo-element. Like Internet Explorer, these earlier versions of Opera don't recognize the :first-child pseudo-element when used as part of a selector and, therefore, ignore the rule following. In the following example code, the style assigned to #navSection is hidden in Opera, version 6 and earlier, and Internet Explorer on Windows:

```
head:first-child+body #navSection {
  background-image: url("navbar.gif");
}
```

If you must limit the style rule masking to just Opera 6, a combination of the Be Nice to Opera Hack and Simplifield Box Model Hack (referred to by John Albin Wilkins, creator of the Owen Hack, as the Be Mean to Opera Hack) is required:

```
html>body #navSection {
  bac\kground-image: url("navbar.gif");
}
```

This concept of nesting hacks is an important one and can help you hone in on specific browser versions you need to address.

Applying Conditional Comments

In the eyes of many designers, a CSS hack is thought to be outlaw code. This feeling persists even if the modification validates, maybe because the hack is not officially sanctioned. With conditional comments, Web designers finally have a hack they can feel good about—a filter straight from the browser developers.

Recent versions of Internet Explorer have included the ability to conditionally include code. The conditions are evaluated according to the type of browser being used. This code used to apply this browser-detection feature is referred to as a *conditional comment*. Windows versions of Internet Explorer 5 and higher can detect and react to conditional comments.

Although such a focus on one browser may seem limiting, the current dominance of the Internet Explorer browser makes the technology worth knowing. Moreover, conditional comments provide an authorized path to correcting CSS oversights in one specific browser version, or a range of versions. As you'll see in this chapter, you also have the ability to include code even if the visiting browser is not a recent version of Internet Explorer.

About Conditional Comments

Microsoft incorporated the very aptly named conditional comments feature in Internet Explorer starting with version 5. A conditional comment is an HTML comment that determines whether the enclosed code is ignored or read by the browser. Conditional comments provide built-in browser detection capable of detecting recent Internet Explorer major and minor versions alike.

What does a conditional comment look like? Here's a basic example:

```
<!--[if IE]>
<p>You're using an Internet Explorer browser,
version 5 or later.</p>
<! [endif]-->
```

Another use would be to conditionally attach a style sheet, like this:

```
<!--[if IE]>
<link href="ie_styles.css" media="screen" type="text/css" />
<![endif]-->
```

The beauty of conditional comments is in the structure. Because the code is inside a standard HTML comment tag, two benefits are gained. All browsers other than Internet Explorer 5 or higher disregard both the code within the comment tag and whatever the code wraps around. Recent Internet Explorer browsers, however, evaluate the code within the opening comment tag ([if IE] in the example) and, if true, renders the code up to the closing comment tag. The comment-based syntax ensures that, for the most part, conditional comments validate against HTML and XHTML standards.

Note You'll learn about the non-valid type of conditional comments in a section later in this chapter titled "Working with Non–Internet Explorer Browsers."

It's important to realize that conditional comments are an HTML construct. Conditional comments must be included in an HTML page and cannot be inserted in an external CSS style sheet. The code enclosed by a conditional comment must also be HTML and not pure CSS. To convey CSS information, you must use the style tag, like this:

```
<!--[if IE]>
<style type="text/css">
p { color: red; }
</style>
<![endif]-->
```

Tip There's no need for the traditional comment tags within the style tag itself. These comment tags are used to hide the non-HTML CSS style declarations from older browsers, a problem that Internet Explorer 5 and higher does not have.

Microsoft uses the term *uplevel browser* to refer to any browser that supports conditional comments. Internet Explorer 5.x and Internet Explorer 6.x for Windows are uplevel browsers. The term *downlevel browsers* refers to any other browser, whether it's from an earlier version of Internet Explorer or from another company.

Note The implementation of conditional comments is another discrepancy between the Windows and Macintosh versions of Internet Explorer browsers. Even though Internet Explorer 5 for the Macintosh was released a year after the equivalent Windows version, conditional comments are not supported on the Mac. In other words, Internet Explorer 5 for the Macintosh is considered to be a downlevel browser.

Although the focus of this chapter is on surrounding style tags and CSS declarations with conditional comments, keep in mind that conditional comments can also be used for any HTML code on the page.

Showing/Hiding Styles from Individual Versions

Conditional comments can be targeted just as precisely (or as broadly) as necessary. You can reveal or disguise CSS styles from Internet Explorer versions 5, 5.5, and 6. You can even narrow the focus further to minor version numbers such as Internet Explorer 6.0290, the version released with Windows XP Service Pack 2 (SP2).

Note It's somewhat difficult to test conditional comments on different versions of Internet Explorer. The best way to do it is to have multiple machines each with a different major version. If you manage to install more than one version on the same system, Internet Explorer relies on the latest version installed to view the conditional comments. For example, if you have both Internet Explorer 5 and Internet Explorer 6 installed, you'll only see conditional comments for Internet Explorer 6 or greater, regardless of how you code your comments.

To show the code if a specific browser version is present, the conditional comment is written with a major and minor version number, like this:

```
<!--[if IE 5.5]>
<style type="text/css">
h1 { text-decoration: none; }
</style>
<![endif]-->
```

This code results in two different outputs: a heading without an underline for Internet Explorer 5.5 and a heading with an underline for every other browser, as shown in Figure 4-1.

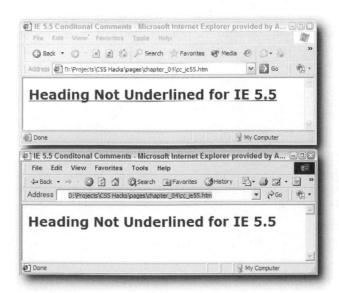

FIGURE **4-1:** The underline style in the conditional comment is hidden from the top browser, Internet Explorer 6, and revealed to the lower one, Internet Explorer 5.5.

Although I've said that we're targeting a specific browser version, this conditional comment code returns true for any Internet Explorer version from 5.500 to 5.599. To be as specific as possible, you'll need to take the version number to four decimal places, like this:

```
<!--[if IE 5.500]>
```

Practically speaking, you'll almost always never want to be this specific. Most corrections made to the most minor of revisions are bug fixes and corrections for security issues, especially where Internet Explorer is concerned. Generally, it's better to target the major versions of Internet Explorer, which, as of this writing, are 5, 5.5, and 6.

So far, you've only seen examples of revealing code if the specified browser is present. Hiding code from a specific browser is an equally important technique. The key is to use the Boolean Not operator (!) before the browser name and version number, like this:

```
<!--[if !IE 5.500]>
<style type="text/css">
h1 { text-decoration: none; }
</style>
<![endif]-->
```

This conditional comment is read "if this page is *not* viewed with Internet Explorer 5.5, apply the following style." Use this type of conditional comment when you need to hide CSS style declarations from the specified browser version. As with other hacks or filters, you often need to think of style rules in pairs when working with conditional comments.

Showing or Hiding a Range of Versions

Some CSS problems run across multiple versions of a browser. The Holly Hack, for example, detailed in the Chapter 3 section "Revealing the Peekaboo Bug," should be applied to Internet Explorer versions 5.5 and 6 to fix common float bugs. With conditional comments, you can address the desired range of Internet Explorer versions, like this:

```
<!--[if IE gte 5.5]>
<style type="text/css">
.innerDiv {height: 1%;}
</style>
<![endif]-->
```

The new element in the opening conditional comment tag (gte) is an *operator*. This particular operator means greater than or equal to. Therefore, the conditional comment can be read "if this page is viewed in an Internet Explorer browser, version 5.5 or higher, apply the following style."

Table 4-1 shows the operators available for use in a conditional comment.

Table 4-1 Conditional Comment Operators

Operator	Description	Example
gt	Greater than	`<!--[if IE gt 5.5]>`
gte	Greater than or equal to	`<!--[if IE gte 5.5]>`
lt	Less than	`<!--[if IE lt 5.5]>`
lte	Less than or equal to	`<!--[if IE lte 5.5]>`
!	Not	`<!--[if !IE gte 5.5]>`

Storing Conditional Comments Externally

Conditional comments are so effective at solving issues with Internet Explorer, you may find that you're using them on every page on your site. Because they are HTML-based, you'll need to ensure that the conditional comments are inserted on each page—which can be a management nightmare if any changes need to be made. An alternative approach is to keep the conditional comments in an external file and add them to your page as a server-side include (SSI).

The SSI file must contain only the necessary conditional comments code; no additional HTML structural tags like html, head, or body should be present. The file can be saved anywhere within the site. (I like to store mine in my styles folder along with the standard CSS files.) The syntax for the SSI depends on where you store your file. If you save the SSI file in the same folder as the page referencing it, use the file attribute, like this:

```
<!-- #include file="cc_ie55.inc"
```

The file attribute should be used whenever you want to specify an include relative to the current page. To refer to a file relative to the site root, use the virtual attribute:

```
<!-- #include virtual="/styles/cc_ie55.inc"
```

Pages including SSIs must be capable of processing server commands. Typically, either an application server such as ASP, ASP.NET, ColdFusion, or PHP is used, or the page is saved with an .shtm or .shtml extension. The latter technique indicates to the Web server that, when requested, any server commands in the page must be executed before the page is served.

You might find it helpful to maintain a library of commonly used conditional comments in SSI format. Use meaningful file names or comments within the file to remind yourself of the conditional comments' functions.

Tip The Boolean Not operator can be combined with any other operator to exclude a range of browsers.

The same rules of browser version specificity covered in the previous section on showing or hiding for an individual browser apply to a browser range. If, for example, you wanted to hide a rule from all browsers from Internet Explorer 5.0 up to, but not including Internet Explorer 6 for SP2, the first line of your conditional comment would look like this:

```
<!--[if IE lt 6.0290]>
```

Working with Non–Internet Explorer Browsers

A variation of the conditional comments syntax can be used to insert styles for browsers other than those specified—including browsers not from Microsoft. Recall that Internet Explorer 5 and above are referred to as uplevel browsers whereas all others are labeled downlevel. The following syntax applies a style for all downlevel browsers:

```
<!--[if !IE]>
<style type="text/css">
#floatBox {
    margin-left: 50px;
}</style>
<![endif]-->
```

Although the code looks similar to a standard conditional comment, there is one major difference: the enclosing tag is not an HTML comment. The dashes are missing from both the opening and closing tags. This code then becomes a proprietary tag and will not validate under either HTML or XHTML specifications. It will, however, render in every intended browser.

Here's how it works. If an uplevel browser views the page with this type of code, it evaluates the conditional statement, just as if it were a standard conditional comment, and reacts accordingly. Downlevel browsers, on the other hand, do not recognize the `<![if... >` or `<![endif]>` tag syntax and ignore those tags while processing the enclosed HTML. In the example shown in Figure 4-2, the standard `margin-left` setting for the floating box (2 pixels) is applied to Internet Explorer 6, while the downlevel browser (Firefox) uses the much larger `margin-left` of 50 pixels, as specified in the conditional comments code.

When working with the downlevel variety of conditional comments, your conditional statement is always going to use the Boolean Not operator (the exclamation point). While its primary purpose is to define styles for downlevel browsers, you could also include one or more uplevel browser versions in your conditional statement. For example, if you wanted to set a CSS declaration to work with all downlevel browsers and Internet Explorer 5.0, your conditional comment code would look like this:

```
<--![if !IE gte 5.5]>
<style type="text/css">
h1 { color: blue; }
}</style>
<![endif]-->
```

The comment-less nature of this conditional comment would force downlevel browsers like Netscape Navigator, Mozilla Firefox, Safari, and even Internet Explorer 5 for Macintosh to set the enclosed CSS declararation, but it would also have the same effect on all Internet Explorer versions below 5.5.

FIGURE 4-2: Although developed by Microsoft, you can use a special syntax of conditional comments to have an effect in browsers other than Internet Explorer.

Practical Applications of Conditional Comments

Now that you understand how conditional comments are used, you can put them to work. The following five CSS bugs are all related to one or more modern versions of Internet Explorer. All of these problems have been discussed, each with their own CSS hack solution, in Chapter 3. These conditional comments–only resolutions provide a viable alternative, using officially sanctioned code.

Three-Pixel Gap

The 3-pixel gap bug typically strikes when designers have oh-so-carefully figured out the proper dimensions for a layout—only to have this Internet Explorer explode their design. This bug often emerges when a layout calls for a floated element (an image or div tag) that is placed next to another content `div`. Both elements are wrapped by a `div` that is set to the exact width needed: the width of the float plus the width of the `content` `div` plus the width of any left or right margins, paddings, or borders. In this example, that width is 502.

```
#floatLeft {
    float: left;
    background-color: #0099FF;
    width: 200px;
}
#content {
    width: 300px;
    border: 1px solid #000000;
    margin-left: 200px;
}
#wrapper {
    width: 502px;
    border: 1px solid #FF0000;
}
```

Internet Explorer mistakenly adds a 3-pixel gap between the float and the `content` `div`. Because the `wrapper` `div` is the exact required width, these additional 3 pixels cause the `content` `div` to fall below the float—ruining the design, as shown in Figure 4-3.

FIGURE 4-3: Internet Explorer's unwarranted extra 3 pixels throw this design out of whack.

If you can't expand the `wrapper div` (and often this is the precise size needed graphically), you must adjust both the right margin of the float and the left margin of `content div`. You'll actually compensate for the additional 3 pixels by declaring a negative `margin-right` value: −3. To make sure the two `div`s butt up against one another, the `content div`'s left margin should be set to 0. Because these changes would wreak havoc on other browsers, a conditional comment is used to apply only to all recent versions of Internet Explorer browsers.

```
<!--[if IE]>
<style type="text/css">
#floatLeft {
    margin-right: -3px;
}
#content {
    margin-left: 0px;
}
</style>
<![endif]-->
```

The difference, as shown in Figure 4-4, is dramatic.

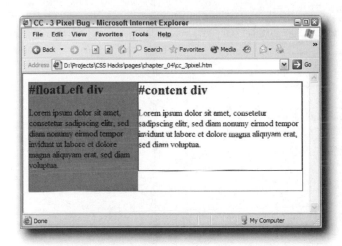

FIGURE 4-4: Adjusting both the right margin of the float and the left margin of the content div in a conditional comment does the trick.

Italics Float Bug

All the various elements that go into making a page are intricately intertwined—especially when it comes to CSS. Another float-related bug is triggered by the one of the least likely suspects: italics. With Internet Explorer 5.5 and 6, a floating container with italicized text is wider than the same container where the text has not been styled with italics. In a tightly designed layout, the wider float causes enough of a shift to have a significant effect, as shown in Figure 4-5.

Numerous ways exist to cope with this issue, but only one maintains the design as specified. If you add an `overflow: visible` declaration, Internet Explorer is forced to keep the original width of the float. Because this bug affects only Internet Explorer 5.5 and 6 on Windows, you'll need to create a conditional comment that incorporates those browser versions, but not Internet Explorer 5:

```
<!--[if gte IE 5.5]>
<style type="text/css">
#floatLeft {
    overflow: visible;
}
</style>
<![endif]-->
```

FIGURE 4-5: The italics float bug emerges when a sizable amount of text is italicized; a smaller amount of text can have the same effect if it is also justified.

As always, the conditional comments are placed in the head region, after the external style sheets are attached. The resulting page puts all the elements in their proper place while staying true to your intended style, as shown in Figure 4-6.

FIGURE 4-6: Making the overflow visible stops floated containers from exceeding their intended width in Internet Explorer 5.5 and 6, regardless of the text formatting.

Note

According to one source, The Nemesis Project (`http://nemesis1.f2o.org`), Internet Explorer 5 also has a similar problem, but a different solution. Rather than declare `over-flow:visible`, the solution for Internet Explorer 5 is to apply `overflow:hidden`. Although I was not able to verify the problem, if you encounter it, the fix is to include another conditional comment, directed at Internet Explorer 5 only:

```
<!--[if IE 5.0]>
<style type="text/css">
#floatLeft {
    overflow: hidden;
}
</style>
<![endif]-->
```

First Letter Bug

Occasionally, a design calls for a heading within a relatively sized container, one that changes size to stay proportional to the width of the screen. If that same design requires letter spacing, your heading will lose its head in Internet Explorer 5.5—the first character vanishes, as shown in Figure 4-7.

FIGURE 4-7: You'd never know that part of your text was missing, unless you tested your page in Internet Explorer 5.5.

Although the design specifications may not be that common, if your design has these requirements, you'll definitely need a fix for Internet Explorer 5.5. The two CSS style declarations used in the example are as follows:

```
.container {
    background-color: #CCCCCC;
    margin: 15px 20%;
}
.innerArea {
    border: 1px solid #000000;
    position: relative;
    letter-spacing: .25em;
    font-family: Verdana, Arial, Helvetica, sans-serif;
    font-size: 2.5em;
    color: #006600;
}
```

The key triggers that cause this problem are the combination of `position:relative` and `letter-spacing: .25em` in the `innerArea` class and the styles assigned (or, rather, not assigned) to the outer `container` class. A number of possible solutions are available that would fix this issue for Internet Explorer 5.5, most of which center around defining a style for the `container` (either a `border-top` or `padding-top` will work) that makes Internet Explorer draw the inner section correctly.

The least-intrusive method that I have found is to assign a 1-pixel top border to the outer container and color it the same as the background color. While this obviously does not have an enormous impact on the design, any intrusion like this is best to limit to where it is absolutely necessary. With an appropriately applied conditional comment, the fix can be targeted just where it is needed, Internet Explorer 5.5:

```
<!--[if IE 5.5]>
<style type="text/css">
.container {
    border-top: 1px solid #FFFFFF;
}
</style>
<![endif]-->
```

Once applied, the first letter is restored to its proper place—and the impact is minimal, as shown in Figure 4-8.

FIGURE 4-8: Although the 1-pixel top border solution is not ideal, it does fix a major problem with a minimum amount of design variation.

Scripting JavaScript and Document Object Model Hacks

JavaScript has long been a partner in the Web's development. Even with CSS in full flower, most common Web effects (such as rollover buttons, expanding/collapsing menus, and calendars, to name a few) are created with JavaScript. As a script-based language, JavaScript can be programmed with nothing more than a text editor. With its low entry barrier, vast library of code, and enormous support community, JavaScript is a multipurpose tool for the savvy Web designer. Best of all, JavaScript plays exceedingly well with CSS.

The standard CSS designs are, at most, two-dimensional: one dimension consists of the default style applied by the designer. Many pages stop there, but others add a second dimension of interactivity, and allow users to pick an alternative style sheet or alter basic elements such as text size. With JavaScript, you can take CSS to the third dimension: programmability. Given any designer-chosen trigger, JavaScript can alter the style of any identifiable element on the page. You could, for example, highlight an answer in a quiz if answered correctly, or reveal a help screen for wrong answers.

The Document Object Model (DOM) is the lifeblood of JavaScript. Through the DOM, JavaScript can get and set values for virtually any page element's properties, including its style. This valuable knowledge can easily be put to use to fine-tune your CSS.

Although some designers resist using JavaScript because users can disable the feature in their browsers, for me there's just too much power here to ignore. Unless your statistics strongly indicate that a large portion of your site's audience does not use JavaScript, you should use it. In this chapter, you see how to determine which browser is currently being used and how to serve the proper style sheet. You also learn techniques for programmatically altering styles to lend more flexibility and power to your navigation and/or page elements.

Dynamically Loading Style Sheets

Browser sniffing is a long-established JavaScript practice. Before CSS came to the forefront, Web developers had to cope with a plethora of browsers, each with its own mix of standard HTML and proprietary tags. Many designers found creating multiple versions of their sites to be an onerous, but necessary, task. Which version of the site was served to the visitor depended on JavaScript code to detect the browser version and redirect accordingly.

The Web has grown wildly in intervening years, and the creation and ongoing maintenance of browser-specific site editions is no longer efficient or necessary. With the rise of standards-compliant browsers, more and more designers have switched to using CSS—a switch that JavaScript is ready to help with. Today, browser sniffers are largely used to detect the current browser so that the proper style sheet can be employed. Maintaining a series of style sheets is far more feasible than keeping up with the updates for a number of variations of an entire site.

Determining Browsers with JavaScript Objects

Two basic approaches to detecting browsers exist. One method depends on the idiosyncrasies of individual browsers and their support of JavaScript objects. This method looks to see if one or more specific objects are supported by the browser currently being used. Depending on the answer, you can figure out the browser name and version. For example, Netscape 4 is the only browser that supports the `document.layers` object, and so this type of code is possible:

```
if (document.layers) {
  // Netscape 4 code goes here
}
```

By calling the JavaScript object itself, either true or false is returned. If true is returned, the object is supported; if false is returned, it's not.

Table 5-1 shows a breakdown of objects and browser support.

Table 5-1 JavaScript Objects in Browsers

JavaScript Object	Found in Browser
`document.images`	Netscape 3 or above, Internet Explorer 4 or above
`!document.images`	Netscape 2, Internet Explorer 3
`document.layers`	Netscape 4
`document.all`	Internet Explorer 4 or above
`document.getElementById`	Internet Explorer 5 or above, Netscape 6 or above
`document.getElementById &&` `!document.all`	Netscape 6 or above

Reading the userAgent Property

The second technique relies on a long-time property of the JavaScript `navigator` object, `userAgent`. When you get the `navigator.userAgent` value, a long string is returned that contains information about the computer platform, the operating system, the browser layout engine, and the browser name, complete with version number.

For example, here's what `navigator.userAgent` returns when I browse a page with my PC:

```
Mozilla/5.0 (Windows; U; Windows NT 5.1; rv:1.7.3) Gecko/20041001
Firefox/0.10.1
```

And here's what I get when I browse the same page from my Macintosh:

```
Mozilla/5.0 (Macintosh; U; PPC Mac OS X; en) AppleWebKit/125.2.2
(KHTML, like Gecko) Safari/125.8
```

To make use of all this information, you'll need to do some additional processing to extract the required data. The typical method is to use JavaScript's `indexOf()` function to search the `userAgent` string looking for a particular value. Here's one technique:

```
var theUA = navigator.userAgent.toLowerCase();
isSafari = (theUA.indexOf('safari') != -1);
```

With this code, the string returned by `navigator.userAgent` is first converted to lower-case to simplify searching, and then assigned to a variable called `theUA`. Then, that variable is searched for a substring, `safari`, which, if found, sets another variable, `isFirefox`, to true. Retrieving the version number is a little more complex and varies from browser to browser. As an example, here's how you would get the current Safari version number:

```
if (isSafari) {
  theVersion = parseFloat(theUA.substring(
theUA.lastIndexOf('safari/') + 7 ));
}
```

Here, the `substring()` function extracts the number values after the term `safari/` and then converts it to a number with the `parseFloat()` function. It's important that the version be in number format so that you can use operators such as less than (<) and greater than (>) to identify the range of browsers. If, for example, you wanted to find out if the current browser was Safari 1.2 or higher, you could use code like this:

```
isSafari1_2up = (isSafari && theVersion >= 1.2)
if (isSafari1_2up) {
  // Safari 1.2 code goes here
}
```

The `&&` symbol is the JavaScript AND operator, so the variable `isSafari1_2up` evaluates to true only if both statements—`isSafari` and `theVersion >= 1.2`—are true.

Many browser-detection scripts on the Web use the `userAgent` method. One of the best I've found is by Chris Nott (`www.dithered.com`) whose Browser Detect script is available under the Creative Commons license.

Note As of this writing, Chris's script is a little out of date (for example, it checks for the original name for Firefox, Firebird), so I've put a more current version on my site at `www.idest.com/css_hacks/files/ch05/browser_detect.js`.

So, which of the two techniques—JavaScript object or `userAgent`—should you use? Although the JavaScript object typically results in more elegant, compact code, I think it's less appropriate for use when setting a style sheet and better suited to more specific programming tasks like determining whether a specific JavaScript function used on the page is available. Moreover, you must keep a constant eye out for browser updates to ensure that availability of a particular JavaScript object has not changed status. The `userAgent` method, on the other hand, while more verbose, is geared toward identifying particular browser versions—a skill highly valued when defining the proper style sheet.

Identifying Opera

Although it has never gained tremendous market share, Opera has long been a favorite browser of many Web designers, especially because of its early and consistent support of CSS. One special feature of Opera is important to note when talking about JavaScript browser detection. To overcome the problem of a browser being blocked from a site if it is not Internet Explorer or another browser, in recent versions the Opera engineers have included a user-selectable preference that allows the browser to disguise itself as a different browser. The disguise takes the form of outputting a different `userAgent` string than normal. Here's how the browser identifies itself if the preference is set to Identify as Opera:

```
Opera/7.54 (Windows NT 5.1; U) [en]
```

However, here's what Opera outputs as the default `userAgent` string:

```
Mozilla/4.0 (compatible; MSIE 6.0; Windows NT 5.1) Opera 7.54 [en]
```

In its default setting, Opera appears to most Web pages as Internet Explorer 6. Other preference settings allow Opera to appear as Mozilla 5, 4.78, or 3.

The good news for designers looking to identify Opera correctly for CSS purposes is that regardless of the preference setting, Opera's `userAgent` string always contains the name "Opera" followed by the version number. When adding code to detect the correct browser, make sure that your JavaScript parses the `userAgent` string instead of relying on another JavaScript property of the navigator object, `appName`. If your detection script includes code like this, Opera users are likely to be served an incorrect style sheet:

```
var browserName = navigator.appName
```

The Browser Detect script from Chris Nott referenced in this chapter handles Opera properly.

Styling for a Detected Browser

Once you've determined which browser is being used, how do you serve the appropriate style sheet? A variety of techniques are available, but perhaps the most common is to rely on the JavaScript function `document.write()`:

```
document.write('<link rel="stylesheet" type="text/css"
href="mainNS4.css">');
```

The same function can be used to dynamically insert the `@import` tag:

```
document.write('@import url("styles/mainIE.css");');
```

The `document.write()` function is put to work in a series of conditional statements or if-then-else clauses. The if-then-else code block cycles through each of the browser-detection statements and, when the current browser is identified, inserts the desired style sheet. Once the style sheet has been dynamically written into the Web page, the code block is exited. Here's a complete code example that first includes a browser-detection script:

```
<script type="text/javascript"
src="../includes/browser_detect.js"> </script>
<script language="JavaScript">
<!--
if (browser.isNS4) {
  document.write("<link REL='stylesheet' HREF='mainNS4.css'
TYPE='text/css'>");
} else if (browser.isIE5xMac) {
  document.write("<link REL='stylesheet' HREF='mainIE5xMac.css'
TYPE='text/css'>");
} else if (browser.isIE55) {
  document.write("<link REL='stylesheet' HREF='mainIE55.css'
TYPE='text/css'>");
} else if (browser.isIE5) {
  document.write("<link REL='stylesheet' HREF='mainIE5.css'
TYPE='text/css'>");
} else if (browser.isIE6up) {
  document.write("<link REL='stylesheet' HREF='mainIE6up.css'
TYPE='text/css'>");
} else if (browser.isSafari) {
  document.write("<link REL='stylesheet' HREF='mainSafari.css'
TYPE='text/css'>");
} else if (browser.isOpera) {
  document.write("<link REL='stylesheet' HREF='mainOpera.css'
TYPE='text/css'>");
}
// -->
</script>
```

The order in which the various browsers are checked is significant. If you're trying to distinguish between two or more different browsers that share a major version number, the rule of thumb is to list the selections from the more specific to the more general. You'll notice in the preceding code that the checks for Internet Explorer version 5 are in this sequence:

```
} else if (browser.isIE5xMac) {
...
} else if (browser.isIE55) {
...
```

} else if (browser.isIE5) {

Because the JavaScript processing stops after an `if` clause is found to be true, it's crucial that the condition is not satisfied too early. If the order were reversed, both Internet Explorer 5 on the Macintosh and Internet Explorer 5.5 browsers would be served the Internet Explorer 5 style sheet.

Switching Style Sheets with the DOM

Previously, you saw how to use JavaScript to automatically serve a specific style sheet based on the current browser. In this section, the focus is on giving users the power to switch between alternative style sheets. This type of control is particularly helpful when designing sites with accessibility requirements in mind. You can, for example, create a style sheet with higher contrasts or larger font sizes to make it more readable for particular users. To enable this type of programmatic styling, you'll need to work with the Document Object Model.

The DOM is a W3C-supported standard, implemented by the current crop of browsers. This standard is supported by most recent browsers, including Internet Explorer 5 and above, Netscape 6 and higher, and Opera 7.x, as well as all versions of Mozilla, Firefox, and Safari.

Understanding the DOM Structure

Every tag in a Web page (including structural tags such as `html`, `head`, and `body`) is a type of node in the DOM called an *element node*. The content within element nodes are also nodes—either other element nodes, text nodes, or comment nodes. This type of structure is often described in parent-child terms: the `html` node is the parent of both the `head` and `body` nodes, while the `head` and `body` nodes are said to be children nodes, which, in turn also have children.

It's important to understand how the DOM relationship is structured so you can develop code that is not page-specific. You can, for example, examine any node to see if it contains child nodes or do the reverse to see what parent nodes are above the current node. Whichever direction you proceed, this process is called *walking the tree*. Through functions of this type, you can control the style on an individual tag level, if necessary. For example to reference the `body` tag via the DOM, you use this code:

```
document.body
```

(Although this could also be written `window.document.body`, the `window` explicit reference is often dropped because it is understood by JavaScript.) The first tag (or child node) within the body is then referred to like this:

```
document.body.childNodes[0]
```

The DOM, like JavaScript, uses zero-based arrays, so the first element in an array is referenced with a 0, the second with 1, and so on.

Another key concept is the use of a DOM method, `getElementsByTagName()`, to gather all the tags of a particular type. For example, to put all the `div` tags in a document into an array, use code like this:

```
var theDivs = document.getElementsByTagName('div');
```

Now each element in the array can be searched for a particular attribute (such as `class`) by looping through the array:

```
for (i=0; i < theStyles.length; ++i) {

  if (theStyles[i].getAttribute('class')== 'legal') {

    //Re-style the all the div tags with a legal class style

  }

}
```

If you know the `id` attribute of a tag you want to modify, you can find it directly with another method, `getElementById()`:

```
var theFooter = document.getElementById('footer');
```

Advanced DOM techniques include modifying text nodes on the fly, creating new nodes of any type, and removing existing nodes.

The DOM provides a structural tree-like view of a Web page where each branch of the tree (referred to as a *node*) can be examined and, in most cases, modified. JavaScript is used to address and, if desired, interact with each node. With style sheet switching, you'll be changing an attribute within nodes representing link tags.

To change style sheets, you'll need to set up a series of link tags to the available style sheets. Typically, style sheets are used in three different ways:

- *Base style sheet*—Contains styles common to all style sheets.

- *Initial style sheet*—Defines the default styles the user sees when first visiting the page.

- *Alternate style sheet*—Provides alternative styles that can be chosen by the visitor.

When the links are inserted in the page, you'll need to use slightly different attributes for each of the three different types. The JavaScript function accesses the DOM to examine the `rel` and `title` attributes; only link tags with both of these attributes can be switched. To ensure that the base styles are always applied (regardless of the user's choice), the `title` attribute is left out of the link to the base style sheet, and the relation to the page (the `rel` attribute) is listed as `stylesheet`:

```
<link href="../../css/basestyles.css" rel="stylesheet"
type="text/css" />
```

The initial style sheet, on the other had, includes the `title` attribute with the identifying value of `default`; again the `rel` attribute is set to `stylesheet`:

```
<link href="../../css/default.css" rel="stylesheet"
type="text/css" title="default"/>
```

Combined, the base and default style sheets create one look, as shown in Figure 5-1.

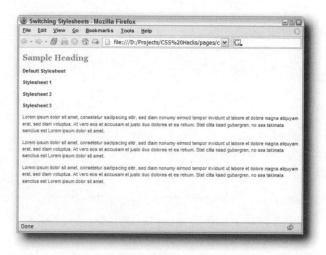

FIGURE 5-1: Whenever the visitor first enters the page, the base and default style sheets are applied.

The alternative style sheets use a different `rel` attribute—`alternate stylesheet`. This value identifies them as user-selectable style sheets to compliant browsers and allows users to change style sheets via the menu. Unfortunately, not many users are aware of this option. In addition the `title` attribute is used to identify each style sheet differently. This same `title` will be used in the JavaScript function to enable the desired style sheet while disabling all others:

```
<link href="../../css/stylesheet1.css" rel="alternate stylesheet"
type="text/css" title="stylesheet1" />
<link href="../../css/stylesheet2.css" rel="alternate stylesheet"
type="text/css" title="stylesheet2" />
```

```
<link href="../../css/stylesheet3.css" rel="alternate stylesheet"
type="text/css" title="stylesheet3" />
```

The individual links that trigger the style sheet changes rely on the `onclick` event to call a custom JavaScript function called `switchStyle()`. The argument passed in the function call corresponds to the `title` attribute in the `link` tag. Here are two examples:

```
<a href="javascript:;" onclick="switchStyle('default'); return
false">Default Stylesheet</a>
<a href="javascript:;" onclick="switchStyle('stylesheet1'); return
false">Stylesheet 1</a>
```

Note The `return false` function added to each `onclick` event stops the browsers from attempting to load a linked page found in the `href` attribute. If you don't prevent this action, some browsers jump to the top of the page, in addition to performing the JavaScript function.

When executed, the `switchStyle()` function runs through this sequence:

1. When the function is called, an argument is established to hold the title passed to it by the `onclick` event of the links.

   ```
   function switchStyle(title)
   ```

2. After declaring two variables, one variable—`theLinks`—is assigned an array of all the `link` tags through the use of the DOM method `getElementsByTagName()`. (See the sidebar "Understanding the DOM Structure" earlier in this chapter for more details on this method.)

   ```
   var i
   var theLinks = document.getElementsByTagName("link")
   ```

3. A loop is established that cycles through each of the `link` tags in the array.

   ```
   for(i=0; i < theLinks.length; i++)
   ```

4. Each `link` tag is checked to see if two conditions are true: that the `rel` attribute includes the string `style` and that a `title` attribute exists.

   ```
   if(theLinks[i].getAttribute("rel").indexOf("style") != -1 &&
   theLinks[i].getAttribute("title"))
   ```

5. If both conditions are met, the `link` tag is first disabled.

   ```
   theLinks[i].disabled = true;
   ```

6. If the title, however, matches the argument passed by the function, the current `link` tag being examined is enabled.

   ```
   if(theLinks[i].getAttribute("title") == title)
   theLinks[i].disabled = false;
   ```

7. After all the `link` tags have been examined—and disabled, with the one requested enabled—the function ends.

Here's the code listing in its entirety:

```
function switchStyle(title) {
  var i
  var theLinks = document.getElementsByTagName("link")
  for(i=0; i < theLinks.length; i++) {
    if(theLinks[i].getAttribute("rel").indexOf("style") != -1 &&
theLinks[i].getAttribute("title")) {
      theLinks[i].disabled = true;
      if(theLinks[i].getAttribute("title") == title)
theLinks[i].disabled = false;
    }
  }
}
```

You can see the two results of the function at work in Figure 5-2 and Figure 5-3. To see this page in action, visit www.idest.com/css_hacks/pages/chapter_05/ stylesheet_switch.htm.

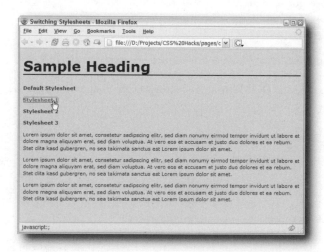

FIGURE 5-2: Stylesheet 1 has a different background, different fonts, and coloring than the default style sheet.

Tip You can trigger multiple style sheets by giving each of them the same `title` value.

A further enhancement to this technique would be to remember the user's style sheet preference and restore it the next time he or she visited the site. Typically, this functionality is achieved through the use of cookies. You could easily incorporate a bit of code to store the title of the last chosen style sheet in a cookie, and then use another function to check for the cookie whenever the page is loaded.

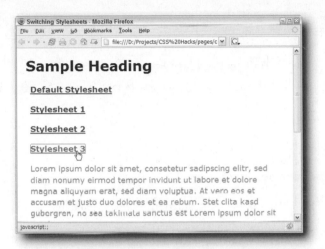

FIGURE 5-3: Stylesheet 2 exemplifies the use of a larger font with a greater contrast.

Another use for this same style sheet–switching technique is to provide an on-screen font size selector. Although most modern browsers provide a menu option for changing the font size, it's often left unfound and unused by browser users; more importantly, browsers take a shotgun approach to changing font sizes. With individual style sheets, you can more tightly control how the increase or decrease of given content is handled; you can even change background images to handle different content requirements.

Style Value Switching for Interactivity

One of the most effective combinations of JavaScript and CSS is centered on `div` tag style with CSS positioning. `div` tags have gained tremendous popularity in programs such as Macromedia Dreamweaver and Adobe GoLive because of their flexibility: `div` tags can be hidden or revealed, change position on the screen, and even appear behind or in front of other `div` tags. Most importantly, all of this activity can be placed under user control.

The basic tool is, once again, the DOM. Through the DOM, individual style attributes can be altered from one value to another. The key is to pinpoint the exact attribute within the desired `div` tag you want to change. For this reason, it's best to work with ID-defined styles for your `div` tags rather than class selectors. Even if you are acting on a group of `div` tags (as is the case in the upcoming example), you often don't want to change the same attribute to exactly the same value for all tags.

The JavaScript code specifies the style attribute for the tag you want to change and a new value. For example, if I wanted to move a 300-pixel-wide div tag named sideNav to the left so that only 10 pixels are showing, I would use code like this:

document.getElementById('sideNav').style.left = "-290px";

As you can see, the DOM getElementById() method is used to declare the desired div and the left CSS style property is specified. Note that a negative margin is declared to move more of the div tag off the page.

Note This particular technique requires DOM-compliant browsers such as all Mozilla-based browsers, Internet Explorer 5 and above, Safari 1.2 and higher, and Opera 7.5. You can, with a minor amount of manipulation, also address Netscape 4 browsers.

Any such combination of CSS and JavaScript will require four primary elements:

- *CSS styles*—Used to define the styles for the div tags. Any type of CSS style (inline, in-page, or defined in an external style sheet) can be used.

- *div tags*—The styled containers that are manipulated by the JavaScript.

- JavaScript functions—Code that modifies elements of the DOM when triggered.

- Event handlers—JavaScript methods inserted into an anchor tag, a, to call the required JavaScript function. Typical event handlers are onClick, onMouseOver, and onMouseOut.

To demonstrate how these parts work together, following is a look at how a sliding sidebar (often used to show and hide navigation) is constructed.

Tip If you want to see how this page works, visit www.idest.com/css_hacks/pages/ chapter_05/slide_side.htm. To keep the concepts clear and the code simple, this page is only intended for DOM-compliant browsers.

The idea for this example is to have a single navigation area that slides mostly off the page when an HTML link within a div is clicked. In addition to moving the navigation section off-stage, a previously hidden div with a second link is revealed while the first link is hidden. The process is reversed when the second link is clicked: the navigation area moves to its original position and the second link is hidden while the first is revealed again (see Figure 5-4).

The first task is to construct the needed CSS styles. For this task, you'll need one for each div tag: the navigation area, the handle that shows when the navigation section is on the page, and the handle that is displayed when the navigation area is off the stage.

```
#sideNav {
        background-color: #FFFF66;
        border: 1px solid #000000;
        position: absolute;
        height: 150px;
        width: 300px;
        left: 0px;
```

```
    top: 60px;
    z-index: 1;
}
#onHandle {
    background-color: #FF0000;
    position: absolute;
    height: 20px;
    width: 5px;
    top: 120px;
    left: 290px;
    z-index: 10;
    visibility: visible;
}
#offHandle {
    background-color: #00FF00;
    position: absolute;
    height: 20px;
    width: 10px;
    top: 120px;
    left: 291px;
    visibility: hidden;
    z-index: 10;
}
```

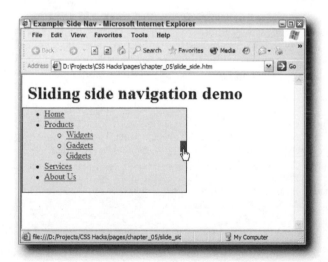

FIGURE 5-4: By combining CSS, JavaScript, and the DOM, you can set the navigation area to slide in and out of the page at will.

The most important properties to notice here are those that deal with position, depth, and visibility. Here, all three ID selectors are declared with the position property set to absolute; it's entirely possible to achieve the same effect with position defined as relative, but absolute is more common. The depth is set with the z-index value; div tags styled with higher z-index values appear to be on top of those with lower z-index values. In this example, the two handles are above the navigation area and have the same z-index. Because they both are on the same plane, as it were, which one is seen is controlled by the visibility property. As you can see, the initial state is for the #onHandle style to be shown while the #offHandle style is hidden.

Next, you'll need to create the three div tags to host these styles. I've used simple X's in the handles to make the structure clearer—you could certainly substitute an image or other object:

```
<div id="sideNav">
  <ul>
    <li><a href="#">Home</a></li>
    <li><a href="#">Products</a>        <ul>
        <li><a href="#">Widgets</a></li>
        <li><a href="#">Gadgets</a></li>
        <li><a href="#">Gidgets</a></li>
     </ul>
    </li>
    <li><a href="#">Services</a></li>
    <li><a href="#">About Us</a> </li>
  </ul>
</div>
<div id="onHandle">X</div>
<div id="offHandle">X</div>
```

Two different JavaScript functions are used to achieve the desired effect: slideSide() and changeVisibility(). Each has a single argument to indicate a current relevant state. For the slideSide() function, the argument dir indicates the direction requested, either in or out. In the changeVisibility() function the divOn parameter tells which of the two handle div tags should be shown. Here's a look at the slideSide() function first:

```
function slideSide(dir) {
  if (dir == "in") {
    document.getElementById('sideNav').style.left = "-290px";
    document.getElementById('onHandle').style.left = "0px";
    document.getElementById('offHandle').style.left = "0px";
  } else {  //direction is out
    document.getElementById('sideNav').style.left = "0px";
    document.getElementById('onHandle').style.left = "290px";
    document.getElementById('offHandle').style.left = "290px";
  }
}
```

As you can see, when the navigation area is to be moved in, the sideNav left style is set to a negative value, moving it off the left side of the page. Additionally, both handles are set to the edge of the page, where they remain visible.

The changeVisibility() function is similarly structured:

```
function changeVisibility(divOn) {
  if (divOn == "onHandle") {
    document.getElementById('onHandle').style.visibility =
"visible";
    document.getElementById('offHandle').style.visibility =
"hidden";
```

```
    } else { //show offHandle
       document.getElementById('onHandle').style.visibility =
"hidden";
       document.getElementById('offHandle').style.visibility =
"visible";
    }
}
```

It's important to note that both of these functions are considerably specific to the page. If you were designing these functions for more general use, additional arguments would be used to indicate the IDs affected, as well as the values required.

The final step connects the styled div tags to the JavaScript functions. JavaScript event handlers with the proper function calls are added to links within the onHandle and offHandle div tags:

```
<div id="onHandle">
  <a href="#"
onclick="slideSide('in');changeVisibility('offHandle')">X</a>
</div>
<div id="offHandle">
  <a href="#"
onclick="slideSide('out');changeVisibility('onHandle')">X</a>
</div>
```

Figure 5-5 shows the page with the navigation area off-screen, ready to be moved back whenever needed. Additional enhancements could be added to move the sideNav div tag over time, resulting in an animation effect.

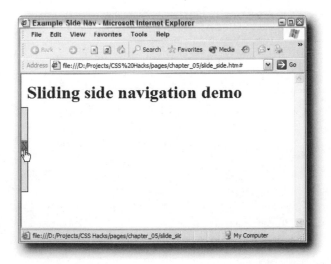

FIGURE 5-5: A click on the link within the now-visible offHandle div tag reverses the position of the navigation area, as well as the visibility of the two handle sections.

Coding Server-Side Solutions

Application servers take Web site development to a whole other level, even where Cascading Style Sheets are concerned. All the top server models (including ASP, PHP, and ColdFusion) provide mechanisms to dynamically control the CSS output.

As you saw in Chapter 5, much of this same functionality is available through JavaScript, but at a price: the user must have JavaScript enabled. Server-side CSS processing ensures that the desired style sheet will be delivered to all site visitors, regardless of their JavaScript settings.

Application servers are often used to serve particular content depending on one or more variables. If a user is not authorized to view a requested page, an alternative page is presented. If, on the other hand, another user with administrative privileges browses to the same initial page, the page requested is sent with additional administrator-only content. In this circumstance, the variable is the login name (the same variable could easily be used to affect the styling of a page). Such variables don't have to be under user control. Server variables, including the one containing the identifying name of the browser version, may also be used to determine content.

This chapter discusses how to make each of the server models covered affect the CSS in two ways: through both user-based variables and server variables. The techniques are essentially the same for all the server models discussed, but the particulars are quite different. Example methods are provided for the top three server models: ASP, PHP, and ColdFusion.

Styling with ASP

Typically, an external style sheet linked into a page is given a `content-type` of `text/css` in this manner:

```
<link href="../styles/mainstyle.css" type="text/css"
```

With ASP, the `content-type` parameter (an attribute that tells the browser what kind of file is being included and, thus, how to handle it) can be specified through the `ContentType` property of the `Response` object.

This capability provides ASP developers with the power to specify an ASP page as an external style sheet, thereby permitting the full range of ASP server-side processing. In this situation, the `link` tag would look like this:

```
<link href="../styles/mainstyle.asp" type="text/css"
```

The ASP page linked as an external style sheet would then include the following code at the top of the page:

```
<% Response.ContentType = "text/css" %>
```

Styles passed from a dynamically created page appear no different than those included from a standard .css file, as shown in Figure 6-1.

FIGURE 6-1: Your visitors will never know that an .asp file is behind your CSS styles.

Note In my testing, I discovered that setting the `ContentType` property was not always necessary. With IIS 5.0, the code can be left out of the dynamic CSS file and will still process properly. However, I recommend keeping the code in the file to ensure forward-compatibility and cross-compatibiltiy with other ASP servers.

Once you're working with an ASP page as your style sheet, the entire world of dynamic processing is available.

A browser-detection script (similar to the JavaScript routine illustrated in Chapter 5, in the section, "Reading the userAgent Property") can be constructed in ASP and included in the style sheet, like this:

```
<!--#include file="detectBrowser.asp"-->
```

Such browser detection would assign Boolean (true or false) values to variables like isIE6 or isNS4, which, in turn, could then be used to specify styles. For example, the following code excerpt reads the server variable HTTP_USER_AGENT and puts it into a string variable, strUserAgent, which is then used to parse to see if the browser is Internet Explorer 6 or Netscape 4:

```
<%
Dim strUserAgent
Dim isIE4, isIE5, isIE55, isIE6, isNS4, isNS6, isMoz, isSafari,
isFF

strUserAgent =
LCase(cstr(request.ServerVariables("HTTP_USER_AGENT")))

isIE4 = FALSE
isIE5 = FALSE
isIE55 = FALSE
isIE6 = FALSE
isNS4 = FALSE
isNS6 = FALSE
isFF = FALSE

If InStr(strUserAgent, "msie 6") Then
  isIE6 = TRUE
ElseIf InStr(strUserAgent, "mozilla/4") Then
  isNS4 = TRUE
End If
%>
```

Note   The preceding code is greatly simplified and does not demonstrate testing for all browsers.

Once the browser is identified, another code routine sets the styles necessary for a given browser:

```
<% If isIE6 %>
body {
     font-family: Verdana, Arial, Helvetica, sans-serif;
     color: #666666;
}
<% Else If isNS4 %>
body, div, p, blockquote, ol, ul, dl, li, dt, dd, td {
     font-family: Verdana, Arial, Helvetica, sans-serif;
     color: #666666;
}
<% End If %>
```

Tip Naturally, if you'd prefer to just switch from one style sheet to another, the variables returned from your browser-detection script could easily be used to link to the desired style sheet. Here's an example:

```
<% If isIE6 %>
<link href="../styles/mainstyleIE6.css" type="text/css"
}
<% Else If isNS4 %>
<link href="../styles/mainstyleNS4.css" type="text/css"
}
<% End If %>
```

Another approach can be used in combination with the dynamically built style sheet to vary styles according to user-based parameters. One technique is to read a previously defined session variable into the style sheet. Suppose you want to present different styles for authorized viewers, according to their access level. Viewers with an access level of `visitor` would see a page styled one way, while those with an `administrator` access level would see another. Typically, the authorization level would be gathered from a recordset and held in a session variable (such as `authLevel`). The ASP code in VBScript to get the current value of such a session variable would be included at the top of the dynamic style sheet:

```
<%
Dim theLevel
theLevel = cStr(Session("authLevel"))
%>
```

What possible impact could you hope to accomplish by changing styles? Although there are many different possibilities, one very real option is to hide or show content. Suppose the Web application being used has an entire level of text designed to help guide those new to the site. In this scenario, the dynamically created style sheet might include a section like this:

```
<% If theLevel = "visitor" Then %>
.helpText { display: block; }
<% ElseIf theLevel = "administrator" %>
.helpText { display: none; }
<% End If %>
```

The result is pretty clear, as shown in Figure 6-2 and Figure 6-3.

Session variables are not the only way to affect CSS styles, although they may be the most effective. You could also trigger styles based on previously stored cookies that are read directly into the dynamically created style sheet.

Note It's vital that the server-side code in your CSS file be correct. One little mistake in your ASP code and none of the styles in the style sheet will render, regardless of whether or not they are altered by the server-side code. I recommend you embed your styles in the head area, complete with server-side code, until it is thoroughly debugged.

FIGURE 6-2: This browser window shows an example page where the authorization level, stored in a session variable, is set to visitor. Here the help text is exposed.

FIGURE 6-3: When another visitor with a higher authorization level sees the page, the help text is hidden.

Controlling CSS with PHP

By default, a standard PHP Web page is identified with a MIME type of text/html. The MIME type is also referred to as the content-type. When a CSS page is linked, the content-type is set to text/css through the type attribute in the link tag:

```
<link href="../styles/main.css" rel="stylesheet" type="text/css" />
```

To execute PHP commands within a CSS file, you'll need to link to a PHP page. On the linked PHP page, you'll also need to reset the content-type attribute to text/css through the PHP header function, like this:

```
<?php header("Content-type: text/css"); ?>
```

With this minor bit of code placed as the first line of your external style sheet, you can execute any PHP command, including taking advantage of the date/time functions. You could, for example, display a different color scheme for Sundays:

```php
<?php header("Content-type: text/css"); ?>

#special {
    font-family: Verdana, Arial, Helvetica, sans-serif;
    color: #000000;
    padding: 5px;
    float: right;
    height: 200px;
    width: 100px;
    border: thin solid #FF0000;
}
<?php if (date( "l" ) == "Sunday") {?>
#special {
    color: #FFFFFF;
    background-color: #FF0000;
}
<?php } ?>
```

Figure 6-4 shows the results of such a dynamic style sheet.

FIGURE 6-4: Change your style sheet on different days of the week with PHP.

Another (potentially more widespread) approach would be to use PHP functionality to detect the browser and react accordingly. In PHP, the userAgent property of the HTTP header is accessible through the $HTTP_USER_AGENT variable. This string can be parsed to determine which browser the page visitor is using with a function such as `strpos()`. For example, the following code sets particular variables to true depending on whether Internet Explorer 6 or Netscape 4 is found:

```php
<?php
$strUserAgent = strtolower($HTTP_USER_AGENT)
if (strpos($strUserAgent, 'msie 6') == true) {
  $isIE6 = true
} else if (strpos($strUserAgent, 'mozilla/4') == true) {
  $isNS4 = true
}
?>
```

Naturally, this type of code functionality should be extended to embrace the full range of browser versions.

With the browser known, that information can be used to load in the appropriate styles or style sheets. In the latter situation, dynamically modified style sheets are not necessary, but can be used if desired. Here's how you might use variables returned from an included PHP browser sniffer to serve the appropriate style sheet to an Internet Explorer 6 or Netscape 4 browser:

```php
<?php if (isIE6) { ?>
<link href="../styles/mainstyleIE6.css" type="text/css"
}
<?php else if (isNS4) ?>
<link href="../styles/mainstyleNS4.css" type="text/css"
}
<?php } ?>
```

Within the dynamically generated style sheet, session variables or cookies could be used to vary the design. As with the ASP example earlier in this chapter, content could be hidden or revealed according to the authorization level of a logged-in user. In this scenario, helpful text is shown only if the user has an authorization level of `visitor` as designated by the value of a session variable named `authLevel`. The relevant code in the external PHP style sheet is as follows:

```php
<?php header("Content-type: text/css"); ?>

.helpText {
  display: none;
    background-color: #FFFF00;
}

<?php if ($_SESSION["authLevel"]=="visitor") { ?>
.helpText { display: block; }
<?php } ?>
```

Figure 6-5 and Figure 6-6 illustrate the two different conditions.

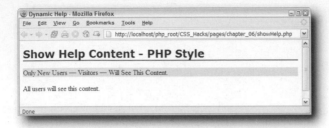

FIGURE 6-5: Users browsing the page with an authorization level of visitor see helpful text.

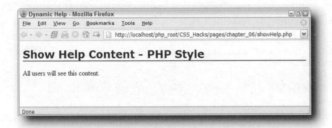

FIGURE 6-6: Page viewers who have an authorization level other than visitor do not see the supplementary text.

ColdFusion Integration with CSS

As with ASP and PHP, ColdFusion has a mechanism for creating external style sheets dynamically. The same basic technique of linking to a dynamic page as the style sheet while using server-side code to alter the page content-type is available in ColdFusion. Code like this is used to link to the style sheet:

```
<link href="../css/mainStyle.cfm" rel="stylesheet" type=
"text/css" />
```

In the external style sheet, the following code is applied as the first line in the file:

```
<cfcontent type="text/css">
```

Once the cfcontent tag changes the content-type to text/css, the code resulting from the server-side execution is treated as CSS. To illustrate the potential of this technique, suppose your client wants to display different backgrounds to a page section depending on the time of day: in the morning, a sunrise image is shown (see Figure 6-7), whereas in the evening, a sunset image displays (see Figure 6-8). A separate image is used for other times.

FIGURE 6-7: Visitors to the site from 5 a.m. until 11 a.m. will see a sunrise image.

FIGURE 6-8: Should the same visitors come back from 5 p.m. until 11 p.m., they'll see a sunset graphic.

```
<cfcontent type="text/css; charset=ISO-8859-1">

#header {
      background-image: url(../../images/standard.jpg);
      background-repeat: no-repeat;
      padding: 5px;
      height: 140px;
      width: 100%;
}

<cfset currentHour=DatePart("h", Now())>
<cfif currentHour GTE 5 AND currentHour LTE 12> #header {
  background-image: url(../../images/sunrise_wide.jpg);
}
</cfif>
<cfif currentHour GTE 17 AND currentHour LTE 21> #header {
  background-image: url(../../images/sunset_wide.jpg);
}
</cfif>
```

Browser detection is easily handled in ColdFusion—and, in some ways, more efficiently than in either ASP or PHP. The userAgent property of the HTTP header is examined to determine the current browser. ColdFusion includes a variable that can be used for this function, HTTP_USER_AGENT:

```
<cfset strUserAgent = #HTTP_USER_AGENT#>
```

As in the other server models, you can parse the string to see if it contains a particular value to test for a given browser version. The findnocase() string function is useful here because it automatically disregards case. If the specified substring is found, its position in the string is returned (a zero means that the string was not found). Here's how you would apply those principles to look for Internet Explorer 6 and Netscape 4:

```
<cfset strUserAgent = #HTTP_USER_AGENT#>
<cfif (#findnocase("msie 6", strUserAgent)# GT 0)>
  <cfset request.isIE6 = true>
<cfelseif (#findnocase("mozilla/4", strUserAgent)# GT 0)>
  <cfset request.isNS4 = true>
</cfif>
```

What makes the ColdFusion brand of browser detection more efficient is the possible use of the Application.cfm file. By including this code in the Application.cfm file, all the resulting browser variables are accessible to any page in your application. To switch between externally linked style sheets, you can address those variables directly with code like this:

```
<cfif request.isIE6>
  <link href="../styles/mainstyleIE6.css" type="text/css"
<cfelseif request.isNS4 >
  <link href="../styles/mainstyleNS4.css" type="text/css"
</cfif>
```

The previous routines you've seen in the ASP and PHP sections of this chapter for displaying or hiding content depending on a session variable adapt well to ColdFusion. As in the other server models, once the authorization level is set as a session variable, the dynamically generated style sheet can use the display property to show help content when appropriate. If the registered user has an authorization level of visitor, the display:block rule is applied (see Figure 6-9); otherwise, the display:none rule is enforced (see Figure 6-10).

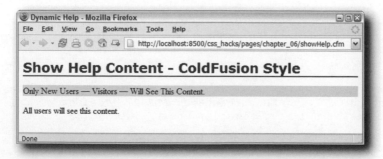

FIGURE 6-9: The typically hidden text is revealed when the session variable containing the authorization level is set to visitor.

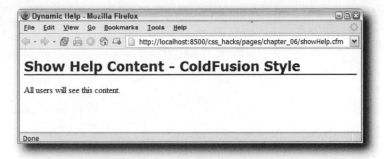

FIGURE 6-10: When users with any authorization level other than visitor hit the page, the extra text is gone.

The external style sheet, linked as styleHelp.cfm, uses this code:

```
<cfcontent type="text/css">
h1 {
  font-family: Verdana, Arial, Helvetica, sans-serif;
  font-size: 24px;
  border-bottom: 2px solid #333333;
}
.helpText {
  display: none;
  background-color: #FFFF00;
}
<cfif if (Session.authLevel IS "visitor")>
  .helpText { display: block; }
</cfif>
```

Note If you run into problems testing this technique, be sure you've cleared out the cache; I recommend unchecking the Save Class Files in the Caching section of the ColdFusion Administrator.

Enhancing Graphics and Media with CSS

When support for Cascading Style Sheets was first available in browsers, the focus was on text. As soon as designers saw the potential, the push for layout control began in earnest with CSS-P (P for positioning the result). But what about one of the key elements that makes the Internet the far more accessible World Wide Web? What about images?

Although you may not be aware of it, there's a quiet revolution under way at the intersection of CSS and graphics as designers push the boundaries of what's possible with media without sacrificing CSS standards. A great deal of work has been done in the controversial area of image replacement: automatically substituting standard text headlines for better quality typographic images. Other CSS-savvy designers have focused on extending the range of graphic effects on the Web. Another area of Web graphic interest has been more flexible integration of images into the page. Examples of all these explorations are contained in this chapter.

Most of the techniques described herein are cutting-edge and require one or more CSS hacks to work properly cross-browser. Some are even further out and will only work with a limited number of browsers. Images aren't the only media that is benefitting from intense CSS interest. You'll find an extremely interesting CSS-related technique for replacing text with Flash movies at the close of this chapter.

Styling Images for Controlled Layout

Many images are floated either directly or placed within a floated `div` or other element. Floats provide a way for text to flow around an image: float the image to the left and the text flows on the right; float to the right and the text wraps around the left. The basic use of float with images is the equivalent of the `align` attribute. However, you do have additional control with float. You can, for example, move the floated image away from the containing element's edge by specifying a `margin-left` or `margin-right`. Likewise, you can make space between a floated image and text without adding the same amount of space to the opposite side—as was the case with the `hspace` and `vspace` attributes.

The core problem with floating an image is the same as aligning it left or right. Regardless of the technique used, an image is still seen as a rectangle and the text wraps around it in a block-like fashion, as shown in Figure 7-1. Web designers look upon print designers—who can flow text along the outline of the actual image rather follow the dimensions of the file—with a high degree of layout envy.

FIGURE 7-1: No matter which way you float it, a standard image retains the file's rectangular shape.

Eric Meyer started the ball rolling with his CSS experiments involving floated sliced images (`http://meyerweb.com/eric/css/edge/curvelicious/demo.html`). Although the technique works, it's fairly labor-intensive and a visitor on a slow connection is likely to see many small images loading in. Jack Baer, architect of bigbaer.com, came up with a more designer-friendly approach. Rather than slice an image into floated elements, Baer places the image in the background of a content area along with a series of stacked floated `div` tags. He refers to these as *sandbag divs* because of the way the text flows around them like water.

Note You can explore the BigBaer's exploration of flowing text at `http://www.bigbaer.com/css_tutorials/css.image.text.wrap.tutorial.htm`.

The key to using these floated `divs` is to also apply a `clear` property to each. Clearing each `div` in the same direction as the float keeps the `divs` in a top-to-bottom stacked formation. To simplify the CSS code, you can group all `divs` into one selector:

```
#flow01, #flow02, #flow03, #flow04, #flow05, #flow06, #flow07,
#flow08 {
  float: left;
  clear: left;
  margin: 0 .5em 0 0;
}
```

A small right margin (.5em) is used to give the image a little breathing room while maintaining the curving shape of the graphic. When styling each of the floated divs, all that is needed is just a width and a height:

```
#flow01 {width:297px; height:36px;}
#flow02 {width:314px; height:60px;}
#flow03 {width:250px; height:21px;}
#flow04 {width:231px; height:28px;}
#flow05 {width:153px; height:76px;}
#flow06 {width:127px; height:24px;}
#flow07 {width:97px; height:26px;}
#flow08 {width:66px; height:12px;}
```

Because each div is cleared, there's no reason to define positions for them, which makes the HTML coding simplicity itself:

```
<div id="content">
  <div id="flow01"></div>
  <div id="flow02"></div>
  <div id="flow03"></div>
  <div id="flow04"></div>
  <div id="flow05"></div>
  <div id="flow06"></div>
  <div id="flow07"></div>
  <!-- Start content here -->
</div>
```

The resulting page definitely breaks the white space barrier surrounding images, as shown in Figure 7-2. A thin border has been added to help you see the width and height of each div.

You'll find that you'll need to tweak the width and height of the divs to get the optimum flow, but you shouldn't adjust them until you finalize the text size. It's important to address both the font-size and line-height of the wrapping text. A smaller font-size value coupled with a slightly larger line-height allows for the optimum flow, as shown in Figure 7-3.

If you want to flow the text between a left-floated image and a right-floated one, you'll need to interweave the divs from one side with those of the other in the HTML. For example, if your divs on the left are defined with #floatLeft and your divs on the right are #floatRight, the opening HTML would look like this:

```
<div id="flowLeft01"></div>
<div id="flowRight01"></div>
<div id="flowLeft02"></div>
<div id="flowRight02"></div>
<div id="flowLeft03"></div>
<div id="flowRight03"></div>
```

This practice prevents Gecko-based browsers from rendering all the `divs` on one side and then all the other ones on the other side.

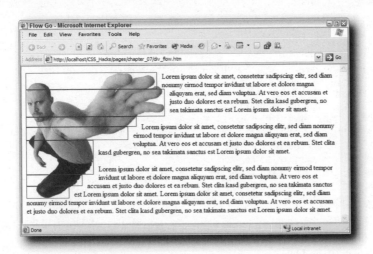

FIGURE 7-2: A series of stacked, empty div tags shape the flow of the text around the image.

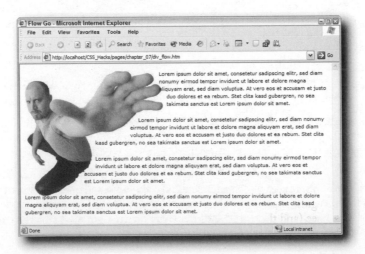

FIGURE 7-3: With a font-size of 11 pixels and line-height of 17, the text just pours around the final image.

Replacing Styles with Images Automatically

One of the biggest frustration designers have wrestled with since the beginning of the Web is typography. Because only fonts common to their users' systems can be used in HTML, body text and headlines were essentially rendered in a lowest common denominator—which severely restricts a designer's creative options. You cannot, for example, style an h1 tag in a Magneto font and expect all visitors to your site (who may be PC, Macintosh, or Unix users with a wide range of operating systems) to have the font installed. The proper font is the least of a typographer's desires. Any graphic artist working with type has the full palette of size, kerning, tracking, and color, not to mention other decorative flourishes.

The earliest work-around was to use a graphic for headlines. To show a headline in Magneto, just create an image with that font and insert it as a GIF or JPEG. However, the rise of CSS with its emphasis on separating document structure coupled with intense interest in fully searchable pages and legislated accessibility requirements has pushed the images-as-text method out of favor.

Dedication (or maybe it was frustration) won out, however. As early as 1999, a designer named C. Z. Robertson described a way to use CSS to replace a heading with an image, retaining both structural integrity and document searchability. The technique didn't really gain notice, however, until spring of 2003 when Douglas Bowman wrote a tutorial on implementing Fahner Image Replacement (FIR), named after Todd Fahner, who suggested the concept independently of Robertson. FIR really took off when it was written about by Jeffrey Zeldman.

The core FIR technique is, surprisingly, very straightforward. Include a span within heading or other block element in your HTML:

```
<h1 id="fir"><span>Welcome!</span></h1>
```

Define a style with a background image depicting the heading set to the same height as the image and set the span within that heading to display:none:

```
h1#fir {
  background-image: url("../images/welcome.gif");
  background-repeat: no-repeat;
  height: 36px;
}
h1#fir span { display: none; }
```

The result is pretty dramatic, as shown in Figure 7-4, and must have appeared very promising to designers committed to CSS. It became apparent, however, that the method wasn't without its drawbacks, especially in regard to accessibility. The majority of screen readers used by the visually impaired would not see (and thus read) the hidden heading. Moreover, there is no alt attribute associated with a background image to rely on.

FIGURE 7-4: The top portion displays a standard h1 tag, styled to 36 pixels, while the bottom portion shows the same markup where the heading is replaced by an image.

It was a powerful concept, however, and numerous other CSS-savvy designers offered their solution. Two, Stuart Langridge and Seamus Leahy, came up with the same basic idea at roughly the same time. Rather than use display:none to conceal the image, their technique focuses on reducing the height of the text to 0 and hiding the overflow. A padding-top value is added to match the height of the replacement image. Because the text is present but not visible, it is read by screen readers. Another key benefit to this approach is that it dispenses with the need for an additional span tag.

```
h1#fir {
    overflow: hidden;
    background-image: url(../../images/welcome.gif);
    background-repeat: no-repeat;
    padding-top: 36px;
    height: 0px;
}
```

Note You can investigate Langridge and Leahy's original articles at http://www.kryogenix.org/ code/browser/lir/ and http://www.moronicbajebus.com/playground/cssplay/ image-replacement/, respectively.

Although this method works pretty well across browsers, it requires a CSS hack for it to work correctly with Internet Explorer 5.x. The Comment After Selector Hack, discussed in Chapter 3, works well since you're just modifying a single property, height:

```
h1#fir {
  overflow: hidden;
  background-image: url(../../images/welcome.gif);
  background-repeat: no-repeat;
  padding-top: 36px;
  height: 0px !important;
  height /**/:36px;
}
```

The !important property is added to ensure a zero value is applied by most browsers.

Dave Shea of mezzoblue.com has come up with an excellent enhancement. By adding a title attribute to the HTML element, a tooltip appears over the graphic and screen readers are doubly covered:

```
<h1 id="fir" title="Welcome to our site.">Welcome!</h1>
```

 You could also use a conditional comment to solve this problem. Conditional comments were discussed in Chapter 4.

Image replacement is a powerful concept, but must be used with some caution. One possible scenario is for users to have their images disabled. Because the CSS is still executed, visitors will see neither graphic nor text in this situation.

Scaling Images for Accessibility

If you've worked on making your sites accessible, you know that font resizing is an important item on your checklist. When testing, you probably noticed that, while your text changes sizes, the images do not. Although it can be argued that accessibility statutes only call for text to be resizeable, the intent of the regulation is to make all Web content on a page more visible. A number of methods have been developed to allow your images to scale right alongside the resizing text.

Anyone who has set up a page to resize under user control knows that the trick is to use percentage-based font sizes rather than fixed-size units like pixels or points. The same holds true when setting up images to scale. Perhaps the best approach is to specify the dimensions in ems rather than pixels. I first saw this method described on the bigbaer.com site at http://www.bigbaer.com/css_tutorials/css.scale.image.html.tutorial.htm.

Suppose you have an image floated right that is normally 296 pixels wide by 224 pixels high. You can roughly convert pixels to ems by using the formula 1 em = 16 pixels. The 1:16 ratio is true for most systems, although you probably will need to tweak the values somewhat to get a more precise match. In the following example, the image was best represented at 17 ems wide by 12.75 ems high:

```
#ringImg {
  width: 17em;
  height: 12.75em;
```

```
    float: right;
    padding-bottom: .5em;
    padding-left: .5em;
}
```

I generally set up my pages with a body font-size of 62.5 percent. This has the effect of making 1 em equal to 10 points and it makes it easier for me to set sizes using ems, but thinking in points. For example, my standard text size is 11 points, which translates quite easily into 1.1 ems. When applied to a page with an image dimensioned by ems, the graphic is reduced in size by a little more than a third. In this example scenario, this is acceptable because I want the image to scale with clarity, as shown in Figure 7-5.

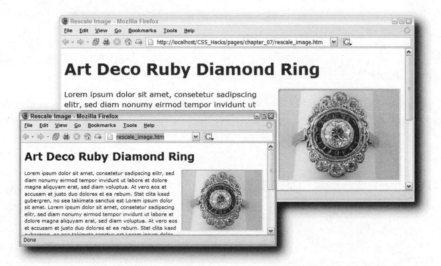

FIGURE 7-5: With the image set to scale in ems, the top browser view shows what happens when the text size is increased.

Note If you're designing with Opera in mind, and you want to match your users' default settings, you should use a value of 100.01% rather than 100%. Some versions of Opera have a bug that computes 100% to be 1 pixel smaller than it should be. In certain circumstances this can mean that text becomes microscopic, since all subsequent font sizes are based off a base font that is too small. Why not use 101%? Because this can cause problems in Safari.

Making Rounded Rectangles with CSS

The Web, by and large, is made up of rectangles. Each of the building blocks of a page— images, `divs`, block elements—are rectangular. Given that variety is the lifeblood of most designers, it's no wonder that the search for the perfect rounded rectangle has been taken up by so many.

Here's an area where the Mozilla project bore early fruit with its proprietary CSS property -moz-border-radius. While all other techniques rely on inserting masking images to reproduce a corner, the -moz-border-radius property simply draws the border with a curved shape. In its simplest variation, the -moz-border-radius property applies the same value to each of the border corners. For example, consider a 200-pixel-wide div, a -moz-border-radius value of 25, specified like this:

```
-moz-border-radius: 25px;
```

This provides a nicely rounded border, as shown in Figure 7-6.

FIGURE 7-6: You can get a rounded border without images, but only in Gecko-based browsers for now.

By specifying two values instead of one, you can realize a differently curved shape. Consider the following code:

```
-moz-border-radius: 25px 10px;
```

This results in a slanting rounded rectangle, as shown in Figure 7-7.

This property, while valid in all Gecko-based browsers, cannot be replicated in other browsers currently, although there is a superset of this functionality included in the CSS3 specifications still in progress.

FIGURE 7-7: A slight variation is possible
by adding a second, different value.

The only other way (admittedly, a major hack) to create rounded rectangles currently is to use
images. The type of graphics used depends on the desired effect. If you just want to create a
simple rounded rectangle with a set width, you can use the image-based approach. You can find
variations of this method on the current Macromedia site and many others. This techique uses
three images: one for the top, another for the middle, and a third for the bottom of the rectangle. You can see how each image is used together, as well as an exploded view in Figure 7-8.

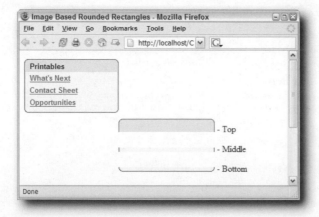

FIGURE 7-8: Each of the three graphics is bound to particular
content in this rounded rectangle.

Each image is embedded as a background image in the style for the content. For example, in the top area of the rounded rectangle depicted, an h3 tag is always used, so the style is defined like this:

```
#roundedBox h3{
  padding: 5px 0px 2px 10px;
  background-image: url(../../images/corner-head.gif);
  background-repeat:no-repeat;
}
```

The middle section places a background image that forms the side border wherever a link is used. This technique works well because this particular pod is intended for navigation.

```
#roundedBox a:link, #roundedBox a:visited, #roundedBox a:hover {
  background-image: url(../../images/corner_bg_nav.jpg);
  font-weight: bold;
  padding: 3px 0px 3px 10px;
  color: #21536A;
  display: block;
}
```

To complete the rounded rectangle, style a class that holds the bottom image:

```
.cornerBottom {
  background-image: url("../../images/corner-bottom.gif");
  background-repeat:no-repeat;
}
```

This class will be applied to a div tag. Because this area is not expected to contain any viable content, a non-breaking space ( ) is needed in the div:

```
<div class="cornerBottom"> </div>
```

For more elaborate rectangles, you'll need to increase the number of images and adopt a different approach to the rectangle's structure. One method that works well across browsers relies on the (thankfully) well-supported CSS property background-position. With background-position, you can specify where in the background you'd like your image to display; among the accepted values are constructs like top left, top right, bottom left, and bottom right. Your styles then look like this:

```
.upRight {
  background: url(../../images/topRight.png) top right no-repeat;
}
.upLeft {
  background: url(../../images/topLeft.png) top left no-repeat;
}
.downRight {
  background: url(../../images/bottomRight.png) bottom right no-
repeat;
}
.downLeft {
  background: url(../../images/bottomLeft.png) bottom left no-
repeat;
}
.upRight, .upLeft, .downRight, .downLeft {
```

```
    margin: 0;
    padding: 0;
}
```

Notice that each of the `div` classes also set both `margin` and `padding` to 0. Failing to do this will cause the graphics to display in a variety of ways. To keep the text or images within the rounded rectangle away from the border edges, apply padding—but no margin—to the content `div`:

```
.content {
    margin: 0;
    padding:1em 2.5em 1.5em;
}
```

Typically, four over-sided images are used to keep the box size flexible. An extra-large image works in the background because only the amount of the graphic needed to display the content is shown. The graphics are not, as you might expect, just the four corners. To depict both an optional background color and border, the full rectangle is sliced up and saved as separate images:

- *Top right* —Includes the top-right corner, along with the top and right borders and, optionally, the body of the rectangle, as shown in Figure 7-9.

- *Top left* —Includes the top-left corner and the left border.

- *Bottom right* —Includes the bottom-right corner and the bottom border.

- *Bottom left* —Includes just the bottom-left corner.

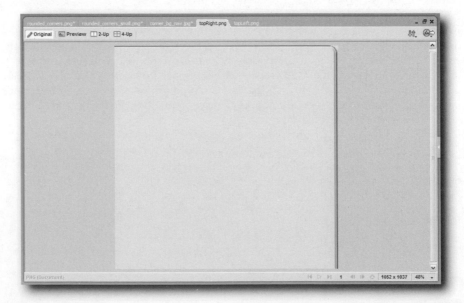

FIGURE 7-9: The full top-right graphic is much larger than will actually be depicted to allow flexible box sizes.

Each of the divs used to hold the images is nested within one another, with the actual text or other content in the innermost region. An outer wrapper sets the position, as well as the dimensions of the rectangle.

The order of the divs—and thus the graphics in the background—is critical. From outermost to innermost, the sequence is as follows:

1. Outer wrapper

2. Top Right

3. Top Left

4. Bottom Right

5. Bottom Left

6. Content

The code for the rounded rectangle depicted in Figure 7-10 shows the nested nature of the div tags clearly:

```
<div id="wrapper">
  <div class="upRight">
    <div class="upLeft">
      <div class="downRight">
        <div class="downLeft">
          <div class="content">
            <h2>Tricked Out Box</h2>
            <p>Lorem ipsum dolor sit amet, more consectetuer
adipiscing elit, sed diamnonummy nibh euismod tincidunt ut
dolore.</p>
          </div>
        </div>
      </div>
    </div>
  </div>
</div>
```

This particular example applies the same color to the body's background-color property as to the rectangle to achieve a quasi-embossed look. You could just as easily use a different color for the rectangle graphics for a completely different feel.

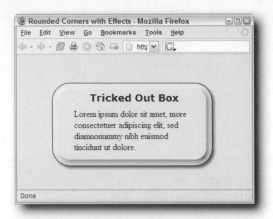

FIGURE 7-10: With multiple images carefully nested in separately defined divs, you can achieve a rounded rectangle with numerous effects applied.

Adding Drop-Shadow Styles

The drop-shadow effect seems to be perpetually sliding in and out of designer favor. Although a drop shadow does help an image jump off the page, it's also been heavily used and is considered by many to be passé. Most modern graphics editors provide some method for easily adding a drop shadow with various characteristics, but the process is labor-intensive, especially when dealing with a gallery of images. A CSS technique makes it possible to add (and remove) subtle drop shadows through code alone, without reprocessing the images themselves.

Note Although CSS includes a `text-shadow` property, it is only supported in Safari 1.1 and higher.

This technique, which was written about by Sergio Villarreal on A List Apart (`http://www.alistapart.com/articles/cssdrop2/`) and based on earlier work by Dunstan Orchard (1976design.com) relies on three low-weight images:

- *shadow.gif*—The actual drop-shadow image. This image is placed in the background of an outer `div` enclosing another `div`, which contains the image.

- *edgeShadow.png*—An inverse shadow used to soften the bottom-left and top-right edges of the shadow. This file, in PNG format, is applied to the background of a `div` wrapping around the image.

- *edgeShadow.gif*—A second file, identical to the PNG inverse shadow file, but in GIF format to optimize the display in Internet Explorer 5.

All three images are over-sized at 800 pixels wide by 800 pixels high. The larger size provides more flexibility and allows the same technique (and images) to be applied to a range of images with varying shapes and sizes. Although the dimensions of the files are quite large, the focus on just the shadow aspect reduces the file weight considerably. All three files are just over 11 KB. This figure becomes quite significant if the same shadow technique is applied to a gallery of images. The files are only downloaded once and rendered multiple times.

The drop shadow applied in this example is quite subtle, as shown in Figure 7-11. You can, of course, make the effect more pronounced by changing the graphic files.

FIGURE 7-11: The soft shadow, as well as the border, surrounding the image is applied via CSS. Several hacks are used to get the same effect cross-browser.

The HTML required to display this image clearly shows the multiple divs used:

```
<div class="shadow">
  <div>
    <img src="../../images/starRing.jpg" alt="The dog Star"
width="335" height="239" />
  </div>
</div>
```

The outer div, shadow, includes shadow.gif as a background image based in the lower-right corner. It also uses the Important Hack to send different margin values to Internet Explorer on Windows. You'll remember that most modern browsers (with the exception of Internet Explorer on Windows) will use any declaration with the !important property in place of a later declaration.

```css
.shadow {
  float: left;
  clear: both;
  background: url("../../images/shadow.gif") no-repeat bottom
right;
  margin: 14px 0 0 17px !important;
  margin: 14px 0 0 8px;
}
```

The inner `div` uses the same Important Hack to set different edge-shadow images for Internet Explorer on Windows than other browsers because Internet Explorer does not offer PNG alpha transparency channels (32-bit) support. The background images are positioned in the upper left so that correct areas of the drop shadow (the top right and bottom left of the image) will be softened.

```css
.shadow div {
    float: left;
    background: url("../../images/edgeShadow.png") no-repeat left
top !important;
  background: url("../../images/edgeShadow.gif") no-repeat left
top;
  padding: 0px 6px 6px 0px;
}
```

In reality, the GIF image referenced will only be applied to Internet Explorer 5. Another hack, enclosed in conditional comments, uses a proprietary Microsoft filter to enforce alpha transparency:

```html
<!--[if gte ie 5.5000]>
<style type="text/css">
.shadow div {

filter:progid:DXImageTransform.Microsoft.AlphaImageLoader(src='../
../images/edgeShadow.png',
sizingMethod='scale');
    background: none;
  padding: 0px 6px 2px 0px;
}
</style>
<![endif]-->
```

Note The hack used to display PNG alpha channels in Internet Explorer is discussed in more depth in the following section of this chapter.

Since a conditional comment is already being used, the padding is adjusted as well to compensate for Internet Explorer's Box Model problems.

Tip Another, more simplified, approach would be to use a single image for the shadow in PNG format. In this technique, you'd have to create the shadow the exact size needed for your images. Although this method is more restricted in terms of the different types of images it could be used with, it's great for galleries of thumbnails where the images are all the same size.

Extending PNG Support

Recently, the ability to use graphics in the PNG format completely and unabashedly on the Web has been getting tantalizingly close to reality. The last great holdout from a browser perspective is Internet Explorer 6, which doesn't provide PNG alpha channel support natively. With this browser's overwhelming market penetration, this lack of support has pretty much killed widespread adoption of PNG on the Web.

Although the PNG format has many advantages over GIF (including better compression and automatic gamma correction), its main claim to fame is variable transparency made possible by each pixel's alpha channel. While GIF offers only a binary type of transparency—either a pixel is transparent or it is not—PNG allows varying degrees of transparency, up to 254 levels for use on the Web. While this facility allows for a great deal of artistic freedom, perhaps the primary benefit of PNG's variable transparency is portability. A PNG file with alpha channel transparency enabled can safely be inserted in a page regardless of the background, as shown in Figure 7-12, without the ghosting shadow so noticeable if you try the same thing with GIF images.

FIGURE 7-12: The variable transparency possible in a PNG format allows the drop shadow of the flowers to blend seamlessly, even against a riotously colored background.

Unfortunately, if you try to look at the PNG-based file in Internet Explorer 5.5 or higher, you'll get a completely different and unusable result. Not only does the drop shadow appear monotone, but the entire background is no longer transparent at all, as shown in Figure 7-13.

FIGURE 7-13: Internet Explorer's inability to support PNG's
alpha channels is immediately apparent.

Microsoft has provided its own solution to the PNG problem, although somewhat "round-a-boutly." If you read the previous section, you'll have noticed that the method for enabling PNG transparency in Internet Explorer is to use a proprietary Microsoft filter, AlphaImageLoader. Although the technique used in the "Adding Drop-Shadow Styles" section is fine for a single image, it's really unworkable for multiple images. Applying the AlphaImageLoader filter requires that the PNG file to be loaded is specified each time. This process is tedious at best and a nightmare to manage with a large site.

A solution has been developed by Erik Arvidsson of WebFX. By relying on another proprietary Internet Explorer function, behavior, Erik was able to craft a file that automatically applies the AlphaImageLoader filter for every PNG image found on the page. You can invoke the behavior function in your CSS:

```
img {
    behavior: url("pngbehavior.htc");
}
```

All browsers except Internet Explorer will ignore the proprietary behavior property. There are two other requirements to implement this behavior: the pngbehavior.htc file (which contains the behavior code) and a blank.gif file (a tiny transparent GIF file). Both must be uploaded to the same folder as your page. As you can see in Figure 7-14, the extra bit of effort is well worth it.

FIGURE 7-14: Once the pngbehavior.htc and blank.gif file are in place (and your CSS style is included on the page), you'll get the same results with PNG graphics in Internet Explorer 5.5 and higher as with other modern browsers.

You can download the necessary files to make Internet Explorer PNG-aware at the WebFX site, http://webfx.eae.net/dhtml/pngbehavior/pngbehavior.html.

Note If Internet Explorer 5 is a concern for you, use conditional comments to replace the PNG image with a GIF version for that browser.

Implementing Flash Replacement

Earlier in this chapter, you learned how an image could be substituted for a heading to achieve a better quality of typography on the Web. The major problem with the technique described is that each heading must have an image replacement created in advance in a graphics editor like Adobe Photoshop or Macromedia Fireworks. How does the busy, often harried, designer set up a page to automatically include the best quality representation of the heading text specified? Enter Flash.

Numerous developers have worked independently and together to make Flash text replacement a reality. Mike Davidson created a one-of-kind solution to complement his work on ESPN.com in 2001. Two years later, Shaun Inman figured out a more general way to approach the problem via the Document Object Model (DOM), JavaScript, and Flash Player 6 called Inman Flash Replacement. Two other developers, Tom Werner and Rob Cameron, brought support for multiple text lines in a heading, CSS, and accessibility. Unfortunately their technique required Flash 7, which is not as omnipresent as the earlier version.

Again, with necessity proving the driving force, Mike Davidson returned to the project and created Scalable Inman Flash Replacement (sIFR). sIFR is a technique that allows automatic generation of Flash headings (in single or multiple lines), properly sized to replace your CSS-styled text and needing only Flash Player 6. Another programmer, Tomas Jogin, helped with making sIFR as flexible as possible and yet another, Mark Wubben, has been instrumental in getting the latest version, 2.0 as of this writing, out the door.

As you can see by the headline in Figure 7-15, the results are very crisp and distinctive. In this example, I was able to use one of my favorite fonts, Palatino, in the banner title. Amazingly enough, this text can be highlighted and copied, just like standard text.

FIGURE 7-15: Each of the headlines here, including the banner, are actually Flash elements, substituted by sIFR.

How does sIFR work? Here's a walkthrough of the process:

1. When the requested page is loaded in the browser, a JavaScript function detects if the proper version of Flash (6 or greater) is available. If Flash is not found, the page is rendered with standard HTML text.

2. If Flash is present, the CSS class `sIFR-hasFlash` is assigned to the HTML tag. This action effectively hides all the elements that are children of `html. sIFR-hasFlash` that have been styled with a `visibility:hidden` property. These are the elements that will be replaced with Flash.

3. A JavaScript routine traverses the DOM and gathers all the replaceable elements. For each element found, the space occupied (width and height) is calculated and an sIFR-generated Flash movie is inserted in that space.

4. Starting at a large point size (96), the Flash movie systematically resizes itself until it matches the bounding box of the given element.

Although there is a lot going on, it all happens in the blink of an eye. One of the beauties of this method is that if users don't have the appropriate Flash player enabled, they see standard text. Another advantage is that any sIFR-hasFlash class selector is available to be replaced, not just headings.

To implement sIFR in your Web pages, you'll need to complete the following steps:

1. Download and unpack the sIFR files from http://www.mikeindustries.com/blog/archive/2004/08/sifr. Currently, another link on that page points to the latest version.

2. Open sifr.fla in Flash MX, Flash MX 2004, or Flash MX 2004 Professional. Double-click the movie clip on the page to edit it. When it opens for editing, select any font you desire from the Properties inspector.

3. Publish the SWF file containing your revised font choice to your site. I recommend using the font name as the name of the SWF file. You can change the name in File ⇨ Publish Settings.

4. In the head of your Web page, include the bundled JavaScript file, sifr.js. At the bottom of the page, in a script tag, call the sIFR JavaScript function, replaceElement(), as described later in this section.

5. Set up your CSS as you would normally. In addition, you'll need to establish style rules to change the visibility to hidden. These style rules use the sIFR-hasFlash class, like this:

```
.sIFR-hasFlash h2 {
   visibility: hidden;
   letter-spacing: -9px;
   font-size: 55px;
}
```

As mentioned earlier, you can specify any selector, not just heading tags.

The replaceElement() function specifies which selectors are to be replaced with which Flash SWF file and much more. The basic function call looks like this:

```
if(sIFR != null && sIFR.replaceElement != null){
  sIFR.replaceElement("h1", "palantino.swf", "#000000", "#000000",
"#999999", null, 0, 0, 0, 0, "textalign=center&offsetTop=6");
}
```

You can replace as many elements as desired. The replaceElement() function is only executed if the sIFR object is found and if the proper function defined. In all, 12 arguments are available to replaceElement():

Argument	Type of Value	Example
Selector	String	h3#pullquote
FlashSrc	String	palantino.swf
Color	String	#000000
LinkColor	String	#0000CC or null
HoverColor	String	#FF0000 or null
BgColor	String	#000000, transparent or null
PaddingTop	Number	0
PaddingRight	Number	10
PaddingBottom	Number	0
PaddingLeft	Number	10
FlashVars	Name/Value pairs (Optional)	textalign=center&offsetTop=2
Case	String (Optional)	upper or lower

It's important that the padding values declared in the replaceElement() function match any padding defined in the CSS style to ensure that the size of the Flash replacement is precise.

Although not recommended for every situation (in many circumstances, the standard fonts available are just what the client ordered), sIFR definitely has its place in the Web designer's palette.

Maintaining Accessibility with CSS

In a very real sense, accessibility is the heart of Cascading Style Sheets. The very nature of separating content and presentation pushes designers toward structuring Web pages with increased readability. Moreover, the use of style sheets opens the door for the Web content to be presented in different formats according to need. A *print style sheet*, for example, might reformat the material without repetitive navigation sections.

The World Wide Web Consortium (W3C), bearer of the CSS standard, is deeply involved in accessibility. A separate committee, called the Web Accessibility Initiative (WAI), guides the accessibility-related recommendations for Web sites, Web-authoring tools, and browsers. Additionally, combined efforts by the Cascading Style Sheets working group and the WAI seek to find ways to achieve better accessibility through CSS. Currently, you can find a note detailing CSS2 features in this area at http://www.w3.org/TR/CSS-access. Unfortunately, key areas of the recommendations have been ignored by browsers. For example, currently only one browser, Linux's Emacspeak, recognizes and supports aural style sheets.

All assistive devices used to make sites accessible work the same way with regard to CSS: they depend on the browser. If the host browser does not read a particular CSS rule, the screen reader or other device cannot translate it. If, for example, you bolded a certain phrase in a rule that excluded Internet Explorer 6, a screen reader working with Internet Explorer 6 would not emphasize that phrase, whereas others would.

Note You want to be especially careful with your stylings in respect to Internet Explorer. The prevalence of the Internet Explorer browser is even higher for those using screen readers than it is for the general population.

This correlation between what the browser and screen reader see means that, for the most part, any CSS hack you apply for a particular browser is transparently translated for the screen reader. There are, however, particular techniques that can be used in conjunction with a CSS to help your sites work better with assistive technology such as text re-scaling and screen readers. These techniques form the basis for this chapter.

Cross-Reference Accessibility is fast becoming integrated into everyday Web design. Consequently, a number of accessibility-related topics have been covered elsewhere in this book. One key technique, style sheet switching, is mentioned in Chapter 5.

Setting Up for Accessible Text

The term "visually impaired" covers a wide range of disabilities. People with the poorest vision (or no vision at all) rely on screen readers to understand the content on the Web. Another, much larger group, simply needs help seeing the often tiny type designers find aesthetically pleasing. All major browsers now include mechanisms for increasing a page's font size (as shown in Figure 8-1), either via menu, keyboard shortcut, or both. However, a great number of Web sites are not set up properly to take advantage of these tools.

FIGURE 8-1: Text resizing is a critical function to help those with less-than-perfect vision. The top browser window displays the standard font size, while the bottom shows the same page with the font size increased.

This disconnect between the Web page and browser is partially because of the initial push for pixels by Web-standard pundits like Jeffrey Zeldman. When faced with the choice of which font-size measurement unit to use, Zeldman and others came firmly out for pixels. Pixels, like points, are a fixed measurement unit and, thus, very appealing to designers who want to control the complete look-and-feel of their sites. Unfortunately, pixels cannot be resized using the browser's built-in font scaling options across the board, most notably in Internet Explorer. Rather, a proportional measurement system such as percent, ems, or (best of all) keywords (large, small, smaller, and so on) must be used.

Although using ems as a base unit works, this method has a major flaw: compounding. Suppose you want your p and td tags to look the same, so you create a style like this:

```
p, td {
   font-size: .9em;
}
```

Text in a p tag outside of a table will render at .9em. However, if you place a p tag within a td tag, the text actually renders at .81em (as .9 x .9 = .81). You can get around this by specifically defining that condition, like this:

```
p td {
   font-size: .9em;
}
```

The trick to using ems as a measurement unit is to declare all possible combinations. Although this is possible, it's a fair amount of work.

Note Numerous designers have worked on the text resizing problem and documented a variety of solutions. A notable article by Todd Fahner appeared on A List Apart (http://www. alistapart.com/articles/sizematters/). Mark Pilgrim from Dive Into Accessibility condensed this technique and provided valuable work-arounds for a wide range of browsers (http://diveintoaccessibility.org/examples/fontsize.html). The following discussion is based on his work.

Keywords arguably offer the best approach to text resizing—but there are, as psychologists and software designers say, issues. First, Netscape 4 doesn't really support keywords in a usable fashion. The changes in each keyword size are too big to be really workable. However, Netscape 4 does adequately support text resizing with a pixel-based measurement. So, the first task is to set the p tag to a standard medium size, 12 pixels:

```
p {
   font-size: 12px;
}
```

Next, you must define styles for every browser except Netscape 4. The Comment Hack discussed in Chapter 2 is perfect for this. Declaring a more specific rule will cause all modern browsers to override the initial p declaration:

```
/* Start hiding from NS4 */
/*/*/
body p {
```

```
   font-size: x-small;
}
/* Resume showing to NS4 */
```

If you're concerned about Opera 5 for Macintosh, you'll need to add an empty rule after the opening part of the Comment Hack. The following code (bolded for emphasis) provides a "toss-away" rule that then allows Opera 5 for Mac to process the next rule declared:

```
/* Start hiding from NS4 */
/*/*/a:{}
body p {
   font-size: x-small;
}
/* Resume showing to NS4 */
```

Why did we pick the keyword x-small? In a perfect world, the choice would be small—which in most browsers is the same as 12 pixels. However, in the real world, Internet Explorer 5 renders x-small as 12 pixels, not small. Therefore, the technique is to initially set the declaration for the exception and then provide the rule, along with a hack to hide it from the problem browser. The Tantek Hack fits the bill perfectly:

```
/* Start hiding from NS4 */
/*/*/a:{}
body p {
   font-size: x-small;
   voice-family: "\"}\"";
   voice-family: inherit;
   font-size: small;
}
/* Resume showing to NS4 */
```

The Tantek Hack (originally developed to handle Box Model problems) puts out a closing curly bracket that, despite being escaped, is read by Internet Explorer 5. Almost all other modern browsers ignore it and apply the font-size: small declaration.

The only other browser version that had the same problem with escaped brackets as Internet Explorer 5 is Opera 5. Because Opera 5 renders x-small as 10 pixels, if you left the problem untreated, text would appear too small in that browser. The final hack is intended to be applied by Opera 5 only:

```
/* Start hiding from NS4 */
/*/*/a:{}
body p {
   font-size: x-small;
   voice-family: "\"}\"";
   voice-family: inherit;
   font-size: small;
}
html>body p {
   font-size: small;
}
/* Resume showing to NS4 */
```

All your bases are now covered and the font should appear the same across all browsers. Best of all, it will resize the same when required.

> **Note** If at all possible, run usability tests for your site, especially if there is a concern that the standard font size is smaller than normal. You may find that the page is difficult to read for a large percentage of your audience.

Handling Print Media Style Sheets

Although print media style sheets are not directly mandated in the Federal Rehabilitation Act's Section 508 guidelines on accessibility, they certainly are in keeping with its spirit. The ability to specify different style sheets for different media makes it a tremendous boon to granting access to content, regardless of the device used to view it. Although establishing a print style sheet is not as difficult as balancing a dozen or so browser variations, there are general guidelines to follow—and specific "gotcha's" to avoid.

Attaching a Print Media Style Sheet

As with many other areas in a CSS, the sequence in which you declare a print media style sheet matters. One factor that many designers tend to overlook is that a standard `link` or `import` statement attaching your standard style sheet—if a media type is not specified—applies to *all* media, including print. To override styles, the print media style sheet must be attached after the main style sheet, like this:

```
<style type="text/css">
  @import "main.css";
</style>

<link rel="stylesheet" type="text/css" media="print"
href="mainprint.css" />
```

> **Note** Some designers work around this issue by specifying media styles for all declared style sheets, (for example, `media="screen, handheld, projection"`). This works as well, but may be an unnecessary step if you're redesigning an existing step to include a print media style sheet.

As when working with different style sheets for different browsers, it's important to restyle the same selectors in your print style sheet as in your overall style sheet. You wouldn't, for example, want to just change the `color` attribute of the body tag to `black` in the print style sheet when the basic style sheet includes a style `#sidebar p` that sets `background-color` to `black` and `color` to `white`.

Defining General Properties

Obviously, the overall presentation in print is quite different from the screen. To take advantage of the benefits in print, you typically want to make sure three basic components are addressed: margins, color, and font size.

Although many designers zero out their margins for a Web page viewed on a monitor, printers need margins. Unless you're attempting a fancy layout for print, the cleanest way to present your text is to set the width to auto and margin to a value around 10% to 15%. By avoiding using a set pixel size for the margins, your print output remains more flexible. Standard U.S. letter size paper will look just as good as A4 sizes found elsewhere.

Printer paper is typically white, so defining the general background color to white and the text color to black results in the sharpest contrast:

```
body {
  background-color: white;
  color: black;
}
```

You'll probably also want to remove any background images for the best reproduction, as shown in Figure 8-2.

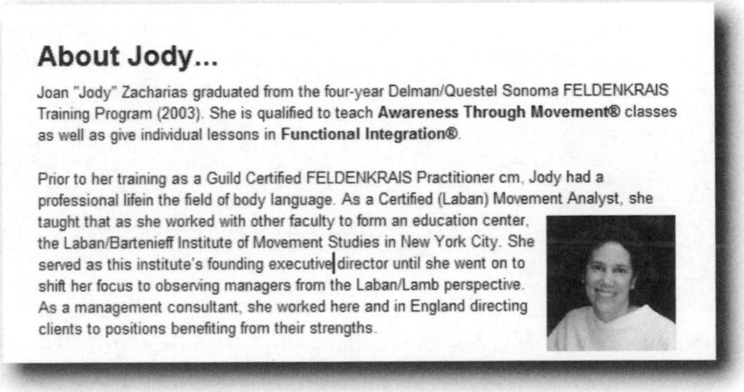

About Jody...

Joan "Jody" Zacharias graduated from the four-year Delman/Questel Sonoma FELDENKRAIS Training Program (2003). She is qualified to teach **Awareness Through Movement**® classes as well as give individual lessons in **Functional Integration**®.

Prior to her training as a Guild Certified FELDENKRAIS Practitioner cm, Jody had a professional life in the field of body language. As a Certified (Laban) Movement Analyst, she taught that as she worked with other faculty to form an education center, the Laban/Bartenieff Institute of Movement Studies in New York City. She served as this institute's founding executive director until she went on to shift her focus to observing managers from the Laban/Lamb perspective. As a management consultant, she worked here and in England directing clients to positions benefiting from their strengths.

FIGURE 8-2: By selectively removing unnecessary elements such as navigation, you are one step closer to prepping your page for print.

To ensure that the white background of the page is displayed, use the transparent property. Suppose that the .sidebar class typically has a graphic as well as a differentiating color. The print style sheet neutralizes both like this:

```
.sidebar {
  background-image: none;
  background-color: transparent;
}
```

Clients and designers alike tend to go a little smaller with font sizes on screen. I generally set my overall font-size to 12 points. Although points as a measurement unit are not well suited for the Web, they're perfect for print.

Correcting Print-Specific Problems

Certain Web page elements are meant only for the Web, while others malfunction when sent to print. Most designers feel that menu navigation has no real use in a print version of a page. To hide the navigation (or anything else) use the `display: hidden` declaration. For example, assume your navigation is contained within a `div` with the ID of `#navbar`. To keep the navigation buttons from printing, your print style sheet would include a style rule like this:

```
#navbar { display: none; }
```

Note

If you think ahead, you can also print content that is not displayed on the Web page. Some companies want to include copyright or legal notices on every printed page. The content must be included in your Web code with `display: none` defined for the general style sheet and `display: block` declared in the print media style sheet.

Gecko-based browsers have a potentially destructive problem with floats. In recent versions of Mozilla, Netscape, and Firefox, if a floated container spans a page break when printed, some or all of the content after the page break vanishes. The issue seems to be related to the float property. Another reported issue occurs when the top of a floated element coincides with a page break. In Internet Explorer, the floated element doesn't print at all. To resolve these problems, declare `float: none` for the appropriate styles.

Note

Designing a print style sheet requires a fair degree of experimentation. You may find that, in addition to declaring `float: none`, you also need to adjust the left margin of an adjacent element to zero.

Links present a particular challenge when making the jump to print. Typically, a link within a paragraph is assigned to a related word, but not the entire link itself. It's not too often these days that you literally see `Visit http://MyDolphinsHome.com/index.html`. It's far more common to use something like `Visit My Dolphin's Home` and the link is assigned to the text. Advanced capabilities of CSS2 and the still under-proposal CSS3 provide the power to print the `href` value following the link.

The first task is to style the link so that it displays the same whether or not it has been previously clicked:

```
a:link, a:visited {
  background: transparent;
  color: black;
  text-decoration: underline;
}
```

To display an actual URL following the selected link, you must use the `:after` pseudo-element to generate the content. One of the properties of the `:after` pseudo-element is the ability to render the value of any attribute listed. The following code puts the `href` value of the link in parentheses:

```
a:link:after, a:visited:after {
  content: " (" attr(href) ") ";
  }
```

The additional spacing around the parentheses ensures that the URL won't be placed directly after the link text. When applied to our example, the output would look like this:

```
Visit My Dolphin's Home (http://MyDolphinsHome.com/index.html).
```

Not all links, of course, are fully formed. Many links internal to a site use document-relative (such as `../../docs/policies.htm`) or site-root-relative (`/docs/policies.htm`) links. When site-root-relative links are found, you can create a fully formed link by prepending the name of the site. A CSS3 attribute selector targets the first letter of an attribute's value and, if there's a match, can be used to generate content. If the site uses site-root-relative links, add this style to your print media style sheet, substituting the name of your site:

```
a[href^="/"]:after {
 content: " (http://www.yourSite.com" attr(href) ") ";
}
```

Currently, this proposed CSS3 attribute selector is supported by Gecko-based browsers, Opera 7, and Safari.

Unfortunately, there's nothing similar that can be done to provide a complete link for document-relative links.

Adding CSS Hacks for Screen Readers

Listening to your Web page be read by a screen reader is an eye-opening exercise that every Web designer should undertake. It's especially beneficial if you happen to experience it in the company of someone who actually uses such an assistive device regularly. The speed at which someone accustomed to screen readers navigates the page is astonishing—and so is the frustration when a non-accessible page is encountered.

Navigation can be a real sore point for people relying on screen readers. Typically, site navigation is positioned near the top of the code, as well as the page. As one of the first elements encountered, a screen reader reacts to a standard navigation bar by saying something like the following:

```
Link Home
Link Products
Link Services
Link Contact Us
Link About Us
```

 Note If you've never encountered a screen reader, you can see them in action at the University of Wisconsin–Madison's site. As part of a vast amount of accessibility research, the University produced a number of videos that demonstrate how screen readers are used and offer insightful advice for Web designers on accessibility. You can find the videos at `http://www.doit.wisc.edu/accessibility/video/`. If you want to experience it for yourself, download a trial version. JAWS for Windows offers a 40-minute trial version at `http://www.freedomscientific.com/fs_downloads/jaws.asp`, and you can get a 30-day trial version of IBM HomePage Reader from this page, `http://www-306.ibm.com/able/solution_offerings/hpr.html`.

Although links are important to navigating a site for any visitor, the initial recital of links can be a hindrance to the screen-reader user, especially on repeated visits. To make it easy for screen-reader users to get to the content, a special link is placed at the top of the page that connects to a named anchor at the top of the actual content. This special link is referred to as a *skip link* and typically uses this code:

```
<a href="#content">Skip Links</a>
```

Many designers find such a link, even if it is styled discreetly, to be a visual blot on the page. For quite some time, the typical solution was to establish a style rule that used the display: none declaration to hide the links. Accessibility experts such as Joe Clark feel that concealing the skip link is counterproductive, because it is useful to many different people, not just the visually impaired. Another accessibility and CSS guru, Bob Easton, has discovered (with the help of others) that screen readers (such as CSS-compliant browsers) also cannot see content hidden with display: none declarations. When you realize that screen readers are only interpreting what the browser sees, this makes perfect sense. The condition with display: none is currently the case with the top three screen readers: JAWS, Window Eyes, and IBM Home Page Reader.

You should, however, think twice before you move to hide the skip link form your page. Some people (such as the elderly who may not be facile with keyboard navigation or others with physical impairments who may be using a device other than a mouse) rely on them to quickly get to the content of a page.

Note   You can review Bob Easton's research at http://css-discuss.incutio.com/?page=ScreenreaderVisibility.

Luckily, another solution has emerged and tested successfully. Instead of using CSS to not render the skip link, you can create a CSS rule that displays the skip link off the visual screen. The standard way of doing this is to style a rule that puts the content off the left edge of the screen, like this:

```
.off-left {
  position: absolute;
  left: -999px;
  width: 990px;
}
```

Once declared, the same class can be used for any amount of accessibility-related text you want to convey to the screen-reader user, but not to the visitor experiencing the Web page visually. In addition to a skip-to-content link, you might also include a skip-to-navigation and/or skip-to-search link.

Integrated CSS Hack Layouts

L ayouts are perhaps the most frustrating CSS techniques to master. Just when you think you've got everything working correctly, one small modification to the page can bring massive unwanted changes. Much of the blame for the fragility of modern CSS layouts should be attributed to browser implementations. For example, suppose you want a particular element to always be 10 pixels above the bottom of its container and so you position your element with the value of bottom: 10px. This is fine for every modern browser, except Internet Explorer—which would place the element 10 pixels above the bottom of the browser window.

The goal of this chapter is to provide you with a series of working CSS layouts that you can adapt and use for your own work. The initial sections of the chapter dive into the specific building blocks of CSS layout: positioning and floats. Both CSS concepts require special attention—and a variety of CSS hacks, both previously discussed and newly uncovered—for their use to be brought into reality on the Web. The balance of the chapter is devoted to the core challenges facing a CSS layout designer: two- and three-column pages, a well-behaved footer, and consistently centered content. Each layout will incorporate CSS hacks as needed to get the job done.

Positioning with CSS

The positioning functions defined by CSS2 gave Web designers tremendous control over their page layouts—and a really big headache. The rules governing the position property appear complex and difficult to master. However, once you understand a few key concepts, you'll be able to re-create the most sophisticated table-based layout without convoluted table code. Then you'll be ready to make any needed adjustments to compensate for browser inconsistencies.

Perhaps the most common misunderstood aspects of the position property are the accepted values: static, relative, absolute, and fixed. The first value, static, is the default position value for all elements. If you remove all positioning from a document, the layout of the page will look exactly the same as if you had assigned `position: static` across the board. This static representation is known as the normal document flow. Each of the other three values can potentially adjust an element's place within the flow. In other (more practical) words, you only have to be concerned with three values.

Position: Relative

Another major positioning concept is the *containing block*. When you specify an offset value (such as `left: 10px` or `top: 20px`) for a relative-, absolute-, or fixed-positioned element, the offset is in relation to the containing block. The primary difference between the three values is that the containing block is different for each one.

The containing block for a `position: relative` element is the element itself where it would normally appear in the document flow. For example, consider specifying a style like this:

```
#content {
    position: relative;
    left: 10px;
    top: 10px;
}
```

Here, you're moving the `#content` element 10 pixels down and 10 pixels to the right from its current position, as illustrated in Figure 9-1.

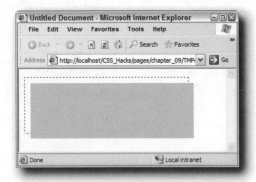

FIGURE 9-1: The dotted outline represents the element's original position in the document flow; the solid rectangle shows the new position after the offset values have been applied.

What uses does a `position: relative` declaration have? One example is to offset a pull-quote box without allowing the text wrapping that goes with using a float. This has the added advantage of changing position properly if the text size is increased or decreased. A `position: relative` element retains its place in the flow, whether it is offset or not.

As far as browser support is concerned, `position: relative` works correctly in all fifth-generation browsers, including all Gecko-based browsers and Internet Explorer 5 and up. The declaration is not recognized by Netscape 4.

The `position: relative` declaration does bring one major advantage to the table, however. Its use corrects many problems in Internet Explorer 6. Theoretically, delaring `position: relative` without specifying any offsets should have no effect on the page rendering. You are, in essence, defining the style to remain in place in the flow. For some unknown reason, applying a `position: relative` declaration to a troublesome selector fixes the problem in Internet Explorer 6 without breaking it anywhere else—the perfect definition of a CSS hack!

To see this effect in action, take a page that has three `div`s: an outer one with a background color, an inner one that contains floated items, and a clearer `div`. Here's what the CSS would look like:

```
#main {
      background-color: #99FFFF,
}
#container {
  border: 1px dashed red;
}
.item {
  float: left;
  background-color: #000000;
  padding: 3px;
  margin: 5px;
}
#spacer {
  clear: both;
}
```

Any text in the outer `div`, #main, disappears when Internet Explorer 6 first loads the page, as shown in Figure 9-2. If you refresh the page by scrolling, resizing the browser window, or going to another application and then returning to Internet Explorer, the text suddenly appears. Pretty strange, right?

How do you serve the page as intended, cross-browser? Add a `position: relative` declaration to your content selectors. For example, if your heading is in an h1 tag, you could add this CSS rule:

```
#main h1 { position: relative }
```

Suddenly, your title is present, first time, every time (see Figure 9-3).

Note As with any miracle cure, you must also administer a grain of salt when applying `position: relative`. Be sure to test your pages thoroughly to make sure what is fixed in Internet Explorer is not broken somewhere else. Internet Explorer 5 for Mac is particularly sensitive to `position: relative` issues.

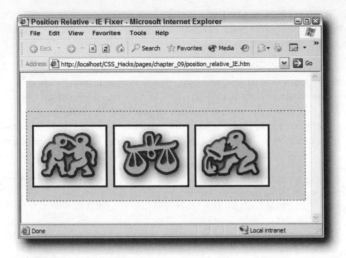

FIGURE 9-2: It's what you don't see—the text above the three zodiac signs—that's important in Internet Explorer 6.

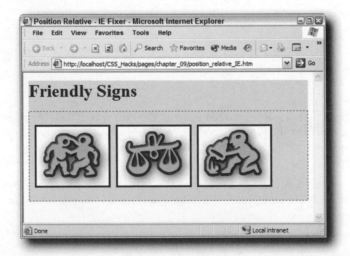

FIGURE 9-3: Applying position: relative to the text makes it appear in Internet Explorer 6, without any ill effects in other browsers.

Beyond serving as a general cure-all for Internet Explorer 6 display woes, the real power of the position: relative declaration is apparent when it is used in conjunction with another positioned element, typically one that has been absolutely positioned.

Position: Absolute

When designers are first introduced to the concept of absolute positioning, they're generally ecstatic. Finally, here's a way you can create pages the way you want to, just like pasting cutout boxes on a layout. The bad news is that it's not that easy. The good news is, once you understand the two ways in which `position: absolute` can be used, you'll have more control than you ever considered.

Once again, the key to understanding this positioning property is the containing block. For `position: absolute`, the containing block is the nearest ancestor element with a `position: absolute`, `position: relative`, or `position: fixed` property. If no such element exists, the containing block is considered to be the document's root element, the `html` tag. This latter case is the one most designers are familiar with. Suppose a designer applies a style like this to a `div` tag:

```
#sidebar {
  position: absolute;
  left: 20px;
  top: 90px;
  width: 125px;
  height: auto;
}
```

The expectation is for a box to appear 20 pixels from the left edge of the document window and 90 pixels from the top. The box is absolutely positioned with respect to the document window—when the page scrolls the box scrolls with it, as shown in Figure 9-4.

FIGURE 9-4: The events listing sidebar is absolutely positioned and uses the html tag as its containing block.

However, the Web isn't a static medium like print, where each page is printed one way and one way only. Many factors could cause elements to shift size or position. Assume, for example, that a visitor to the page had a slightly higher font-size setting. If the navigation text is set to be resizable, soon your absolutely positioned box is absolutely in the way, as shown in Figure 9-5.

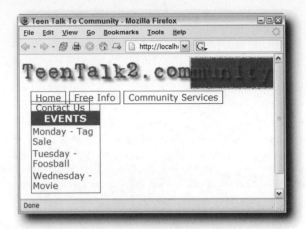

FIGURE 9-5: When an absolutely positioned object is tied to the html tag, undesired overlaps are entirely possible.

By taking advantage of the containing block definition, you can have the best of both worlds. Rather than relying on the html tag to be the containing block, in many cases it's best to define another style with a position: relative declaration to wrap around the absolutely positioned div. You'll need to adjust the left and top properties within the absolutely positioned style, however. Because the container div is in the flow of the document, chances are your left will be much less, if not zero. To ensure that the absolutely positioned element flows downward when necessary, you'll also need to set the top property to auto. The relevant portion of the style sheet now looks like this:

```
#container {
    position: relative;
}
#sidebar {
    position: absolute;
    height: auto;
    width: 125px;
    left: 0px;
    top: auto;
    border: 1px solid #006699;
}
```

Note If you want to add some consistent space between the relatively positioned container and the absolutely positioned element, apply a margin-top value to the absolutely positioned style.

Now, even if the text size is increased significantly, the absolutely positioned element stays right where you want it, correctly placed in the flow of the document, as shown in Figure 9-6.

FIGURE 9-6: To maintain both positioning and flexibility, wrap your absolutely positioned styles with a position: relative style.

Several ways exist to size an absolutely positioned element, but you have to use caution if you decide not to go with the `width` property. An alternative approach is to use the `left` and `right` properties. For example, if your outer container has a width of 400 pixels, setting the `left` property to 10% pixels and the right to 20% would create a box 280 pixels wide (assuming all margins, padding, and borders are at zero). Although this might seem like a method for keeping your absolutely positioned box a constant size, it's problematic in both Opera and Internet Explorer. Both of these browsers tend to reduce the size of a box defined in this way to fit the content—a process referred to as *shrink-wrapping*. A better method to maintain a consistent ratio between an inner box and a container of variable size is to set the inner box style to a percentage width, like this:

```
#sidebar {
    position: absolute;
    height: auto;
    width: 80%;
    left: 0px;
    top: auto;
    border: 1px solid #006699;
}
```

All browsers display styles with a percentage width at their full width regardless of the amount of content.

Note

Internet Explorer 5 for Mac has a particular problem handling the `right` property in absolutely positioned styles, often leaving unwanted gaps and generating unnecessary horizontal scroll bars. If Internet Explorer 5 for Mac is a targeted browser, you're better off defining your width through another method.

Position: Fixed

The position: fixed declaration is exactly like position: absolute with one difference: the containing block. Whereas position: absolute can use either the html tag or another ancestor element as its containing block, position: fixed only has one option—the browser screen or *viewport*. When the HTML document scrolls within the viewport, any element that has been fixed in position stays in place. This facility gives position: fixed frame-like behavior without the drawbacks of frames.

Note   The viewport changes according to the medium in use. With a monitor and browser, the viewport is the browser screen. When printing, the viewport is each page printed.

Sounds too good to be true? It is—Internet Explorer 5 or greater on Windows, the world's most used browser, doesn't support the fixed attribute. However, there is a way to trick Internet Explorer into scrolling only part of the screen. In fact, with the aid of conditional comments, you can use the position: fixed declaration successfully on most modern browsers, in either quirks or standards mode.

The first task is to set up your page properly. Each region to be fixed (as well as the scrolling content) should be in its own region, typically separated with a div tag. The example used in this section has two fixed sections: a header and a sidebar. Abstracted, the HTML for the page shown in Figure 9-7 looks like this:

```
<div id="header">
[Header image and navigation goes here]
</div>
<div id="sidebar">
[Sidebar content goes here]
</div>
<div id="content">
[Main content goes here]
</div>
```

In the CSS declaration for the body tag, use padding (not margins) to position the scrollable content correctly. Because the example fixes both a header and a left sidebar, the content is placed down and to the right:

```
body {
    padding: 100px 0 0 160px;
    margin: 0;
}
```

As part of the work-around to get the concept to work across browsers, the two fixed areas are initially positioned absolutely:

```
#header {
    position: absolute;
    top: 0px;
```

```
      left: 20px;
      height: 100px;
}
#sidebar {
      position: absolute;
      top: 105px;
      left: 20px;
      height: auto;
      width: 125px;
}
```

FIGURE 9-7: You'd never know it from first glance, but both the header and sidebar are fixed in position.

Using the Child Selector Hack, which excludes Internet Explorer on Windows, the two styles are now fixed in place:

```
html>body div#header { position: fixed; }
html>body div#sidebar { position: fixed; }
```

At this stage, the page will render as expected in all Gecko-based browsers, Opera, Internet Explorer 5 for Mac, and Safari (see Figure 9-8).

FIGURE 9-8: Both fixed areas stay in place while the content scrolls.

To get it to work on Internet Explorer on Windows, you'll need to supply two different hacks, one for Internet Explorer 5 and another for Internet Explorer 6 and above. The styles used set up the content area to scroll, if all of it cannot be shown on the screen at once (a condition known as *overflow*), while hiding the overflow from the main document element. For Internet Explorer 5, the main document element is considered to be the body tag; for Internet Explorer 6, it's the html tag:

```
<!--[if IE 5]>
<style type="text/css">
body {
    overflow: hidden;
}
div#content {
    height: 100%;
    overflow: auto;
}
</style>
<![endif]-->

<!--[if gte IE 6]>
<style type="text/css">
html {
    overflow: hidden;
}
body {
    height: 100%;
```

```
        overflow-y: auto;
}
</style>
<![endif]-->
```

The two-conditional-statement technique allows designers to create pages in standards mode, as shown in Figure 9-9.

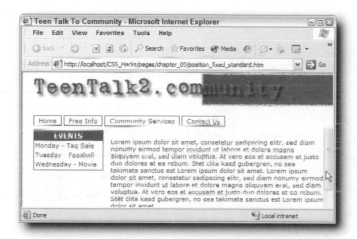

FIGURE 9-9: Even Internet Explorer can be made to display fixed elements properly with a little CSS hackery.

If your page is in quirks mode, you only need one conditional comment to affect all Internet Explorer versions:

```
<!--[if IE]>
<style type="text/css">
body {
        overflow: hidden;
}
div#content {
        height: 100%;
        overflow: auto;
}
</style>
<![endif]-->
```

Note Much of the technique discussed in this section is culled from the work by Anne van Kesteren, a designer in the Netherlands. He has numerous examples posted on his site at `http://annevankesteren.nl/archives/2004/07/fixed-positioning`.

Managing the Float

The float property is one of the most powerful in CSS, so it only makes sense that it is also one of the most problematic. Any element styled with a float value of left or right is moved to one side of its parent element, allowing the content of the parent to flow around it. In its simplest form, the float property mimics that of align when applied to images—but float is much more powerful. Many layout designs rely on the float property as a key element.

It will come as no surprise to hear that most of the problems with the float property stem from Internet Explorer on Windows. While the bugs are many, common solutions appear to solve a great deal of them. When you encounter an issue with floats, try these fixes first:

- If possible, always define a width or height dimension for the parent element containing a float. This is particularly important when the float touches a clearing element. The Holly Hack (which gives the parent of a floated element a height of 1%) resolves this problem for Internet Explorer on Windows; Internet Explorer 5 for Mac floats require an explicit width. The Holly Hack is detailed in Chapter 3.

- Although it is not always possible, you can avoid numerous issues when floating text elements by assigning a width to the element style.

- Conversely, avoiding widths on elements following floats also prevents display problems.

- If you're using negative margins on a float to create an effect such as the cut-out drop-cap in Figure 9-10, you might see a slight clipping of the text in Internet Explorer. To work around this issue, add position-relative to the floated style.

- To put space between floated text and the wrapping text, apply increased margin values to the float rather than on the text following the float. Unfortunately, Internet Explorer on Windows doubles the outside margin for floats. For example, if you use a float: left with a margin-left of 3 pixels, Internet Explorer renders that as 6 pixels. You can defeat the doubling up by adding a display: inline declaration to the float.

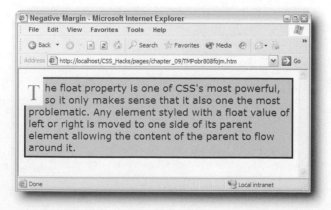

FIGURE 9-10: Floats can be positioned with negative margins to create cut-out effects—but you may run into problems with Internet Explorer.

A number of browser bugs appear when you attempt to *clear* a float. When a floated image or other element is placed before one or more paragraphs of text, the standard behavior is for the text to flow to the right or left of the floated element. If there is enough text, the words continue to wrap all the way around the image and then expand to the full width of the containing element. If you want to ensure that the next text or content does not wrap around the float, add a `clear` property to the style, like this: `clear: both`. The use of the `clear` property allows you to wrap some, but not all, content, as shown in Figure 9-11.

FIGURE 9-11: With the clear property applied, the quote will always display below the floated image.

It's important to understand what the `clear` property does, because it's handled differently in all modern browsers and Internet Explorer. When you apply a `clear` declaration to an element, the browser increases the top margin as much as necessary to push the cleared element below the floated element. When the cleared element is pushed down, it brings the surrounding container (if any) down with it. The problem emerges when you take the cleared element away—and Internet Explorer acts as if it is still there, as shown in Figure 9-12.

Naturally, this behavior could be standardized across browsers by simply adding a clearing element. However, one of the goals of good CSS practice is not to add unnecessary markup just for the sake of a fix. In addition to being inelegant, additional markup is a chore to manage and maintain. The ideal solution to this dilemma is to automatically add a clearing element that doesn't impact the page in any unwanted way.

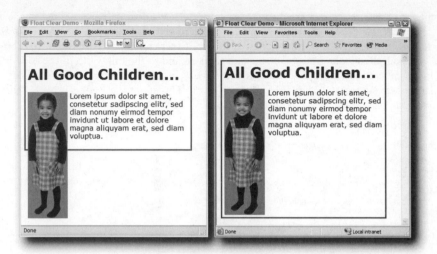

Figure 9-12: Even without a clearing element, Internet Explorer expands the container to enclose the float.

Designers John Gallant and Holly Bergevin have documented an excellent way to clear a float without additional markup. The key is the :after pseudo-element, which is used to generate a tiny bit of hidden content (a single period) that includes a clear: both declaration. The :after pseudo-element is used in conjunction with a defined class so that the style can be used as needed on a page. You'll need to make sure the class also has display: block declared as the default because display: inline does not work with the clear property.

```
.clearItem:after {
  content: ".";
  clear: both;
  height: 0;
  visibility: hidden;
  display: block;
}
```

The class is applied to the container element. Once both the CSS and the assigned class are in place, the container will expand around the float in all browsers, even ones like Firefox that follow the specifications closely (see Figure 9-13).

While this is a dramatic improvement over the previous solution of inserting a div tag with a clear property defined, there are a few complications. If your containing element does not include a width or height, Internet Explorer will not automatically wrap around the float. Moreover, Internet Explorer does not recognize the :after pseudo-element. A great way to handle this is with a variation on the Holly Hack (discussed in Chapter 3) applied to the previously styled clear class:

```
/* Start Commented Backslash Hack \*/
* html .clearItem, * html .clearItem * {height: 1%;}
/* Close Commented Backslash Hack */
```

FIGURE 9-13: With CSS inserting and then hiding generated content with a clear: both property, no additional clearing element markup is required to get the desired effect.

You'll remember that the Commented Backslash Hack (discussed in Chapter 3) is used to hide the style rule from Internet Explorer 5 for Mac. The bolded second selector in the Holly Hack ensures that any element within the container with the float also has the `height: 1%` declaration applied. This clears up any difficulties Internet Explorer has displaying the hover state of links without affecting any other aspect of the area.

One final hack is needed to bring Internet Explorer 5 for Mac into the fold. As with many other CSS displays, Internet Explorer 5 for Mac properly handles containers without floats, so it will not automatically enclose the float like Internet Explorer on Windows will. Unfortunately, it also does not understand the `:after` pseudo-element. To get the Mac browser to enclose the floated element, you'll need to add a `display: inline` to the clearing class—and then you'll need to reset it once again for the rest of the browsers. Luckily, part of the Holly Hack has the Mac filtering mechanism already built-in. Your relevant CSS will ultimately look like this:

```
.clearItem:after {
  content: ".";
  clear: both;
  height: 0;
  visibility: hidden;
  display: block;
}
```

```
.clearItem { display: inline; }

/* Start Commented Backslash Hack \*/
* html .clearItem, * html .clearItem * {height: 1%;}
.clearItem { display: block; }
/* Close Commented Backslash Hack */
```

Crafting Two- and Three-Column Designs

The primary CSS-related goal of designers these days is to completely replace table-based layout. Though tables still have their place within the layout, using them to structure the page is not one of them. Layouts, although widely varied in their final look, are largely based on a few core designs: two columns (with the main content area on the left or right) or three columns (with the main content in the middle). Often, these pages have a header that spans all columns.

In this section, you'll bring together what you've learned in this and earlier chapters to create basic layouts that look the same in all modern browsers and, if desired, as good as possible in Netscape 4.

Two-Column Layouts

Two-column layouts are very popular because they give prominence to two separate sections, while breaking up the page for greater visual interest. Often, designers use one column for navigation and another for their primary content; each column can, in turn, include other page elements for a varied look.

One of the two columns is almost always significantly smaller than the other. Two-column layouts equal in width are rare. Designers are equally split between placing the smaller of the two columns on either side. It's good to know how to do both to vary your sites. You'll also want to be able to create fixed-width layouts as well as layouts that expand or contract with the browser window. A layout that adjusts to the browser window size is said to be *liquid* or *fluid*. Once you have a basic structure and styles created, it's fairly easy to switch between fixed-width and fluid layouts.

Note Project Seven (http://www.projectseven.com) has been and continues to be a tremendous resource for CSS, especially for those designers using Dreamweaver. Much of the discussion in this section is based on their research.

Fixed Width, Main Content on Left

Let's start with a fixed-width, two-column design. The example page includes a header, a main content column on the left, and a sidebar column on the right. You'll need to create styles for each of the primary elements: #header, #mainColumn, and #sideColumn. To be able to position the side-by-side columns together, you'll also need a #wrapper style. All of these styles are applied to div tags to form the primary divisions of the page. Figure 9-14 shows the completed version.

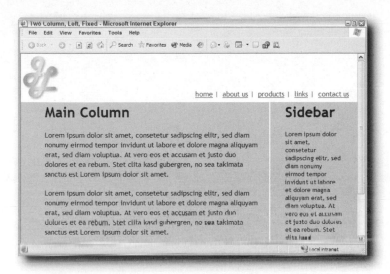

FIGURE 9-14: A wrapper helps to keep the columns centered.

In this design, the page's background color (as applied to the body tag) serves as the background for the content and sidebar. By using the page's background color for the columns, you don't have to worry about one column being shorter than the other—the color will always be consistent. The header is given another background color to differentiate it from the columns and it also includes a logo and some navigation. The header height matches that of the logo image, while the width is omitted and will be automatically adjusted to fill the page. To avoid a portion of the header's background color disappearing should the browser window be reduced to require a horizontal scroll bar, a minimum width is defined. You want to keep the header the true width of the wrapper, which you can calculate by adding its width plus the left and right padding (720 + 10 + 10 = 740 pixels). The header style looks like this:

```
#header {
    height: 110px;
    background-color: #FFFFFF;
    min-width: 740px;
}
```

The min-width property is not supported by Internet Explorer on Windows, so you'll need to take two actions to work around this problem. First, wrap the logo in the header in an h1 tag (you could use any block-level element). Second, in a conditional comment, set the width of the #header h1 selector to the same value as the minimum width:

```
<!--[if IE]>
<style type="text/css">
  #header h1 { width: 740px }
</style>
<![endif]-->
```

This page will require a number of CSS hacks for Internet Explorer. Ultimately, all of these could be put into an external style sheet and then linked to the page from within a conditional comment.

The #wrapper div that is placed around the two columns is given a fixed width and centered by setting the left and right margins to auto. A little bit of padding moves the content in equally on both sides:

```
#wrapper {
  width: 720px;
  margin: 0 auto;
  padding: 0 10px;
}
```

Internet Explorer 5 does not recognize the margin: 0 auto technique for centering page elements, so you'll have to add two rules to a conditional comment. The first centers all elements via the body tag with the text-align property and the second resets individual elements so that the element is centered, but the text is left-aligned:

```
<!--[if IE 5]>
<style type="text/css">
  #body { text-align: center }
  #header, #sideColumn, #mainColumn {
    text-align: left;
  }
</style>
<![endif]-->
```

Both of the columns are positioned using the float: right declaration and define pixel widths. By floating both elements, browsers render them tightly next to each other and padding is used to set the desired separation. For a page in which the sidebar is on the right, it comes first in the HTML (so it will appear furthest right) and it is padded on its left.

```
#sideColumn {
  float: right;
  width: 160px;
  padding: 0 0 0 15px;
  font-size: .9em;
}
```

The main content, which is displayed on the left, defines a similar padding on its opposite side to keep separation from the other column.

```
#mainColumn {
  float: right;
  width: 520px;
  margin: 0;
  padding: 0 15px 15px 0;
  border-right: 2px solid #fff;
  font-size: 1em;
}
```

A border is added on the right of the main column to delineate the two columns.

Folowing is a summary of this technique to highlight the key aspects for creating the fixed-width two-column layout in which the main column appears on the left side:

- *Wrapper*—Set at a specific pixel width equal to the true width of both columns, which includes their stated width, padding, and borders (if any). Centered using the margin auto method.

- *Main column*—Set at a specific pixel width, floated right, padded on the right, and uses a right border.

- *Sidebar column*—Also set at a specific pixel width and floated right. However, the padding appears on the left and no border is specified. The `div` containing the sidebar column must appear before the main column `div` in the HTML code.

Fixed Width, Main Content on Right

With the fixed-width page created, it's actually quite easy to manipulate the CSS to reverse the order of the columns. The `#header` and `#wrapper` styles stay the same, and only the `#mainColumn` and `#sideColumn` styles need to be altered in two key ways. The primary difference is that both styles, instead of floating right, are floated left. Because the `#sideColumn` `div` comes first in the HTML, it will be displayed all the way to the left.

The other changes are to the padding and border properties—in short, everything is switched to the opposite side. In the sidebar column (now on the left), the right side is padded, while in the main column (now on the right), the left side is padded. Also in the main column, the `border-right` property is changed to `border-left`. As you can see in Figure 9-15, these few alterations bring big results.

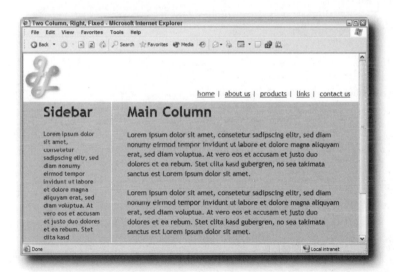

FIGURE 9-15: Switch the two-column styles to float left and reverse the padding to change the layout design.

Fluid Main Column on Right

To convert the fixed-width layout into a fluid one where the main column expands with the browser window, a different series of changes (although equally small) are needed. Three styles are affected: `#wrapper`, `#mainColumn`, and `#sideColumn`.

The #wrapper style, previously set to a pixel width equal to the size of the two columns, is now set to a width: auto. This allows the outer container to grow or shrink in size as dictated by the browser window width. Any additional padding or margins are removed.

```
#wrapper {
  width: auto;
}
```

Likewise, the fixed width is removed from the main column style. The margin property is used to position the column a specific distance from the left edge of the wrapper (which conforms to the browser window width). In this example, the left margin is 200 pixels. Again, a border-left property separates the columns.

```
#mainColumn {
  margin: 0 10px 0 200px;
  border-left: 2px solid #fff;
  font-size: 1em;
}
```

The sidebar retains its fixed width, but is positioned absolutely.

```
#sideColumn {
  position: absolute;
  top: 130px;
  left: 10px;
  width: 160px;
  font-size: .9em;
}
```

No additional CSS hacks are required to make the leap from fixed-width to fluid layout (see Figure 9-16).

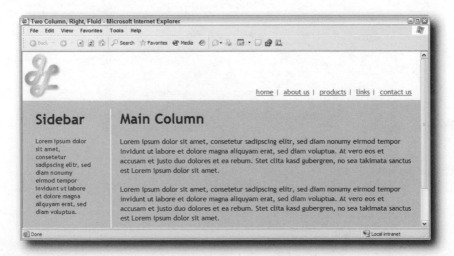

FIGURE 9-16: A fluid layout typically combines one or more static columns with one that grows as needed.

Three-Column Layouts

Once you've mastered two-column layouts (particularly the fluid version), it's a snap to move onto three columns, especially when the two side columns are static and the center fluid. You'll need a number of CSS hacks (especially for Internet Explorer 5 and 6 on Windows) to get the layout cross-browser compatible.

The concept is essentially the same as with the two-column, fluid layout—with a few twists to keep it interesting. For this layout, you'll need the same styles and divs as before: #wrapper, #mainColumn, and #sideColumn. For the sake of clarity, it's best to rename #sideColumn to #leftColumn. One additional style is needed: #rightColumn.

As discussed earlier in this chapter in the section "Position: Absolute," you'll assign a position: relative declaration to the #wrapper style. This declaration allows the two side columns (both absolutely positioned) to be placed correctly. Defining the minimum width keeps the fluid center section from being reduced undesirably.

```
#wrapper {
  width: auto;
  position: relative;
  min-width: 740px;
}
```

Again, to compensate for Internet Explorer's deficiencies, a block element within the center section (the h1 heading) is given a width. This declaration will occur within the conditional comment discussed later in this section.

Both #leftColumn and #rightColumn have a fixed width in addition to being absolutely positioned. The column on the left derives its position from the top and left edge of the wrapper, while the right-side column relies on the top and right edge.

```
#leftColumn {
  position: absolute;
  top: 0px;
  left: 10px;
  width: 160px;
  font-size: .9em;
}

#rightColumn {
  position: absolute;
  top: 0px;
  right: 10px;
  width: 160px;
  font-size: .9em;
}
```

The center column that contains the main content is anchored by the two static side columns. When the browser window is resized, the center adjusts its width, according to the amount of space left by the left and right columns. This size adjustment and initial position is determined by the margin settings. The left and right margins are calculated from the width of the static columns, plus their left and right positioning, as well as the center column's padding and border widths.

```
#mainColumn {
  margin: 0 182px 0 184px;
  padding: 0 10px;
  border-left: 2px solid #fff;
  border-right: 2px solid #fff;
  font-size: 1em;
}
```

That's all that's needed for modern browsers. But what's needed to get the design to work cross-browser? Internet Explorer will have a number of issues to deal with:

- Internet Explorer 5 will misrepresent the Box Model and the two-static-column width will need to be adjusted.

- All layout styles (`#wrapper`, `#mainColumn`, `#leftColumn`, and `#rightColumn`) need the Holly Hack to display properly in Internet Explorer 5 and greater.

- As noted earlier, the `min-width` property work-around must be defined for the `h1` element in the center column.

Building a Basic Netscape-Friendly Layout: Another Approach

Although CSS2 wasn't recommended by the W3C until well after Netscape 4 was on the market, the browser does support the `position` property to a limited degree. To create a two-column layout with the main content on the left in Netscape 4 (and all modern browsers as well), you'll need to structure your page somewhat more simply than if you were targeting only the more modern browsers. Suppose you want to create a fluid two-column layout with a header and primary content on the left. The key technique is to set the left column `width` to a percentage and the absolutely positioned right column `left` value a slightly higher percentage. For example, if the left column was 70% wide, the right column's left value would be 71%. These two declarations will create a small separation between the columns and keep them fluid (see Figure 9-17). Your core styles would look like this:

```
#header {

    height: 100px;

    margin: 0;

    padding: 10px 0 0 0;

}

#leftContent {

    width: 70%;

    margin: 0;
```

```
        padding: 0;

}

#rightContent {

        position: absolute;

        left: 71%;

        margin: 0 0 10px;

}
```

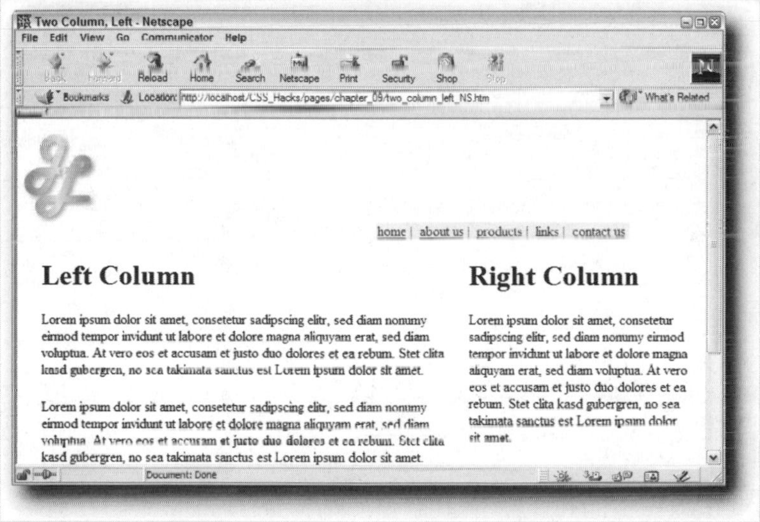

FIGURE 9-17: Create a two-column layout that works in all released browsers,
starting with Netscape 4.

In the HTML, it's important that the `#rightContent` div appears before the `#leftContent`
div; if the placement is reversed, the right column will appear below the left column, not side-
by-side.

If your implementation calls for more advanced features that Netscape cannot support, your
best course is to attach two style sheets to the page, one for Netscape and another for more
modern browsers, as described in Chapter 2.

You can find an all-round good source for Netscape 4.x layouts at http://www.realworldstyle.
com/.

Perhaps the best way to handle all of these problems is to use two conditional comments, one for Internet Explorer 5 specifically and another for Internet Explorer 5 and above:

```
<!--[if IE 5]>
<style>
  #leftColumn, #rightColumn {width: 170px;}
</style>
<![endif]-->
<!--[if gte IE 5]>
<style>
  #wrapper, #mainColumn, #leftColumn, #rightColumn {
    height: 1%;
  }
  #mainColumn h1 { width: 740px }
</style>
<![endif]-->
```

When all the code is in place, you'll have a very flexible three-column layout, as shown in Figure 9-18.

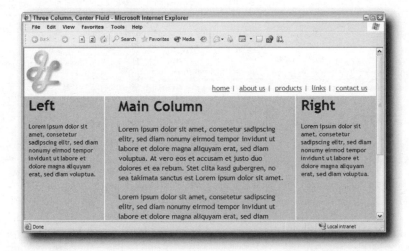

FIGURE 9-18: To get the three-column layout to work properly in Internet Explorer, you'll need a series of CSS hacks.

Placing Footers Correctly

There are essentially two different types of footers: one that appears at the bottom of the longest content and another that is set to the bottom of the viewport, regardless. Both, separately, are fairly easy to achieve. To put a footer beneath the main content, you simply include a separate `div` as a footer at the end of that content. The `position: fixed` property, as discussed earlier, can be used to keep a footer constantly at the window bottom.

The ideal footer, however, incorporates both behaviors. When the content is longer than the viewport, you'd scroll down to see the footer at the end. But when the content is shorter, the footer is always visible, as shown in Figure 9-19.

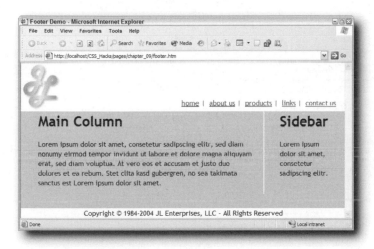

FIGURE 9-19: When the length of the content is shorter than the window, the footer is displayed.

You can incorporate the ideal footer into your pages by creating a parallel container for the page and positioning the footer absolutely within it (at the bottom). You'll also need to ensure that the container is at least as tall as the viewport's height. The first chore is accomplished with two new styles and matching `div`s:

```
#page {
    position: absolute;
    top: 0;
    left: 0;
}
#footer {
    position: absolute;
    bottom: 0;
    width: 100%;
    background-color: #FFFFFF;
}
```

The `#page div` wraps around all the content in the `body` tag, essentially becoming a substitute for the document window. The `#footer div` is placed at the bottom of the HTML, just before the closing tag of the `#page div`.

To ensure the #page container is the same height as the viewport, regardless of the length of the content, the min-height property is used. This works well for Gecko-based browsers (and recently, Safari), but fails in Internet Explorer on Windows. However, the height property in Internet Explorer delivers the same functionality.

```
html, body, #page {
    min-height: 100%;
    width: 100%;
    height: 100%;
}
```

The task now is to reset the height for all non–Internet Explorer browsers. The Child Selector Hack provides just the filter needed:

```
html>body, html>body #page {
    height: auto;
}
```

Some browsers (including earlier versions of Safari) that don't support min-height or apply height like Internet Explorer will not put the footer at the bottom of the viewport when the content is short. Instead, the footer will always appear beneath the longest content.

Centering Page Layouts

CSS hacks aren't always obscure combinations of characters capitalizing on uninterpreted properties. Sometimes a hack is just a particular method or technique that gets a result heretofore thought unobtainable. Centering an item on the page (both horizontally and vertically in the browser), while a piece of cake with tables, has long been elusive in CSS—until a particular hack was found. This particular technique was uncovered and documented by Joe Gillespie, whose site, Web Page Design for Designers (http://www.wpdfd.com/editorial/wpd0103.htm#toptip), has been a valuable resource for years.

You've already seen numerous examples of how easy it is to center an element horizontally. Combining a margin-left: auto with a margin-right: auto (or use the shorthand version, margin: 0 auto) declaration causes almost all modern browsers to take the horizontal space available, split it, and make the side margins equal. Unfortunately, the equivalent declaration to create vertical centering doesn't work.

Note This technique is for fifth-generation browsers and above. If you must center an item for Netscape 4, you'll need to use a combination of tables and the valign attribute.

To center an element on a page both vertically and horizontally, you'll need two styles. The first is applied directly to the element to be centered, while the second wraps around it. The inner style, #content in this example, is positioned absolutely 50% from the left with the top and margin-left values set at a negative amount equal to one-half the centered element's width. For example, if you're trying to center an image that is 396 pixels wide by 396 pixels high, your style rule will look like this:

```
#content {
     height: 396px;
     width: 396px;
     margin-left: -198px;
     top: -198px;
     position: absolute;
     left: 50%;
}
```

The outer style (named #wrapper here) is also absolutely positioned with a top value at 50%; however, that's pretty much the only expected declaration. The width is defined at 100% with a 1-pixel height. Finally, the overflow property is declared to be visible.

```
#wrapper {
     overflow: visible;
     position: absolute;
     height: 1px;
     width: 100%;
     top: 50%;
}
```

What's really interesting about the technique (apart from the results evident in Figure 9-20) is that the outer wrapper is completely generic as far as the positioning elements are concerned. You only have to relate the dimensions of the centered object to the inner style.

FIGURE 9-20: Applying two different styles to divs, enclosing the image, centers the bull's-eye in both directions.

Building Navigation Systems

By far, the bulk of the navigation in use today on the Web is based on JavaScript routines used for swapping two or more images, depending on the visitor's interaction. CSS-based navigation, however, is on the rise, as designers discover the inherent advantages to using CSS.

Perhaps the biggest benefit is speed. The pure CSS menu loads much faster than graphic-based menus. Although button graphics tend to be small, the sheer number of images involved (one per menu item for every mouse state) can increase the page download time significantly. A navigation bar (or *navbar*) with five menu items (each with a different image for link, active, hover, and visited states) requires 20 separate images, in addition to the graphics for the containing element. The same design rendered in CSS may require anywhere from four images to a single image.

CSS also brings enhanced accessibility to the navigation table. Most CSS navigation bars rely on styled unordered lists that can be easily rescaled along with the rest of the page for increased readability. Moreover, screen readers will never have to hunt for `alt` text with CSS-based navigation— and designers won't have to remember to put it in.

Unfortunately, pure CSS navigation menus can only go so far. A major inability of Internet Explorer prevents anything beyond single-level navigation from being constructed using only CSS definitions. However, combining CSS with a minimum amount of JavaScript provides the best of both worlds: CSS sleekness and accessibility, along with advanced, flexible functionality.

Designing CSS Navigation Bars

The primary goal with CSS navigation is to take ordinary text and convert it into a linked button. When the user's mouse hovers over the button, a state change takes place, which alters either the graphic background or the label in the foreground (or both). A series of such buttons makes up a navigation bar, which can be positioned vertically or horizontally on the page.

Although almost any linked block element styled correctly could function as a button, unordered lists are really the perfect fit. More complex navigation areas on a page include subcategories, and may include sub-subcategories. Lists are ideal for conveying this type of expandable, nested structure. For older browsers, CSS-based navigation degrades gracefully into an easily understood unordered list of links.

Both of the following sections (one for vertical navigation bars and the other for horizontal) are built upon lists. Only relatively minor changes are required to switch the navigation bar orientation. Once again, the CSS hacks necessary to get navigation working across modern browsers are primarily applied for Internet Explorer's sake. The hacks are slightly different for the two variations.

Vertical Navigation

The CSS buttons created in this section are comprised of three parts: the HTML list, the CSS styles, and the background images. Although you can build navigation buttons out of pure CSS and HTML, to get the most flexibility in your navigation design, you'll need to create graphic assets, typically one for each state represented. Unlike with graphics-based buttons, these images are only used in the background of the button, and the label is CSS-styled text.

The first step is to make (in your favorite graphics program) a rectangle for each navigation state used. In this example, two states are used: up (the normal button condition) and over (or hover) position. The over state is also used to represent the selected button of the current page in a navigation bar. It's generally a good idea to create your rectangles larger than you would normally. An oversize graphic allows for expansion when the text is rescaled to be larger. The rectangles shown in Figure 10-1 are 300 pixels wide by 60 pixels high, even though the default dimensions will be 200 pixels by 22 pixels.

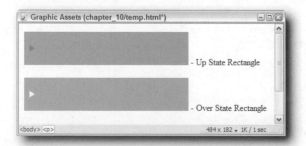

FIGURE **10-1: Create oversize rectangles in contrasting designs to use as the background of CSS navigation buttons.**

Note If your graphics include a square, triangle, or other symbol that is intended to align with the text, center the symbol vertically at either end of the image. Should the text be rescaled, the symbol will be placed properly.

After saving the rectangles as separate images in a Web-oriented format (GIF, JPEG, or possibly PNG), you're ready to define the CSS styles. The techniques used here are really intended to represent a navigation bar in the more modern browsers, and so an external style sheet should be imported rather than linked. This technique then degrades gracefully and displays a bulleted list of links in Netscape 4.

The next (and simplest) element to create and examine is the HTML. An unordered list, consisting of a series of links, is placed within a `div` tag with the `id` of `navholder`.

```
<div id="navholder">
  <ul>
    <li><a href="home.htm">Home</a></li>
    <li><a href="prod.htm">Products</a></li>
    <li><a href="serv.htm">Services</a></li>
    <li><a href="about.htm">About</a></li>
  </ul>
</div>
```

Note You can add as many list items as necessary to create the navigation bar. All list items, however, must be wrapped within an `a` tag and linked to another page or to a null value (such as `javascript:;`).

The first CSS rule creates a containing style that is required to hold the navigation buttons together in a series. Although a variety of techniques can be used to place the navigation bar, one method is to float the navigation holder to the left or right within another wrapper. In this scenario, the wrapper also contains the main content section. For a vertical navigation bar, you also want to establish the initial button width:

```
#navholder {
  float: left;
  width: 200px;
  font-family: Geneva, Arial, Helvetica, sans-serif;
  font-size: 0.8em;
}
```

The next style defined removes the bullets and the standard indentation from the unordered list. You'll need to specify both margin and padding as zero to handle the indent properly for the range of browsers. Set `margin` at 0 pixels to affect Internet Explorer and Opera, and `padding` to 0 pixels for Gecko-based browsers.

```
#navholder ul {
  margin: 0px;
  padding: 0px;
  list-style-type: none;
}
```

Tighten the space around the list items by setting its `margin` to 0 as well:

```
#navholder li {
  margin: 0px;
}
```

The next style is what really turns the linked list into a series of buttons. The basic goal is to change an everyday, run-of-the-mill link into a clickable button area. This is accomplished with the first `important` declaration, which changes any a tag within the navigation container from an inline element to a block element. Once the a tag is a block element, you can assign an image to its background to form the button's graphic. The up state graphic is applied to the generic a tag. To account for potential text rescaling, the background is positioned at 0 percent horizontally and 50 percent vertically. Padding is used to place the text correctly in relation to the graphic. In the example shown in Figure 10-2, a left padding of 25 pixels keeps the text from overlapping the triangle symbol. Finally, a border is assigned to the left, right, and bottom of the a tag's block area—the top border is intentionally omitted to avoid double lines on the buttons.

FIGURE 10-2: Even though the link is very plain at this stage, the entire button area is active.

```
#navholder a {
     display: block;
     background-image: url(../images/up_btn.gif);
     background-repeat: no-repeat;
     background-position: 0% 50%;
     background-color: #599D7E;
     padding: 4px 4px 4px 25px;
     border-right: 1px solid #000000;
     border-left: 1px solid #666666;
     border-bottom: 1px solid #000000;
}
```

Besides the extended link area, a button's other main characteristic is interactivity. Interactivity is handled by specifying styles for the various a tag pseudo-classes: `a:link`, `a:visited`, `a:hover`, and `a:active`. Here, the approach is to present one color of text for the up state (as represented by the `a:link` and `a:visited` pseudo-classes), and another for the over state (`a:hover` and `a:active`). In addition, the background image is changed in the over state. In all instances, the standard underline is removed by setting `text-decoration` to none.

```
#navholder a:link, #navholder a:visited {
  color: #FFFFFF;
```

```
    text-decoration: none;
}
#navholder a:hover, #navholder a:active {
    color: #000000;
    background-image: url(../images/over_btn.gif);
    background-repeat: no-repeat;
    background-position: 0% 50%;
    text-decoration: none;
}
```

One final style is required to replicate common navigation bar functionality. To indicate which page the user is currently on, the up state of the relevant button is altered. While it could be set to a completely different background than seen before, the approach taken in this example (to use the over state background) is not uncommon. To be able to switch the selected link from one page to another, a new id style is created (here, #sellink) and the desired declarations applied to all the ID's pseudo-classes. This locks the button into one look, regardless of the user's mouse position.

```
#sellink a:link, #sellink a:visited, #sellink a:hover, #sellink
a:active {
    color: #000000;
    background-image: url(../images/over_btn.gif);
    background-repeat: no-repeat;
    background-position: 0% 50%;
    text-decoration: none;
}
```

To address issues across the board in modern versions of Internet Explorer, you'll need to address versions 5 and 6 separately. Neither version extends the clickable region beyond the linked text. This can be fixed by assigning a height to the a tag, which causes Internet Explorer to reassess how far the a tag block element extends. The height: 1 em declaration also eliminates the substantial gap between the list item buttons in Internet Explorer 6, but you'll need to specify several more values for Internet Explorer 5 to work properly. The most straightforward way to handle these CSS hacks is through the use of separate conditional comments for each version.

```
<!--[if IE 5]>
  <style>
    #navholder a {
      height: 1em;
      float: left;
      clear: both;
      width: 100%;
    }
  </style>
<![endif]-->
<!--[if IE 6]>
  <style>
    #navholder a { height: 1em; }
  </style>
<![endif]-->
```

When the CSS hacks are inserted, the CSS-based vertical navigation bar works the same across all modern browsers (see Figure 10-3).

FIGURE 10-3: CSS hacks bring button-like behavior to linked lists, even in Internet Explorer.

Horizontal Navigation

Changing your CSS navigation system from a vertical to horizontal orientation really demonstrates the power of Cascading Style Sheets. Essentially, you only need to minimally adjust three CSS styles—two of which only need a change to one declaration—and the required hack.

The first CSS style that must be altered to go horizontal is the one that wraps around the navigation system. You'll recall that with a vertical navbar, a fixed pixel width was used for the `#navholder` rule. For the horizontal version, the width is set to 100 percent; this value allows for any necessary expansion caused by text rescaling for accessibility. The `#navholder` rule now looks like this:

```
#navholder {
    float: left;
    width: 100%;
    font-family: Geneva, Arial, Helvetica, sans-serif;
    font-size: 0.8em;
}
```

More extensive modifications are needed for the list items within the navigation container. To align the list items in a row, the `float: left` declaration is applied in combination with a `white-space: nowrap`. A margin setting adds a bit of room between the text and the bottom of the button, while zeroing out all other settings. Again, the `padding` is set to 0 for Gecko-based browsers.

```
#navholder li {
    float: left;
    white-space: nowrap;
```

```
    margin: 0 0 1em 0;
    padding: 0;
}
```

One final CSS rule is changed to flip the buttons from vertical to horizontal. In the `#navholder a` selector's style, the `display: block` declaration is removed. If left in place, this declaration would keep the buttons stacked one on top of another. In the same selector, the right padding is increased significantly. This alteration increases the size of the buttons and ensures that there is enough room between the text of one button and the start of another.

```
#navholder a {
    background-image: url(../images/up_btn.gif);
    background-repeat: no-repeat;
    background-position: 0% 50%;
    background-color: #599D7E;
    padding: 4px 50px 4px 25px;
    border-right: 1px solid #000000;
    border-left: 1px solid #666666;
    border-bottom: 1px solid #000000;
}
```

The two conditional comments can be combined into one for the horizontal navbar. The key declaration here is to set the `position` property to `relative`.

```
<!--[if gte IE 5]>
<style>
  #navholder a  {
    position: relative;
    height: 1em;
  }
</style>
<![endif]-->
```

With just these few changes in place, the same HTML content can be represented totally differently, as shown in Figure 10-4.

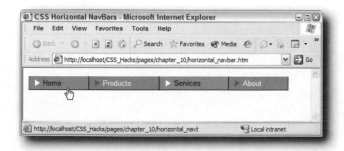

FIGURE 10-4: The horizontal CSS navigation doesn't remotely resemble the bulleted list it is based on.

Creating Multilevel Drop-Downs

The larger a site grows, the greater the need to extend the navigation. A standard solution is to create hierarchical menus. These menus allow visitors to drill down through a range of categories, reveal any subcategories for a particular selection, and choose an item from the subcategory list. One way to depict such hierarchical menus is through an expanded navigation bar with as many drop-down (or fly-out) submenus as needed.

Any attempt to expand the pure CSS navigation system described in the previous sections into multilevel drop-downs hits a major blockade with Internet Explorer. No number of CSS declarations applied in a conditional comment or other CSS hack is sufficient to overcome Internet Explorer's lack of support for pseudo-classes beyond the a tag. To enable CSS-based drop-down lists for Internet Explorer, you'll need to incorporate another technology, either JavaScript or Internet Explorer proprietary behaviors. This example demonstrates how the goal is accomplished using JavaScript. The techniques and JavaScript described here are based on the work of Patrick Griffeths and Dan Webb (`http://www.htmldog.com/articles/suckerfish/dropdowns/`).

Note If you're interested in exploring the method that uses Internet Explorer's proprietary behaviors, you'll find a good example at `http://www.xs4all.nl/~peterned/examples/cssmenu.html`. If you decide to go this route, keep in mind that XP Service Pack 2 requires the MIME type set to `text/x-component` for `.htc` files.

The HTML list structure really proves its worth when the navigation expands to multilevel drop-downs. The key is to nest unordered lists with the parent list item. In the following code, used throughout this example, unordered lists are nested two deep, one under the Products category and another under Gadgets:

```
<ul id="nav">
  <li><a href="#">Home</a></li>
  <li><a href="#">Products</a>
    <ul>
      <li><a href="#">Widgets</a></li>
      <li><a href="#">Gadgets</a>
        <ul>
          <li><a href="#">Gadget 1</a></li>
          <li><a href="#">Gadget 2</a></li>
          <li><a href="#">Gadget 3</a></li>
        </ul>
      </li>
      <li><a href="#">Gidgets</a></li>
    </ul>
  </li>
  <li><a href="#">Services</a></li>
  <li><a href="#">About</a></li>
</ul>
```

The outermost ul tag is given an ID (here, nav) to help specify the required CSS selectors. With the ID attribute in place, you can pinpoint ul and li tags at any level. The first task is to establish the general guidelines for any ul tags within the navigation, including the primary one, #nav. In addition to removing the bullets from the unordered lists and establishing baseline values for padding, margin, and width, the line-height property is set to 1. This declaration overcomes a problem that keeps the nested ul tags from aligning properly. The width of these outer containing elements is determined by the number of main menu items. With four menu items, the width value is 60em; if you had five, the value would more likely be 72em.

```
#nav, #nav ul {
  list-style: none;
  padding: 0;
  margin: 0 0 1em 0;
  width: 60em;
  line-height: 1;
}
```

The list items within all the navigation lists are then floated to the left and kept from wrapping, with minimal margins and padding:

```
#nav li {
  float: left;
  white-space: nowrap;
  margin: 0;
  padding: 0;
  width: 10em;
}
```

To ensure that all the button items are sized the same, a set width is provided for all the a tags within the #nav ID. You'll also need to set the display property to block to achieve the full button-clickable area.

```
#nav a {
  background-color: #599D7E;
  padding: 4px 50px 4px 25px;
  border-right: 1px solid #000000;
  border-left: 1px solid #666666;
  border-bottom: 1px solid #000000;
  display: block;
  width: 10em;
  w\idth: 6em;
}
```

Note the use of the Selector Hack to set a smaller width value for Gecko-based browsers, Internet Explorer, and Safari. The larger width is applied by Internet Explorer 5.x to overcome its misrendering. This technique is used throughout this code.

It's considered a best practice to indicate the availability of any submenus in some way. If your design doesn't call for background images for the buttons, you can use CSS to display such a symbol whenever needed. In addition to the graphic itself, you'll need a CSS class defined that sets the background image to align vertically in the center and to the right, horizontally, like this:

```
#nav a.parentItem {
  background: url(../../images/right_triangle.gif) center right
no-repeat;
}
```

Any buttons with submenus should be given the class of parentItem.

Note For this example, the background images and properties applied to the navigation menus in the previous sections were removed.

If you test your page at this point, all the menu items (including the items intended to be hidden until dropped down) are displayed, as shown in Figure 10-5.

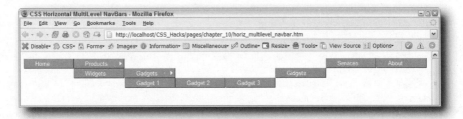

FIGURE **10-5:** The navbar is undesirably spread out because the submenus are still visible. Note the parent items with the right-facing triangle.

To hide and reveal the submenus interactively, you'll need to define a series of CSS rules that rely on the nested li tag's :hover pseudo-class. Because Internet Explorer does not support pseudo-classes on anything except the a tag, it's time to introduce the needed JavaScript. The following script, adapted from the code developed by Griffeths and Webb, programmatically gives each list item within the #nav container a class, subHover. Internet Explorer has no problem styling list items with a standard class. The beauty of this script is that although small (only 12 lines), it applies to all submenu items, regardless of how deep.

```
<script type="text/javascript">
subHover = function() {
    var subEls =
document.getElementById("nav").getElementsByTagName("LI");
    for (var i=0; i<subEls.length; i++) {
        subEls[i].onmouseover=function() {
            this.className+=" subhover";
        }
        subEls[i].onmouseout=function() {
            this.className=this.className.replace(new RegExp("
subhover\\b"), "");
```

```
                }
            }
}
if (window.attachEvent) window.attachEvent("onload", subHover);
</script>
```

JavaScript alone won't do the trick, however. You must define a few CSS rules with some very precise selectors to pull it all together. By default, any nested unordered lists within the navigation should be hidden. As noted elsewhere in this book (for example, see the section "Implementing Flash Replacement" in Chapter 7), the most effective way to hide elements visually and still keep them accessible to screen readers is to position them off-screen to the left. You'll need to set the `position: absolute` declaration to make sure the elements are placed properly, as in this style:

```
#nav li ul {
    position: absolute;
    left: -999em;
    height: auto;
    width: 8em;
    margin: 0;
}
```

While hiding all the nested `ul` tags in one default style is perfectly okay, revealing them all at once is not. You don't, after all, want to show both levels of menus when you hover over the button for just the first. Consequently, a style is defined that moves any nested `ul` tags below the current one off-screen. Because the `li:hover` pseudo-class is required for this selector, you'll also need to include its Internet Explorer equivalent that uses the JavaScript-inserted subhover class.

```
#nav li:hover ul ul, #nav li.subhover ul ul {
    left: -999em;
}
```

To reveal the desired submenu, the `left` property is set to `auto` for items that are being hovered over and their immediately nested `ul` tags. The `left: auto` declaration brings the list buttons back into the proper position. Again, selectors for both `li:hover` and `li.subhover` are used.

```
#nav li:hover ul, #nav li li:hover ul, #nav li.subhover ul, #nav
li li.subhover ul {
    left: auto;
}
```

Note If you expand beyond a two-level-deep drop-down menu, you must add additional selectors to both hide and show the menus. For example, to add another submenu to this example, the CSS rules would look like this (additional material bolded for emphasis):

```
#nav li:hover ul ul, #nav li:hover ul ul ul, #nav li.subhover ul
ul, #nav li.subhover ul ul ul, {
    left: -999em;
}
```

```
#nav li:hover ul, #nav li li:hover ul, #nav li li li:hover ul,
#nav li.subhover ul, #nav li li.subhover ul, #nav li li
li.subhover ul {
     left: auto;
}
```

Although the interactivity is handled, to get the right look, you must style the nested list items, anchor tags, and unordered lists. The following rules work well for the example menu (see Figure 10-6):

```
#nav li li {
  padding-right: 0;
  width: 8em;
}


#nav li ul a {
  width: 10em;
  w\idth: 4em;
}


#nav li ul ul {
  margin: -1.75em 0 0 11em;
}
```

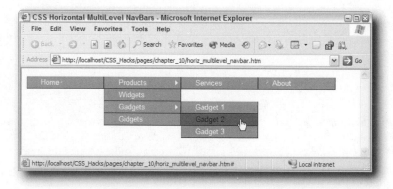

FIGURE 10-6: JavaScript and creative CSS render this drop-down menu properly across all modern browsers.

Naturally, your own CSS styles will vary in width and margin settings to get the optimum fit.

Crafting CSS Tabs

Tabs provide another approach to the problem of multitiered navigation. This type of navigation system relies on the folder tab metaphor. Here, the visitor switches from one main category page to another by clicking on a tab representation. Any subcategories appear below the primary categories, usually in a single line. The technique outlined in this section uses CSS only—no JavaScript is required—with a minimal number of hacks to bring Internet Explorer into line.

Note Many talented designers have created tabbed navigation examples in CSS. Much of the technique covered in this section is based on the work by Adam Kalsey (`http://www.kalsey.com/tools/csstabs/`).

A key benefit to this style of CSS tabbed navigation is compactness. The complete HTML code for navigation (including all categories and subcategories) can be included on every page. The CSS is designed to highlight the tab for the page's primary category and only show the related subcategories. Best of all, the navigation is structured as a highly accessible unordered list, which degrades gracefully to a series of links in older browsers. Here, for example, is the HTML for a site with four main categories, two of which have subcategories:

```html
<ul id="nav">
  <li id="cat1"><a href="#">Home</a></li>
  <li id="cat2"><a href="tabs_products.htm">Products</a>
    <ul id="subcat2">
      <li><a href="#">Widgets</a></li>
      <li><a href="#">Gadgets</a></li>
      <li><a href="#">Gidgets</a></li>
    </ul>
  </li>
  <li id="cat3"><a href="tabs_services.htm">Services</a>
    <ul id="subcat3">
      <li><a href="#">In Office</a></li>
      <li><a href="#">In Home</a></li>
      <li><a href="#">Online</a></li>
    </ul>
  </li>
  <li id="cat4"><a href="#">About</a></li>
</ul>
```

You'll notice that each of the main categories, represented by `li` tags, includes an `id` attribute (cat1, cat2, and so on). Likewise, the two subcategories are identified with their own `id` values, subcat2 and subcat3. The CSS used in this technique relies heavily on being able to pinpoint individual sections via precise selectors. The `id` attribute makes this possible.

As in previous topics in this chapter, the top-level `ul` tag is also given an `id`, nav. The CSS sets the font characteristics for all the main categories as well as the subcategories initially. From a design standpoint, the #nav style is used to establish a common bottom border that will visually tie the primary category tabs together. A `padding-bottom` value positions the border appropriately. The `padding-bottom` value will need to be adjusted for Internet Explorer.

```css
#nav {
  margin : 0;
  font-family: "Trebuchet MS", Arial, sans-serif;
  font-size: 1.25em;
  font-weight: bold;
```

```
  padding-left : 10px;
  padding-bottom : 20px;
  border-bottom: 5px solid #990000;
}
```

The next CSS rule removes the bullets from the unordered list and sets up a linear display. The `margin` and `padding` attributes are zeroed out to provide a baseline from which to position the elements.

```
#nav ul, #nav li  {
  display : inline;
  list-style-type : none;
  margin : 0;
  padding : 0;
}
```

Next, the basic links are styled. A background color (the same as the previously defined bottom border) is applied to achieve a tab-like appearance (see Figure 10-7). The size of the tab is controlled by the `padding` and `line-height`. To represent interactivity, a `:hover` pseudo-class is defined that changes the font color for the main category tabs.

FIGURE 10-7: Combining restyled bulleted list items with a bottom border gives a tab-like appearance.

```
#nav a:link, #nav a:visited  {
  color : #FFFFFF;
  float : left;
  font-size : small;
  line-height : 1.5em;
  margin-right : 8px;
  padding : 2px 10px 2px 10px;
  text-decoration : none;
  background-color: #990000;
}
```

```
#nav a:hover   {
  color : #66FFFF;
}
```

 Note Although this example uses only background and foreground colors, you could easily add background images to these style rules. Any images used should be created oversized to handle rescaled text correctly.

At this stage of development, all the main category buttons look the same. An important aspect of this type of navigation is a clear indication of the current page. You want the tab of the current page to stand out. To achieve this effect (and retain code compactness and portability), you must add a `class` attribute to the `body` tag that identifies the page, like this:

```
<body class="category2">
```

This class is then referenced in the CSS so that whenever a particular page is rendered, its related tab is highlighted. Here's what the CSS rule looks like:

```
body.category1 #nav li#cat1 a,
body.category2 #nav li#cat2 a,
body.category3 #nav li#cat3 a,
body.category4 #nav li#cat4 a {
  background : #fff;
  color : #000;
  border-top-width: 1px;
  border-right-width: 1px;
  border-left-width: 1px;
  border-top-style: solid;
  border-right-style: solid;
  border-left-style: solid;
  border-top-color: #990000;
  border-right-color: #990000;
  border-left-color: #990000;
}
```

In addition to altering the background and font color of the tab, a border is drawn on three sides: top, left, and right. The bottom is intentionally left out so that the design resembles a currently selected folder tab, as shown in Figure 10-8.

The subcategories are next on the list for styling. Initially, these nested unordered lists are hidden. In other sections of this chapter, the secondary navigation links were placed off to the left for accessibility reasons. However, for this type of navigation, only the current page's subcategories are desired. A masking technique is used, which also hides the unneeded subcategories from screen readers, as well as the visual display.

```
#nav #subcat1,
#nav #subcat2,
#nav #subcat3,
#nav #subcat4 {
  display : none;
}
```

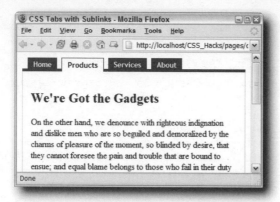

FIGURE 10-8: The highlighted tab changes according to which class is assigned to the body tag. Here, the class is set to category2, Products.

The next step is to define the CSS rules governing the selected subcategories. Again, the class of the body tag determines which nested list is actually rendered with the defined styles. When displayed, the secondary navigation will also be inline, but without the box-like background and a slightly smaller font, as shown in Figure 10-9.

FIGURE 10-9: A different sub-navigation (or none at all) is automatically shown depending on which tab is clicked.

```
body.category1 #nav ul#subcat1,
body.category2 #nav ul#subcat2,
body.category3 #nav ul#subcat3,
body.category4 #nav ul#subcat4 {
```

```
        display : inline;
        left : 10px;
        position : absolute;
        top : 35px;
}

body.category1 #nav ul#subcat1 a,
body.category2 #nav ul#subcat2 a,
body.category3 #nav ul#subcat3 a,
body.category4 #nav ul#subcat4 a {
        background : #fff;
        border left : 1px solid #ccc;
        color : #990000;
        font-weight : normal;
        line-height : 1.2em;
        margin-right : 4px;
        padding : 2px 10px 2px 10px;
        text-decoration : none;
        border: none;
}
```

One final style rule, which sets the :hover color for the subcategories, completes the navigation section of the page. The !important declaration is used to make sure the change is applied.

```
#nav ul a:hover {
        color : #0066FF!important;
}
```

Only a couple of CSS hacks are required to make this navigation work well in Internet Explorer. First, the padding-bottom property is slightly increased (here, by 3 pixels) to compensate for rendering differences. Next, the current subcategories are moved down an equal amount. Both modifications can easily be enclosed in an Internet Explorer conditional comment and your navigation is ready to go (see Figure 10-10).

```
<!--[if IE]>
<style type="text/css">
#nav {
        padding-bottom : 23px;
}
body.category1 #nav ul#subcat1,
body.category2 #nav ul#subcat2,
body.category3 #nav ul#subcat3,
body.category4 #nav ul#subcat4 {
        top : 38px;
}
</style>
<![endif]-->
```

FIGURE 10-10: With the CSS hack in place, the resulting page works as expected, cross-browser.

Troubleshooting CSS

As day follows night, bugs follow CSS-based Web pages—or maybe they just seem inevitable. Although the actual writing of HTML markup and CSS styles can be accomplished with nothing more than a text editor such as Notepad or Simple Text, the actual achievement of satisfactory pages across target browsers is anything but simple. Testing (and especially debugging) CSS-based Web pages is an essential—and often painful—step prior to pushing the site live.

The goal of this chapter is to reduce the duration and stress of CSS-related bug hunting as much as possible. In addition to addressing a specific major Internet Explorer failing (known as the *flash of unstyled content*), this chapter also lays out a general debugging strategy. Finally, you'll find a checklist of the most common bugs and their solutions.

Avoiding the Flash of Unstyled Content

Only Web designers understand that a Web page exists in the dimension of time as well as the two-dimensional (2D) world of the browser window. Any designer who experiences a site over a slow dial-up connection will attest that the time a page takes to display is significant. Generally, CSS-based layouts load much faster than table-based ones. Unfortunately, the speed at which a site appears is not the designer's only concern. How the page is loaded and rendered has also become an issue.

Under certain conditions, users of Internet Explorer browsers (versions 5 and greater) will experience a moment where the raw, unstyled page is visible shortly before the CSS styles are applied. This *flash of unstyled content* (FOUC) was initially documented by Rob Chandanais (http://www.bluerobot.com/Web/css/fouc.asp). Although it only happens for a second, and under very specific conditions, the effect is quite unnerving—especially to any designers who have spent many, many hours crafting their CSS.

What does a FOUC look like? Naturally, it depends entirely on the page and CSS design, but Figures 11-1 and 11-2 illustrate the before and after states of this effect.

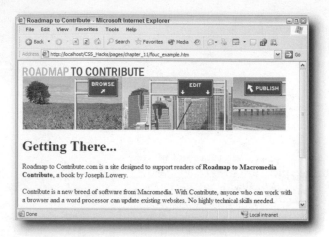

FIGURE 11-1: Just for a second, the page visitor using Internet Explorer 5 or higher sees the page like this. . .

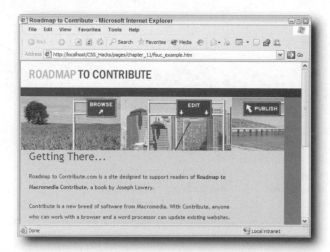

FIGURE 11-2: . . .when it's really intended to look like this.

A Web page exhibits the FOUC when all of the following factors are in play:

- Viewed by Internet Explorer 5 or higher.
- External style sheet is attached with a single @import tag.
- No link tag is used in the head area.

- No other `script` tag is used in the `head` area, aside from the one used for the `@import` tag, or before the content in the `body` area.

- The page is viewed for the first time. Subsequent viewings that cache page elements stop the FOUC from appearing.

It's interesting to note that this phenomenon occurs under the purest of CSS circumstances (that is, with only a single `@import` statement). Ironically, the movement to code to standards and to stop supporting Netscape 4.x has caused many a designer to encounter the FOUC bug. For example, until recently, the articles found on a major international news Web site suffered from FOUC.

Although this FOUC can be quite annoying, it's pretty easy to fix. The condition disappears if you include one or more `link` tags in the `head` area. If your CSS requirements don't naturally incorporate either of these elements, include a link to an alternative CSS file or a media-specific (such as print) CSS link.

Note If you link to an external CSS file to solve the FOUC problem, be sure the file is posted to the server and contains some content—even a single comment will suffice. Failure to link to an existing valid file could cause problems with certain browsers, notably Internet Explorer 5 for the Mac.

An additional `script` tag in the `head` area also prevents the FOUC occurrence. It doesn't matter what the `type` attribute of the `script` tag is assigned to: either `JavaScript` or `VBScript` work equally well.

Debugging CSS Problems

I worked, for a while, as a manager for computer trade shows (anyone remember the Commodore Amiga?). When asked to describe my duties during the actual show, I always replied, "Fireman." I always felt my role was to stop small problems before they became large ones. Although the troubles that arose were, thankfully, never literally fires, they could certainly grow out of control like one if left unattended.

I get the same sense of being a fireman when it comes to debugging CSS. In fact, my overall philosophy for attacking CSS bugs is pretty close to my show management method: do the best job you can during setup and when (not if) a problem arises, isolate it until you can fix it. With CSS, the most important step you can take is to code with CSS-compliant browsers in mind. If you target the most popular browser (Internet Explorer 6), rather than a CSS-savvy one (such as Firefox or Safari), you'll spend much more time trying to bring the rendered page into line, cross-browser.

You should begin testing once you have the first significant portion of your page completed. The longer you wait to view your pages in all your target browsers, the more complex and the more difficult it is likely to be to isolate your bugs. In general, your watchword should be "Test Early, Test Often."

Note   It is critical that you are capable of viewing your pages in all of your target browsers. If you don't have all the necessary versions installed, consider using a service like BrowserCam (http://www.browsercam.com). Its main claim to fame is its Screen Capture Service, which allows you get a snapshot of any submitted URL being rendered on one (or all) of the more than 40 browsers available. The browsers range across platforms, companies, and versions. While the static shots returned by the Screen Capture Service are extraordinarily helpful for layout control, they don't reflect any interactivity. BrowserCam recently added a Remote Access Service that allows you to experience your Web site through another a computer—without having to own it.

Here's a general roadmap to debugging CSS:

1. After you've created a page that looks the way you want in a CSS-compliant browser, view it in all of your target browsers. Note where problems emerge and with what browser.

Note   Because Internet Explorer bugs are among the most prevalent (and the most heavily documented), try to determine if the issues you're seeing fall into that category. One technique is to test in two or more non–Internet Explorer browsers (such as Firefox and Safari), as well as one or more versions of Internet Explorer. If you're not seeing the problem in the non–Internet Explorer browsers, but are in Internet Explorer, you've most likely narrowed down your bug to being Internet Explorer–related.

2. Check to see if any the problems you've encountered are among the most common. (See the section "CSS Usual Suspects Checklist" later in this chapter for a list of the most frequently seen CSS bugs.) If any fall into that category, implement the known solution and retest.

3. For any remaining bugs, make a copy of the page to work on. From this point on, the hunt for bugs intensifies and you don't want to lose work. Reduce the page to its minimal HTML elements that still exhibit the buggy behavior. In other words, scale back the paragraphs of content to a sentence or two, but if the problem only appears when a certain amount of content is applied, keep at least that much content. The goal now is to track down the bug and squash it, so you want to make sure it is always occurring.

4. Transfer any external CSS into style tags embedded in the head area. The reasons to do this are twofold. First, it saves you from going back and forth in two different files, which, in turn, greatly speeds up the process. Second, incorporating the CSS into the Web page eliminates caching problems. Often, when you're viewing the same file over and over again for testing purposes, your browser will cache the previous version of an external CSS file, even if it has been changed. If you forego this step and keep your CSS separate from the Web page, chances are you'll be making changes that should have a physical effect on the page, but you'll never see them—unless you reload. Play it safe and embed your styles in your page where caching is never a problem.

5. Organize your CSS by section affected. Suppose one of your navigation menus is out of alignment. Group the CSS so that all the navigation-related styles are together. Likewise, you would put all the CSS rules affecting the content together and all of the CSS targeting the header together.

6. Now you're ready to actually begin the bug hunt in earnest. The strategy at this stage is to remove sections of the CSS that *don't* affect the bug. You must isolate the bug before you can deal with it. Start by commenting out the largest possible portion that retains the bug. If the section you comment out removes the bug, replace it and comment out the other styles (see Figure 11-3).

```
CSS Horizontal MultiLevel NavBars (chapter_10/tabs_experiment.htm*) (XHTML)
85  #nav li ul ul {
86    margin: 0;
87  }
88  /*
89  #nav li:hover ul ul, #nav li.sfhover ul ul {
90    left: -999em;
91  }
92
93  #nav li:hover ul, #nav li li:hover ul, #nav
    li.sfhover ul, #nav li li.sfhover ul {
94    left: 10px;
95    top: 16px;
96  }
97
98  #nav li ul a:link, #nav li ul a:visited {
99    color: #FF0000;
```

```
<head> <style>                                         4K / 1 sec
```

FIGURE 11-3: Tools that color-code your CSS are great for working with commented-out sections while debugging.

7. Repeat Step 6 as you continue to narrow down the amount of code that exhibits the buggy behavior. Each time you locate the portion of the style sheet that contains the problem, comment out a smaller portion of the styles within that region.

8. When you locate the exact style rule(s) or properties, try applying alternative values to the properties. Keep in mind that although one declaration may appear to be the culprit, the fix may lie in parent areas.

There is often quite a bit of trial-and-error once you've isolated the bug. However, like many other learning curves, the CSS bug hunt becomes less time-intensive after you've begun to see the same problem over and over again.

Note   If you're a Firefox or Mozilla user, there's a great add-on that's perfect for helping in the debugging process. The Web Developer toolbar, created by Chris Pederick, allows you to browse to a page and quickly outline block-level elements, or any other element of your choosing. You can also view the CSS of a page and—best of all—edit it while it is still in the browser. The Web Developer toolbar is freely available at `http://www.chrispederick.com/work/firefox/webdeveloper/`.

CSS Usual Suspects Checklist

One of the axioms of CSS woes is, "Déjà vu, all over again." Although never-seen-before bugs do occur, the chances of you encountering one are much less than you'd think. For the most part, issues that arise have been seen (and dealt with) many times before, by many other designers. Before you engage in a search-and-destroy mission on your own, it's a good idea to double-check the most common bug-related scenarios. For this exercise, you should work from the top (the server) down to the document's CSS level. The broadest categories are not only the most impactful, they are also the easiest to confirm and fix.

Verifying Server-Side Setup

Web servers are responsible for delivering (or serving) a requested page and all its constituent parts, in the proper format. An element's format is determined by its file extension and the associated MIME type, which is set by the server administration. If the MIME type for .css is not set to `text/css`, any external CSS file will be interpreted as plain text or HTML. In either case, your page will not be styled.

Here's a case where the forgiving nature of one browser can lead to the downfall of a more strictly interpreting one. For the most part, Internet Explorer will apply any externally defined CSS files appropriately, regardless of the MIME type set (or not set) on the server. Browsers such as Firefox and Mozilla, however, only render CSS as they're told to render CSS (in other words, only if the server tells them to). This browser split leads to the circumstance where the administrator, viewing your page through Internet Explorer, sees a fine example of a CSS-designed page while you, as the developer using a Gecko-based browser, are only seeing the raw, unstyled HTML.

Although this problem is admittedly pretty rare, it's a core issue and must be resolved. You'll most likely encounter this issue when working with a new client or moving to a new server. The .css MIME type must be set to `text/css` either directly through the server settings, or, if you're working with a commercial host, it's possible (but not certain) that you can add the .css MIME type through the administration interface. You'll most often see this feature when you are working with an Apache server. This process inserts an .htaccess file at the server root with the following code:

```
AddType text/css .css
```

If you have Telnet access to your Apache-hosted site, you can accomplish the same goal manually.

Approaching Document-Level Issues

With the server squared away, it's time to turn to the document. The concerns to watch out for in this section are general problems that could easily trip you up when you're tearing apart your CSS styles looking for a particular property. Always remember to step back and take a look at the forest before examining each individual CSS-defined tree.

Handling the XML Prolog

When XHTML began to become popular, many designers (including myself) mistakenly included an XML prolog at the top of our new pages. An *XML prolog* is used in XML files to declare the version of XML used, declare the encoding, and define specific namespaces, if any, like this:

```
<?xml version="1.0" encoding="iso-8859-1"?>
```

My excuse, poor workman that I am, is to blame my tool: Macromedia Dreamweaver MX. In this release of the program, Macromedia began support for XHTML and each new page in that format included the XML prolog. Unfortunately, Internet Explorer 6 interprets the XML prolog as a request to enter quirks mode—which basically makes Internet Explorer 6 render like Internet Explorer 5. Macromedia's next release, Dreamweaver MX 2004, corrected this problem and the XML prolog is no longer automatically included with every new XHTML page.

If you do want to force Internet Explorer 6 into quirks mode, it's best to use the doctype switching technique and remove any XML prolog from your pages. Numerous ways exist to ensure quirks mode is engaged. One technique is to declare a transitional DTD for HTML 4.01 transitional and leave out the referring URL:

```
<!DOCTYPE HTML PUBLIC "-//W3C//DTD HTML 4.01 Transitional//EN">
```

To use the same doctype, but set Internet Explorer 6 into standards mode, include the URL, as follows:

```
<!DOCTYPE HTML PUBLIC "-//W3C//DTD HTML 4.01 Transitional//EN"
"http://www.w3.org/TR/html4/loose.dtd">
```

You can also set standards mode by declaring a doctype for XHTML or HTML 4.01 strict.

Applying Media Types Correctly

The ability to address different media types is a key concept in the W3C's philosophy on Cascading Style Sheets. With CSS, you can render the same content differently (and appropriately) on different media by specifying a media type (such as screen, print, or projection). There are two ways to declare a target for a specific style sheet: @media and @import.

If you're using @import, the basic syntax looks like this:

```
@import url(mainstyle.css) screen;
@import url(pagestyle.css) print;
```

Internet Explorer, along with all other modern browsers, understands the @import rule, but not when a media type is declared within it. Any such rules are ignored by Internet Explorer, versions 6 and below. To use @import, making sure that your style sheet is read by these browser versions and applied correctly for the proper medium, rely on the media attribute in the style tag:

```
<style type="text/css" media="screen">
<!--
  @import url(mainstyle.css);
-->
</style>

<style type="text/css" media="print">
<!--
  @import url(pagestyle.css);
-->
</style>
```

Although this approach is more verbose, it gets the job done, cross-browser. Another strategy is to specify `@media` rules for those declarations that must be specifically changed for a different medium:

```
<style type="text/css">
  @media print {
    body {background: white; color: black; }
    #nav {display: none; }
  }
</style>
```

Internet Explorer interprets `@media` rules correctly.

Validating Your Document

Some Web designers regard a Web page that validates under both HTML and CSS guidelines as the Holy Grail. I prefer to think of validation as an extremely useful tool, but not a religion. CSS validation, however, is suited perfectly for debugging your code. A lot of designers hand-code their CSS rules, and it's perfectly understandable how an opening or closing brace (or curly bracket) could be left out. CSS validators, however, can catch these types of syntax errors (see Figure 11-4) and many others.

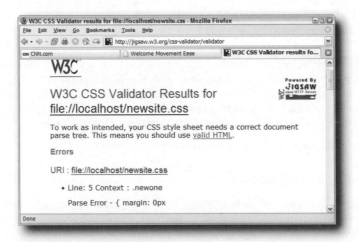

FIGURE 11-4: Validate your CSS to check for syntax errors such as omitted closing curly brackets.

Note
Numerous CSS validation services are available. I use the one from the W3C located at `http://jigsaw.w3.org/css-validator/`.

Remember that CSS and HTML work together to create your page. You'll also want to ensure that your HTML is error-free. To validate your HTML, visit `http://validator.w3.org/`.

Avoiding General CSS Errors

Although there are plenty of browser-related bugs you should be aware of, missteps that you take in your coding can cause CSS problems all on their own. Some issues arise because the designer is overlooking a key CSS principle, whereas others are based on incorrectly held assumptions. Regardless of the root cause, ensure that all your own ducks are in a row before you begin hunting down browser-based bugs.

Getting Specificity Right

Have you ever found yourself changing a CSS property in the code only to have the effect never appear? If you're sure you're working with the right selector, chances are there is another declaration with a higher specificity—and the same property—that is overriding your changes. Say, for example, you're trying to change the color from blue to red for the p tags within the div with an ID of content and you make the change to this CSS rule:

```
#content p {
  color: red;
}
```

You make the change to red, but nothing happens; the paragraphs still render blue. After a little exploration of your CSS file, you find another rule:

```
div#content p {
  color: blue;
}
```

The selector on the second rule, div#nav p, will always control the properties because it is more specific. Specificity is listed as a series of four values, each in its own column:

- *Styles*—If a selector uses the style attribute (commonly known as an *inline style*), the first column is equal to 1; otherwise it is 0.

- *IDs*—The number of IDs in the selector makes up the second column.

- *Classes and pseudo-classes*—The total number of classes and pseudo-classes used in the selector is represented in the third column.

- *Elements and pseudo-elements*—The fourth column is equal to the number of elements (or tags) and pseudo-elements found in the selector.

Specificity is generally shown as four columns separated by dashes or hyphens (for example, 0-1-0-1). Once you calculate the specificity of your selectors, it's easy to see which one is higher:

```
#content p { }
/* One ID and one tag;        specificity= 0-1-0-1 */

div#content p { }
/* One ID and two tags;        specificity= 0-1-0-2 */
```

If two selectors address the same property, the property value for the selector with the higher specificity is rendered.

Another CSS concept related to specificity is the !important property. When !important is added following a property's value, the given value always overrides any applicable declaration, regardless of specificity ranking. For example, in the contest between these two styles, the first one—with the less-specific selector, but with the !important property—will be the rendered style:

```
#content p {
  color: red !important;
}
div#content p {
  color: blue;
}
```

Note Be very careful not to overuse the !important property because it will even override user-defined styles, which are often implemented for accessibility reasons.

Setting Up Proper Paths

Web pages (whether HTML, XHTML, or generated by an application server) rely on external documents including CSS files. Often, the path to the external style sheet is stated relatively, like this one:

```
@import url(styles/mainstyles.css)
```

Translated into English, this path would read "import the mainstyles.css file in the styles folder that's in the same directory as the current Web page." Suppose you're upgrading a page that includes an inline div tag with a background image. The code would look like this:

```
<div id="sidebar" style="position:absolute; left:100px; top:200px;
width:300px; height:150px; z-index:1; border: 1px none #000000;
background-image: url(images/sidebar.jpg);"></div>
```

Note that the background image, sidebar.jpg, is in a folder called images; the images folder is also in the same directory as the current file. When you're converting inline styles to external style sheets, you must take extra care to get the path correct. The external style sheet will, in this case, have a different path than the inline style:

```
#sidebar {
  position; absolute;
  left: 100px;
  top: 200px;
  width: 300px;
  height: 150px;
  z-index: 1;
  border: 1px none #000000;
  background-image: url(../images/sidebar.jpg);
}
```

Because the images and styles folders are situated on the same level of the directory tree, to properly locate the background image, you must go up a level from the location of the CSS file (styles) and back into the images folder. Put simply, if you use relative paths, ensure that the path to your external style sheet is relative to your Web page, and the paths to all CSS-inserted images is relative to the CSS file.

There's one other "gotcha" associated with CSS-declared paths. While it may seem natural to use single quotation marks with the url() syntax, Internet Explorer 5 for the Mac does not recognize it and will not render the defined style.

Ordering Pseudo-Classes Properly

Another factor that is involved in determining the actual property value applied is the style order. If the specificity is the same—and the !important keyword is not used—the rule presented last in the file is given precedence. Pseudo-classes (such as a:link, a:hover, and so on) are among the areas most likely to be affected, primarily because they are used together so often.

The four different pseudo-classes associated with links must be defined in the following order: a:link, a:visited, a:hover, and a:active.

```
a:link {
  color: blue;
  font-weight: bold;
  text-decoration: none;
}
a:visited {
  color: purple;
  font-weight: bold;
  text-decoration: none;
}
a:hover {
  color: red;
  font-weight: bold;
  text-decoration: underline;
}
a:active {
  color: yellow;
  font-weight: bold;
  text-decoration: underline;
}
```

Tip The abbreviation LVHA is often suggested to help designers remember the proper sequence, along with the somewhat cynical mnemonic LoVe, HA! An alternative for ultra-geeks to consider is Lord Vader Has Anakin.

If you don't put your definitions in this order, you won't get the effects you desire across all browsers. Internet Explorer browsers tend to be more forgiving in this area, but sticking to the proper sequence will ensure that your intentions are preserved in every browser that supports pseudo-classes. (You might remember that Netscape 4 doesn't support the a:hover pseudo-class.)

Another pseudo-class affected by code position is :focus. Suppose you want to really highlight the last clicked link, more than all the other links previously clicked, but have the highlight vanish when the link is about to be clicked again. By combining the :focus and :hover pseudo-class, you could achieve the proper effect—but only if you define them in the following order:

```
a:focus { background: yellow; }
a:focus:hover { background: none; }
```

Declaring Measurement Units

Many CSS properties require a numeric value, and almost all of these properties allow a wide range of measurement units. You can, for example, specify padding in pixels, points, centimeters, millimeters, inches, picas, ems, exes, or percentages. Because all browsers do not require a measurement unit for zero values, it's easy for designers to mistakenly leave the measurement unit off the other values for the same property.

Suppose you're setting the margin for a content area and you want a zero margin for top and bottom, but you do want to specify left and right margins. You might, in error, define the margin property this way:

```
#content { margin: 0 150 0 20; }
```

The results for such a declaration would vary widely across browsers. To get the desired effect, you'd have to remember to declare unit measurements for the non-zero values:

```
#content { margin: 0 150px 0 20px; }
```

Targeting Design Problems

Recognizing common CSS bugs only comes with a fair amount of experience under your belt. Table 11-1 is designed to give you a leg up in this area and help you track down (and resolve) your CSS woes faster and easier. Many of these bugs have been covered in detail in this book. Rather than repeat the associated information, a reference to the chapter and section is provided.

Table 11-1 CSS Design Problems

Bug	Browser	Reference Chapter and Section
Zero margins ignored on block elements.	Netscape 4.x	Chapter 2, "Adjusting Margins and Borders"
Gap between background color and border.	Netscape 4.x	Chapter 2, "Working through Background Problems"
Size and/or color applied to bullet but not list text.	Netscape 4.x	Chapter 2, "Correcting List Issues"
Table cells not picking up styles applied to tables.	Netscape 4.x	Chapter 2, "Handling Table Discrepancies"

Bug	Browser	Reference Chapter and Section
Box elements appear smaller in one browser than others.	Internet Explorer 5+ (Windows)	Chapter 3, "Understanding Internet Explorer's Box Model Problem"
Content in div tag disappears when page loads, but appears when page is refreshed.	Internet Explorer 6	Chapter 3, "Revealing the Peekaboo Bug"
Margin of floated element is twice what it should be.	Internet Explorer 5+ (Windows)	Chapter 3, "Solving the Doubled Float-Margin Problem"
Content in float extends beyond float boundary.	Gecko-based browsers	Chapter 3, "Float Clearing with the :after Pseudo-Element"
Floated element shifted to one side.	Internet Explorer 5+ (Windows)	Chapter 4, "Three-Pixel Gap"
Italic text breaks out of floated container.	Internet Explorer 5.5+ (Windows)	Chapter 4, "Italics Float Bug"
First letter in heading disappears.	Internet Explorer 5.5 (Windows)	Chapter 4, "First Letter Bug"
Absolutely positioned block not moving when text resizes.	All modern browsers	Chapter 9, "Position: Absolute"
Nested box collapses to content.	Internet Explorer 6	Chapter 9, "Position: Absolute"
Fixed-position areas moving.	Internet Explorer 6	Chapter 9, "Position: Fixed"
Float touching clearing element rendering badly.	Internet Explorer 5+ (Windows)	Chapter 9, "Managing the Float"
Negative margins on floated element not aligning properly.	Internet Explorer 5+ (Windows)	Chapter 9, "Managing the Float"
Min-width property not rendering.	Internet Explorer 5+ (Windows)	Chapter 9, "Fixed Width, Main Content on Left"
Page elements not centered.	Internet Explorer 5 (Windows)	Chapter 9, "Fixed Width, Main Content on Left"

Implementing CSS Hacks in Dreamweaver

The lion's share of the world's professional Web developers use Macromedia Dreamweaver at some stage of their site-building process. Some designers create Web pages from scratch in Dreamweaver's Design view, while others work only in Code view. Dreamweaver's ability to handle dynamic applications has increased markedly in recent years. Now, whether you code for ASP, PHP, ColdFusion, or .NET—or static HTML—you can work in Dreamweaver.

Dreamweaver has always supported some degree of CSS. Even the first version (released in 1997) allowed designers to attach style sheets and define styles. In recent releases, the focus shifted to the rendering of applied CSS in Design view. Although not perfect, Dreamweaver MX 2004 made great strides in this regard.

What about CSS hacks and Dreamweaver? Although there is no real native support for applying hacks, there are numerous techniques that simplify the process. However, you really must understand how Dreamweaver works to make the most of them.

This chapter begins with an exploration of CSS in Dreamweaver from top to bottom: from setting CSS preferences so Dreamweaver will continually write CSS code the way you want, to working at maximum speed with the Relevant CSS panel. You'll also find an in-depth discussion of one of Dreamweaver's most useful power tools, snippets.

Working with CSS in Dreamweaver

There is no single CSS panel or menu in Dreamweaver. Rather, CSS is infused throughout the program. For designers, this omnipresence of CSS is a double-edged sword. On one hand, you have many CSS access points with numerous ways to apply styles, and even various approaches to modifying an existing style. This open access allows designers to decide how they work best. On the other hand, it's difficult for designers to uncover all the available options, and they often end up working harder than they should.

Even if you think you know all the CSS tricks that Dreamweaver offers, I urge you to give this section a thorough read. More likely than not, you'll discover—or rediscover—the true CSS power that will save you time and frustration.

Setting Up CSS Preferences

CSS support in Dreamweaver began to dominate in Dreamweaver MX. Up until that time, Dreamweaver's engine stressed table-based layout with HTML tags like font for formatting. You can switch between these two modes through Preferences. Choose Edit ⇨ Preferences (Dreamweaver ⇨ Preferences on the Mac) to display the Preferences dialog box. In the General category, make sure that the "Use CSS instead of HTML tags" option is chosen. If you ever are working on an unfamiliar system and Dreamweaver is mysteriously using font tags instead of CSS classes to format your text, you're either working with an older version of Dreamweaver, or this option is unchecked.

Note One sure sign that Dreamweaver is set to use HTML tags and not CSS is apparent in the Property inspector. (The Property inspector is discussed in greater detail later in this chapter in the section, "Applying Style Rules.") Place your cursor within any text styled by CSS. If the text's characteristics (font name, size, color, and so on) are not displayed in the Property inspector, you're in HTML tag mode.

Two-thirds of the remaining CSS-related options in Dreamweaver's Preferences are strictly design-time tools. You can enable or disable CSS code hints and you can also control the color scheme you see when editing CSS rules in Code view. Both of these settings are useful for personalizing your experience of working with CSS in Dreamweaver. The third preference, however, directly affects how Dreamweaver writes your code. Thus, it has a much longer-lasting impact. Before you see how to control Dreamweaver's CSS output, the following sections take a look at the code coloring and hints options.

CSS Syntax Coloring

Like standard HTML or XHTML code in Dreamweaver, CSS code is colored according to its syntax. Eight different syntax types are definable: @import, @media, comments, !important, properties, selectors, values, and strings. You're probably familiar with all of these concepts except the last. A *string* is anything within quotation marks or parentheses (such as the path to a background image or a font family). To set the look-and-feel of any of these syntax types, follow these steps:

1. Select the Code Coloring category in the Preferences dialog box.

2. Choose CSS from the Document type list.

3. Click Edit Color Scheme.

When the Edit Coloring Scheme for CSS dialog box opens (see Figure 12-1), you'll be able to choose the syntax type you want to alter, and then change the text color, background color, and various styles (bold, italic, and underline). The preview area at the bottom of the dialog box displays how the CSS looks when your changes are applied. Click OK when you're finished. Any modifications take place immediately after you've closed Preferences.

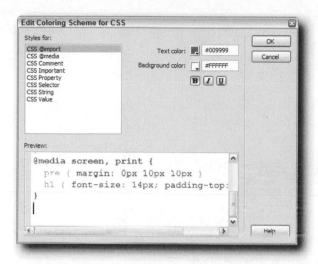

FIGURE 12-1: Your custom palette for CSS code applies to all your CSS styles seen in Dreamweaver's Code view.

Tip   If you don't want your CSS code colored at all, you must go through each of the eight syntaxes and set the text color to the default color, black. On a page-by-page basis, you can disable coloring by entering into Code view and toggling off the View ➪ Code View Options ➪ Syntax Coloring menu item. This option is also accessible from the Document toolbar under the View Options menu button.

CSS Code Hints

If you like to hand-code your CSS styles in Dreamweaver, you're probably familiar with code hints. A *code hint* is a type of advanced tooltip that appears to remind you of available properties and their values. When you first start defining a new CSS declaration, a list of available properties appears (see Figure 12-2). Every time you type a letter, the list moves to the properties that start with that letter. Each new letter you type moves the list to the first matching selection. For example, if you type **b** the list highlights background, add an **o** and border is now selected. To choose a selected entry, press Enter (Return). You can also move up or down the list using the respective arrow keys at any time. Not only does this process (called *auto tag completion*) eliminate misspelled properties, it makes the whole process very fast.

When it comes to property values, code hints are even more valuable. After you type the colon that follows the property name, the attributes list appears in the code hint pop-up. Typically, the items in the list are true hints, intended to provide guidelines of expected values rather than the values themselves. For example, after you've entered **border:**, you'll see two code hint entries: `'border-width' 'border-style' 'color'` and `inherit`. In the case of properties expecting color values, the code hint consists of a pop-up color-picker; with URL-related properties, you'll see an option to Browse. Choose this item to open a Select File dialog box.

FIGURE 12-2: Code hints are a great way to ramp up your CSS writing productivity.

If you find code hints more annoying than helpful, open Preferences and switch to the Code Hints category. There you'll find options to turn off code hints for CSS specifically, or all code hints in general. You can also globally disable auto tag completion. Finally, if the code hints are not coming up fast enough, you can adjust the delay before they appear. My personal preference is to set delay to 0. I think they're instantly and constantly useful.

CSS Coding Styles

As a scripted language, CSS is remarkably flexible. Not only can the text-based code be format-ted however you like (with whatever degree of white space you're comfortable with), but many properties offer code-minimizing and time-saving shorthand. You could, for example, set the margins for a selector like this:

```
#container {
  margin-top: 5px;
  margin-right: 0px;
  margin-bottom: 5px;
  margin-left: 0px;
}
```

The same margins could also be written in shorthand:

```
#container {
  margin: 5px 0px;
}
```

Dreamweaver is happy to use shorthand whenever possible—all you have to do is ask. In Preferences, the CSS Styles category is almost exclusively dedicated to managing shorthand, as shown in Figure 12-3. You have the option of (when values allow) using shorthand for the following groupings:

- *Font*—Combines `font-family`, `font-size`, `font-style`, `font-variant`, and `font-weight` values.

- *Background*—Puts the `background-image`, `background-repeat`, `background-attachment`, and `background-position` values on a single line.

- *Margin and padding*—For both margin and padding, combines the `top`, `right`, `bottom` and `left` values.

- *Border and border width*—Groups `border-style`, `border-color`, and `border-width` values.

- *List-Style*—Combines `list-style-type`, `list-style-image`, and `list-style-position` values.

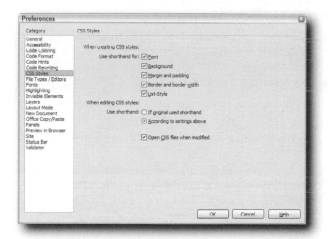

FIGURE 12-3: Compress your Dreamweaver CSS code via the shorthand options in Preferences.

Dreamweaver is smart enough to use shorthand, even if only a couple of the available properties are used. For example, if you declare the `background-image`, `background-repeat`, and `background-position` but not `background-color`, you'll get code like this:

```
#sidebar { background: url(../images/bg_sb.gif) repeat-y center
center;  }
```

You can also control how Dreamweaver handles existing CSS styles that are modified. If you want to keep the styles as written—whether they are in longhand or shorthand—choose the "Use shorthand if original used shorthand" option. If you'd prefer to convert the code to the style chosen according to your preferences, select the "Use shorthand according to the settings above" option. You should note that Dreamweaver will only restructure the CSS styles if they are modified within the program.

One very important option is found in the CSS Styles category that is unrelated to shorthand. The "Open CSS files when modified" option does two things, one obvious and the other somewhat obscure. If selected, whenever you make a change to one of the styles in an external style sheet, that style sheet is opened in another Dreamweaver tab or window. That's the obvious action. What you may not realize is the effect this allows. If a CSS file is open in Dreamweaver, any modification to its style sheet can be undone. If this option is not enabled in Preferences, the change is permanent. For this reason, I make sure that "Open CSS files when modified" is always selected, even though it means dealing with another open file.

Attaching External Style Sheets

One of the first acts many designers take when beginning a new Web page is to attach an external style sheet. Dreamweaver's point-and-click interface allows you to attach a style sheet using either the link or @import method. You can even attach a nonexistent style sheet— and Dreamweaver will create the file for you.

Dreamweaver offers several ways to attach a style sheet (in addition to hand-coding). All methods are accessed through the CSS Styles panel:

- Click the Attach Style Sheet button at the bottom left of the CSS Styles panel.
- Right-click (Control-click) in the CSS Styles panel and choose Attach Style Sheet.
- From the Options menu located at the top right of the panel group, choose Attach Style Sheet.

All three methods yield the exact same result: the Attach External Style Sheet dialog box (see Figure 12-4) appears. You have the option to either link or import the style sheet—and you can even preview the effect any chosen sheet will have on the current page. Clicking Cancel or switching to another CSS file removes the displayed preview.

FIGURE 12-4: Not sure which style sheet to use? Select Preview to get instant feedback.

To attach a style sheet in Dreamweaver, follow these steps:

1. Open the Web page you want to attach the style sheet to in Dreamweaver and make sure it's the current document.

2. If necessary, open the CSS Styles panel by choosing Window ⇨ CSS Styles or pressing Shift+F11.

3. From the CSS Styles panel, click the Attach Style Sheet button or use one of the other menu-based techniques.

4. When the Attach External Style Sheet dialog box opens, click either the Link or Import option.

   Choose Link if you want to insert a link tag and Import if you'd prefer to use the @import method.

5. Enter the path to the style sheet if you know it, or click Browse to open the standard Select File dialog box and locate your style sheet.

   The Select File dialog is preset to filter for files with a .css extension.

6. To see the effect the chosen sheet would have on the current page, click Preview. If that's not the desired style sheet, choose another, or click Cancel to stop the Attach Style Sheet procedure.

7. When you've located the style sheet you want, click OK to write the necessary code.

Assuming your style sheet changes either the layout of the page, specific tags, or classes or IDs already embedded in your HTML, you'll see an immediate effect. Although the CSS rendering in Dreamweaver MX 2004 is good, it's not perfect—particularly when it comes to positioning rules. Preview in one or more browsers to see the page as it will be ultimately rendered.

Note If you're declaring media types for your attached style sheet, you'll need to add that attribute in Code view. Dreamweaver's Code Hints feature makes it pretty easy: just place your cursor in the link or style tag, type an m, and press Return to insert the property media. All the recognized media values (all, screen, print, and so on) are then presented in a code hint.

So, how do you get Dreamweaver to create a style sheet for you if you are really starting from scratch? Attach the style sheet as you normally would, but when it comes time to select a file, browse to the desired folder location and enter the filename you want to use. Be sure to include a .css file extension. You will get an alert from Dreamweaver saying it can't find that file. Click OK to proceed. The file is actually created when you define your first style through the Dreamweaver interface.

The CSS Styles panel is capable of listing all the style sheets you have attached, as well as any internally defined ones. Each is presented in an outline format and can be expanded or collapsed as needed.

Defining CSS Styles

Hand-coding your CSS styles rules is always an option in Dreamweaver. Some designers prefer to hand-code all the time, while others prefer Dreamweaver's point-and-click interface. Both methods can be used interchangeably at any time.

To work in Code view with an attached external CSS file, all you need do is open it. CSS files can be opened, like any other Web page, through the Files panel. Simply locate the desired file and double-click to open it. Unlike other file types, however, CSS files can also be opened another, more direct way. If you right-click (Control-click) on the file entry in the CSS Styles panel and choose Go to Code (see Figure 12-5), the external file is immediately loaded and opened. Better yet, if you select a particular rule and choose Go to Code, Dreamweaver opens the file to the selected rule, ready for editing. This technique works whether the rule is in an external style sheet or included internally in a `style` tag.

FIGURE 12-5: Go to Code is an excellent navigational tool for changing the CSS code directly.

If you'd rather not hand-code, Dreamweaver's alternative point-and-click method is available. Defining a new style through the CSS Styles panel is basically a two-step operation that mirrors the structure of a CSS declaration:

1. Enter the selector or selectors for the new style rule.

2. Set the properties and values for the selector(s).

A separate dialog box is used for each of these major steps. You can begin the style definition process in any of a number of ways:

- Click the New CSS Style button at the bottom of the CSS Styles panel.

- Right-click (Control-click) in the CSS Styles panel and choose New.

- From the Options menu located at the top right of the panel group, choose New.

- In the Relevant CSS panel, right-click (Control-click) and select New Rule.

Note Yet another method of beginning to define a new style rule is through the Edit Style Sheet dialog box. You can find details on using this dialog box later in this chapter in the "Modifying Styles" section.

Setting Selectors

Let's break down the process into its two major components. To define a selector for a new CSS style, follow these steps:

1. Click the New CSS Style button at the bottom of the CSS Styles panel, or use any of the alternative methods listed previously (see Figure 12-6).

FIGURE 12-6: The most efficient approach to defining your selector is to work bottom-up: choose your style destination first, then the type, then the selector name itself.

2. When the New CSS Style dialog box opens, set where the style is to be defined.

- If the style is to be part of an attached external file, select that file from the "Define in" drop-down list. If you want to add the style to an external file currently not attached to the page, choose New Style Sheet File and you'll be given an opportunity to attach a new style sheet.

- If you want the style to be written into the head area of the current document, choose the "Define in this document only" option.

3. Pick the selector category from the three options:

- *Class*—A single CSS class.

- *Tag*—A single HTML tag.

- *Advanced*—Any type of selector other than single classes or single tags. This category includes IDs, contextual selectors, grouped selectors, pseudo-classes, pseudo-elements, as well as universal, child, adjacent-sibling, or attribute selectors.

4. Enter the selector name in the text field, according to the type chosen. Each of the selector types deals with the entered text differently:

- Class names should start with a period. However, if you don't include it, Dreamweaver adds it to the rule declaration.

- A tag name is entered without angle brackets.

- You can enter any type of selector desired in the Advanced field, including tag or classes. If you enter a class, however, you do need to supply the leading period.

5. Click OK to add the selector and curly braces to the desired destination and move on to defining the style's properties and values.

The Advanced field of the New CSS Style Definition dialog is really wide open. Enter any selector or combination of selectors. If Dreamweaver MX 2004 doesn't recognize it as a valid CSS 1 selector, an alert appears. Click Yes to proceed and Dreamweaver will write out the code as requested.

Note If you enter a CSS2 selector (such as `h2[align="left"]`), Dreamweaver allows it without prompting you. You will, however, get the warning when inserting a proposed CSS3 selector.

Defining Style Properties

After you've clicked OK to confirm your selector choices in the New CSS Style dialog box, you're ready to choose needed properties and their values. The CSS Style Definition dialog that is displayed next is composed of eight different categories: Type, Background, Block, Box, Border, List, Positioning, and Extensions. The style may include as many or as few properties as needed.

The following tables detail the available fields on the various categories and list the specific CSS property covered by the option.

Note Just because Dreamweaver allows you to define a property doesn't mean that the property will be rendered correctly in Design view.

Use the Type category to define the appearance and layout of the page's typeface, as shown in Figure 12-7. Not coincidentally, the Type category contains the most supported CSS properties (see Table 12-1), capable of being rendered in Internet Explorer 3.0 and above and Navigator 4.0 and up.

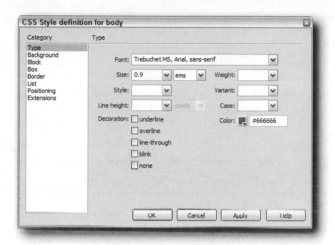

FIGURE 12-7: The first category in the CSS Definition dialog box is one of the most frequently used.

Tip

If you don't find the text properties you're looking for in the Type category, try Block.

Table 12-1 CSS Type Properties

Field	CSS Property
Font	font-family
Size	font-size
Style	font-style
Line Height	line-height
Decoration	text-decoration
Weight	font-weight
Variant	font-variant
Case	text-transform
Color	color

Backgrounds are an essential element to modern CSS design. Modern browsers take advantage of the ability to position a background image precisely as well as control the tiling of the image. Older browsers, such as Netscape 4.x, do not support these properties and must be handled separately. Table 12-2 shows background properties.

Table 12-2 CSS Background Properties

Field	CSS Property
Background Color	background-color
Background Image	background-image
Repeat	background-repeat
Attachment	background-attachment
Horizontal Position	background-position
Vertical Position	background-position

Dreamweaver includes numerous text properties in the Block category. Certain properties (such as vertical-align) are used to position non-text elements. Table 12-3 shows block properties.

Table 12-3 CSS Block Properties

Field	CSS Property
Word Spacing	word-spacing
Letter Spacing	letter-spacing
Vertical Alignment	vertical-align
Text Align	text-align
Text Indent	text-indent
Whitespace	white-space
Display	display

Properties in the Box category define the placement and dimension of CSS styles (see Figure 12-8). Both margin and padding attributes may be written in shorthand if that option is selected in Preferences (see Table 12-4).

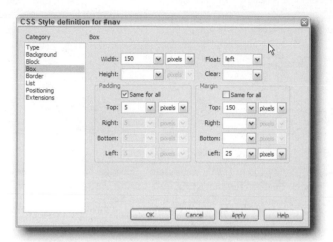

FIGURE 12-8: The Box category is often used to define floating elements.

Table 12-4 CSS Box Properties

Field	CSS Property
Width	`width`
Height	`height`
Float	`float`
Clear	`clear`
Margin	`margin; margin-top, margin-right, margin-bottom, margin-left`
Padding	`padding; padding-top, padding-right, padding-bottom, padding-left`

Any or all sides of a border are set in the Border category (see Table 12-5). If the "Same for all" option is selected, the rule is written with the border property. If "Same for all" is unchecked, the individual border properties (`border-top`, `border-right`, `border-bottom`, and `border-left`) are used as needed.

Table 12-5 CSS Border Properties

Field	CSS Property
Style	`border; border-top, border-right, border-bottom, border-left`
Width	`border; border-top, border-right, border-bottom, border-left`
Color	`border; border-top, border-right, border-bottom, border-left`

Working with list elements has gained considerable importance, because they have increasingly been used to craft navigation bars. Be careful when using bullet images: resizing your list items may cause the bullet images to scale improperly. Table 12-6 shows list properties.

Table 12-6 CSS List Properties

Field	CSS Property
Type	`list-style-type`
Bullet Image	`list-style-image`
Position	`list-style-position`

The Positioning category is heavily used in modern CSS layout techniques (see Figure 12-9). Frequently, these properties (see Table 12-7) are applied to `div` tags or other containers to structure the document.

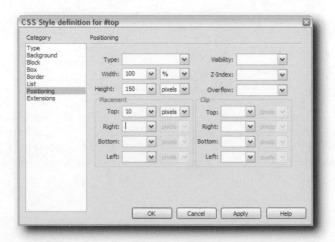

FIGURE 12-9: div tags are often the recipient of styles with properties from the Positioning category.

Table 12-7 CSS Positioning Properties

Field	CSS Property
Type	position
Width	width
Height	height
Visibility	visibility
Z-Index	z-index
Overflow	overflow
Placement: Top	top
Placement: Right	right
Placement: Bottom	bottom
Placement: Left	left
Clip: Top, Right, Bottom, Left	clip: rect(top, right, bottom, left)

The Extensions category is Dreamweaver's catch-all for CSS properties that don't really fit anywhere else (see Table 12-8).

Table 12-8 CSS Extensions Properties

Field	CSS Property
Pagebreak	page-break-before, page-break-after
Cursor	cursor
Filter	filter

Although `cursor` is generally supported in modern browsers, the `page-break` properties are less so. The `filter` property is proprietary to Internet Explorer only, although a semblance of cross-browser compatibility for some filters can be achieved by combining an Internet Explorer–only filter property with a related Mozilla-specific property and an increasingly supported CSS3 property. For example, the following renders the image 50% transparent in Internet Explorer 4 and up, Gecko-based browsers, and Safari:

```
#transparent {
    filter:alpha(opacity=50);
    -moz-opacity:0.5;
    opacity: 0.5;
}
```

Here are a few general tips on using the CSS Style Definition dialog:

- In fields allowing a numeric entry, you can enter the abbreviation for the measurement unit after the number in the same field and press Tab to confirm the entry. For example, if you wanted to set the left property to 15%, instead of entering **15** in the first field and then selecting from the drop-down list, you can enter **15%** in the initial field. Once you press Tab, the measurement unit is selected from the drop-down list and 15 is entered in the first field.

- Any value field that consists of a drop-down list is completely editable. If you'd prefer to type the value into the field rather than choose a value from the list, you're free to.

- If you must change all but one or two aspects of a border, padding, or margins setting to be the same, leave the "Same for all" option checked and enter the most common value in the top field. Then uncheck "Same for all" and change only those values necessary.

Applying Style Rules

Although the process of defining styles in Dreamweaver may be a bit convoluted, the application of those styles is wonderfully direct. Dreamweaver offers a wide variety of methods for applying styles, so you can choose the one that works best for you. You can apply any defined style, whether it is in an external style sheet or embedded, by any of the following methods:

- *Tag Selector*—Right-click (Control-click) any element from the Tag Selector on the bottom of the Document window and two options are immediately available, Set Class and Set ID. Each lists the styles defined in their respective categories.

- *Property inspector*—Select any tag or text in the Document window and the Property inspector displays a visual list of available classes to choose from; you can see at a glance what font characteristics are defined in the style (see Figure 12-10). In the Text Property inspector, classes are listed in the Style list whereas other Property inspectors label the list as Class. Some Property inspectors (such as those for text, table, and div tags) also show a list of possible ID styles; other Property inspectors display a single text field on the upper left where you can enter the ID style manually.

- *Standard menu*—If you're a menu-driven designer, choose Text ➪ CSS Styles to select any of the defined classes.

- *Context menu*—Do you prefer the shortcut menus? Right-click (Control-click) any selection to bring up the context menu and choose CSS Styles to see which classes can be applied. You cannot apply an ID through either the regular or context menus.

- *CSS Styles panel*—With any text or element selected in the Document window, right-click (control-click) a defined class or ID shown in the CSS Styles panel and choose Apply.

- *Relevant CSS panel*—This key Dreamweaver panel, covered later in this chapter, also allows you to apply any defined class. Right-click (Control-click) anywhere in the panel and make your choice from the Set Class list.

FIGURE 12-10: When many CSS classes are defined, the Property inspector's visual listing of classes is extremely helpful.

Of all these methods, I find that the Tag Selector and Property inspector routes are the fastest and easiest for me. With the Tag Selector, I can simultaneously select a tag and set a class or ID. The Property inspector's main benefit is the visual display of classes—very useful for CSS pages with a number of similarly named classes defined. Both the Tag Selector and Property inspector methods allow you to remove any class or ID by choosing None from their available options.

div tags (in addition to all the other methods outlined) have one more way to apply a CSS class, ID, or both. With Insert Div Tag, you can combine multiple steps into one operation. With one command you can create and precisely place a div tag on your page while at the same time assigning it the needed styles.

To use the Insert Div Tag feature, follow these steps:

1. Choose the Insert Div Tag object from the Layout category of the Insert toolbar. Alternatively, you can select Insert ⇨ Layout Object ⇨ Div Tag. The Insert Div Tag dialog box appears, as shown in Figure 12-11.

2. If you want to apply a class to the div tag, choose one from the Class drop-down list or, if the class has not been defined yet, enter it into the field. You do not need to enter a leading period.

FIGURE 12-11: The Insert Div Tag object is an excellent time-saver when constructing CSS layouts.

3. To add an ID to the `div` tag, select defined styles from the ID list. Again, you can enter an ID name directly in the text field. Do not use an initial # character.

4. Select where you'd like the `div` tag to appear in the code. The available options are:

   - Wrap around selection

   - At insertion point

   - Before tag

   - Before start of tag

   - Before end of tag

   - After start of tag

5. If you've chosen a tag relational option, the accompanying list of page elements with IDs becomes active. Select one and click OK to close the dialog.

The option to wrap the `div` around a selection is only present when elements or text were selected before the Insert Div Tag dialog box was opened. This is a great technique for enclosing existing content in a `div` tag, without having to resort to Code view.

Modifying Styles

It's very rare that you define all your styles right the first time. Whether it's your visual sense or your client's wishes that requires a change be made, you can easily make it happen in Dreamweaver. Again, you'll have multiple ways to reach your destination.

Note This section describes modifying style rules with Dreamweaver's built-in tools. However, you're not limited to them. If you have a dedicated CSS editor you'd prefer to work with, open Preferences and, in the File Types/Editors category, select .css from the Extensions listings. Use the Add (+) button to pick the executable for your editor. If it's the only editor chosen for the .css file type, it will be marked as Primary; otherwise, you can select it and click Make Primary. After you've closed Preferences, there's one more step to take. From the CSS Styles panel Options menu, check the Use External Editor choice. Now, whenever you opt to edit a style, your preferred CSS editor opens instead.

If you feel most comfortable with creating styles in Dreamweaver, you can make all your changes through the same CSS Style Definition dialog box. Simply choose the style you want to alter in the CSS Styles panel and click the Edit Style button at the bottom of the panel to the left of the Trashcan. The CSS Style Definition dialog box reopens, ready to be modified. Click Apply to see your changes immediately in the Design view and click OK when you're finished.

Automatically Created Styles

To make it easy for designers new to CSS to get up to speed, Dreamweaver MX 2004 introduced automatically created styles. Although the Dreamweaver engineers fully intended this Property inspector–based feature to be beneficial, it can be a bit of a nightmare to manage. Here's how it works:

1. The designer selects some text in Design view. The text can be a previously styled tag with either a class or an ID—or no style at all.

2. A text-formatting change is applied in the Property inspector. This change can be to the font name, font color, or font size.

3. Dreamweaver automatically creates a class declaration and inserts it into an embedded style sheet in the `head` area of the current document. The class is named incrementally starting with `style1`, followed by `style2`, `style3`, and so on.

4. If the style is applied to more than one place in the document and another formatting change is made, Dreamweaver generates another class style.

5. If the font name, color, and/or size properties of one auto-created style are changed to match another, the latter style is dropped and all instances of the applied style are renamed to match the original style. For example, suppose you have one style that is colored blue and sized at 14 pixels (`style1`) and another that is the same size and green (`style2`). If you change `style2`'s color to blue, Dreamweaver deletes the `style2` class declaration and replaces any class attributes set to `style2` with `style1`.

Numerous difficulties exist with this automated approach. First, it creates an unnecessary amount of classes. Many designers feel that classes should be used sparingly. The classes are also hard to get rid of. If you remove the one and only time a Dreamweaver-defined style is used, the style definition remains.

The style names are also a problem. To be truly effective, the auto-named styles should be renamed to something more meaningful. Although Dreamweaver includes a renaming feature, it's moderately well-hidden and may be overwhelming for the beginner. Perhaps the largest problem of all is Dreamweaver's practice of embedding the new styles rather than placing them in an external style sheet.

All in all, Dreamweaver's automatic style sheet feature is more of a bother than boon, and should be avoided.

Would you like to make your changes by hand? The CSS Styles panel is still your quickest way there. Double-click the style rule you want to change and Dreamweaver reveals the CSS code. If the style is contained in an external sheet, the CSS file is opened in Code view; if the style is embedded in the head area, Dreamweaver changes to Split view and places the cursor at the indicated style, ready for changes.

If you're making a number of changes to your style rules, you might want to work with more of an overview. Select the style-sheet name or root style tag in the CSS Styles panel and then select Edit Style Sheet—it's the same button as the Edit Styles, but its name is contextual. A dialog box with the name of the current style sheet that lists all the defined style rules appears (see Figure 12-12). This dialog box allows you to perform many CSS tasks: attach a new style sheet, create a new style, or edit, duplicate, rename, or delete (remove) an existing one.

The process of renaming a CSS style deserves special attention. The problem with renaming a CSS class or ID is that you must perform the operation in more than one place. Not only must the style definition itself be renamed, but so must all the applied styles. If you're working with an external style sheet attached to many pages in your site, this can be quite a task.

Note You can also start the renaming procedure by right-clicking (Control-clicking) on a style in the CSS Styles panel and selecting Rename.

Dreamweaver accomplishes the heavy-lifting chore of renaming applied styles through its Find and Replace feature. Once you've invoked the Rename command and entered the new name for the style in the dialog box that appears, Dreamweaver checks to see if the style is contained in an external style sheet. If it is, an alert informs you that to rename this style multiple pages would be affected and asks if you want to proceed. Click Yes to proceed. The Find and Replace dialog box opens next, prefilled with proper information to perform the operation. This is significant because regular expressions are used to locate and change just the class attributes with the specified names. The scope of the operation is set to the entire site, and you have the option of making the change one item at a time or using Replace All to do it all at once.

FIGURE **12-12:** The duplicate feature is excellent for crafting a series of styles with mostly similar properties and values.

Dreamweaver Layers

Following Netscape's (the market leader at the time) naming convention, the first version of Dreamweaver introduced the concept of *layers*. To the modern CSS-savvy designer, a Dreamweaver layer is a `div` tag styled inline with absolute positioning. A typical layer looks like this:

```
<div id="Layer1" style="position:absolute; left:68px; top:99px;
width:205px; height:126px; z-index:1; background-color: #FFCCCC; layer-
background-color: #FFCCCC; border: 1px none #000000;"></div>
```

A Dreamweaver-style layer is created whenever the Draw Layer object is used, which (as the name indicates) allows the user to draw out a layer, much like drawing a rectangle in a graphics program. Layers can be dragged anywhere on (or off) screen and their properties modified at will through the Property inspector, in Code view or—to some degree—through the Layers panel.

Although the Draw Layer object is useful for quick prototyping, most designers end up moving the inline style either to an external or embedded style sheet. One of the most prolific early extension developers, Jaro von Flocken, has created an extension called Layer to Style that moves inline code up to the style tag. You can find it on his site, http://www.yaromat.com/dw, in the Layers category.

Using the CSS Relevant Panel

Another (more direct) way to modify existing styles is through Dreamweaver's other CSS interface, the Rules and Relevant CSS panel. This panel changes names (and functions) depending on what is selected. If you select a listing in the CSS Styles panel, you'll see the Rules panel with all the CSS properties and values depicted (see Figure 12-13). There are two views, switchable through the two buttons on top of the panel: the Category view separates the properties into eight categories, paralleling those found in the CSS Style Definition dialog, whereas the List view shows all CSS properties in alphabetical order (except that applied properties are first). Because of the easy access this grants, I tend to stick with List view.

FIGURE 12-13: Switch between rules on the CSS
Styles panel to see (and change) the Rules panel.

When you place your cursor in the Document window (in either Design or Code view), you'll see the Relevant CSS panel with the properties and values applied to the current selection, as well as a listing of all the selectors. Again, the properties panel can be displayed in either the Category or List views. Choose any of the listed selectors and those properties are shown. As you move up the selector tree, you'll notice some of the properties are marked with a red strikethrough (see Figure 12-14). The strikethrough indicates that the value of the property is not rendered in the current selection. If you hover your mouse over the property, a tooltip explains why. Typically, the value is either not inherited or overridden because another selector with the same property has a higher specificity. Not only is the Relevant CSS panel highly instructive, it also serves as a tremendous debugging tool when you're trying to figure out why a style is not rendering as desired.

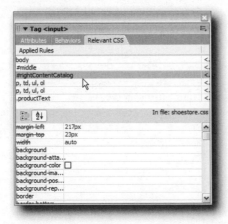

FIGURE 12-14: The Relevant CSS strikethrough indicator is a great CSS debugging tool.

The property portion of the panel (whether it's in Rules or Relevant CSS mode) is not just for show. Any property's value can be changed directly. Just click in the corresponding value field and enter a new value. Depending on the property, the value field changes: some value fields include drop-down lists with pertinent values, color swatches that pop up a color picker, or point to file and folder icons to allow easy selection of files.

In all types of value fields, the value can also be entered by hand. This is especially useful when working with properties that accept compound values (such as `border`). Hover over a property value to see a code hint. After you've inserted your new value, press Enter (Return) or click anywhere to confirm the change. Dreamweaver immediately renders the results.

Working with Design Time Style Sheets

It's not unusual for designers these days to work with a variety of style sheets for a single page, each one applicable to a particular condition. With a little JavaScript or server-side coding, different style sheets can be applied according to which browser is being used, the platform employed, even the screen resolution at work.

The Design Time Style Sheets command enables you to work with a specific style sheet while hiding others. One key use of this command is to utilize a style sheet that is linked from your page dynamically at run-time. Your style sheets, in other words, do not have to be specifically attached to your page for you to be able to use them.

To set up design time style sheets, follow these steps:

1. From the CSS Styles panel Options menu, choose Design Time Style Sheets. Alternatively, you can select Text ➪ CSS Styles ➪ Design Time. Whichever method you choose, the Design Time Style Sheets dialog box (shown in Figure 12-15) is displayed.

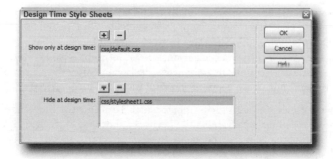

FIGURE 12-15: The Design Time Style Sheet feature is great for fine-tuning dynamically attached style sheets.

2. To show a specific style sheet, select the Add (ı) button above the "Show only at design time" list area and select an external style sheet from the Select File dialog box.

3. To hide a specific style sheet, select the Add (+) button above the "Hide at design time" list area and select an external style sheet from the Select File dialog box.

4. To delete a listed style sheet from either list, select the entry and then choose the Remove (-) button above the list.

5. Click OK when you're finished.

Once a style sheet has been designated to be explicitly displayed or hidden at design time, you'll see the word "design" or "hidden" in quotes following the entry for the style sheet in the CSS Styles panel. The displayed style sheets can be modified as you would normally; hidden style sheets are locked against editing.

Note

Design Time Style Sheets are extremely useful when it comes to compensating for CSS rendering bugs in Dreamweaver.

If you're designing sites for use in Contribute 3, you'll find even more uses for Design Time Style Sheets. In addition to being a great way to render a page that ultimately uses a dynamically added style sheet, Design Time Style Sheets can also be used with pages derived from templates, a common practice in Contribute. If you set up Design Time Style Sheets when you create the template in Dreamweaver and upload the template to the Contribute site, any child pages of that template will use the Design Time Style Sheets settings. Even Dreamweaver MX 2004 can't do that.

Using Snippets for CSS Hacks

One tool in the Dreamweaver feature set is especially useful when it comes to applying CSS hacks: snippets. A *snippet* is a portion of any kind of code, stored in a library and capable of being repeatedly inserted. Dreamweaver's snippets come in two varieties: block and wrap. A *block snippet* is a single block of code inserted at the current cursor position. A *wrap snippet*, on the other hand, consists of two code sections that are placed before and after the current selection, effectively wrapping the selection. Both types of snippets are useful for inserting CSS hacks.

Dreamweaver manages snippets through the Snippets panel. To access the Snippets panel, choose Window ➪ Snippets; alternatively, press the keyboard shortcut, Shift+F9. The Snippets panel organizes the code fragments in an expandable folder structure, as shown in Figure 12-16. Select any defined snippet and a preview area shows what the snippet looks like if it can be rendered in Design view; if it can't, as is the case with CSS hacks, the preview shows the code. Not only can new snippets be added easily, but you can also add new organizational folders and move snippets from folder to folder by dragging them.

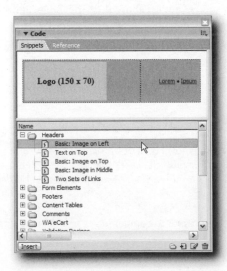

FIGURE 12-16: The Snippets panel comes with a large number of predefined snippets and is easily extended to include CSS hacks.

Dreamweaver comes with a range of standard code snippets, but, as of this writing, none are concerned directly with CSS hacks. The best approach is to create a new folder to hold the new snippets. To do so, follow these steps:

1. Choose Window ⇨ Snippets or press Shift+F9 to open the Snippets panel.

2. If any of the folders or snippets are highlighted, right-click (Control-click) into the open area at the bottom the panel (below all folders) to deselect all items. Click once with the left button in the same location to dismiss the shortcut menu.

   Newly created folders are placed within the currently selected folder. If this happens, you can drag the folder to the root, but, by deselecting all items, the new folder will automatically be created at the base level.

3. Click the New Folder button at the bottom of the Snippets panel.

4. Name your new folder "CSS Hacks" (see Figure 12-17).

Note

Dreamweaver MX 2004 on Windows has an unfortunate sorting bug in the Snippets panel. Any new folders are placed at the top of the listing, out of alphabetical order. A related bug occurs when you create a new snippet or edit an existing one: the snippets are sorted in reverse of the current order. If the snippets are in an A–Z order, they are flipped to display in Z–A sequence. One work-around is to open a snippet in the folder for editing and then click OK without making any changes. I haven't yet discovered a way to fix the sequence of the main root folders.

Figure 12-17: Put your new CSS Hacks folder at the main root level so you can access it quickly.

Creating a snippet is about as easy as making a folder to hold them. Although you can enter the code by hand directly into a dialog box, a far simpler approach exists. If you opt to make a new snippet while some code is selected, that code automatically appears in the New Snippet dialog box. The following steps walk through the process of converting the multipurpose Holly Hack into a snippet:

1. Select the CSS hack code you want to convert into a snippet.

   Here's a typical example of a Holly Hack in use:

   ```
   /* Start Commented Backslash Hack \*/
   * html #container {height: 1%;}
   /* Close Commented Backslash Hack */
   ```

2. In the Snippets panel, select the folder you want to hold your new snippet.

   If there are existing snippets in the folder, you can also highlight one of them.

3. Click the New Snippets button from the bottom of the Snippets panel.

4. When the New Snippet dialog box opens, enter a name to be displayed in the Snippets panel in the Name field. In this case, I'd identify it with "Holly Hack."

5. If you like, you can enter a brief description of the snippet in the Description field.

   Frankly, I never use the Description field. The box used to enter information appears too far to the right of the snippet name to be really useful. Instead, I try to make the names of my snippets as clear as possible.

6. Choose the type of snippet you're creating: Wrap Selection or Insert Block. The dialog box changes depending on your choice. In this case, Insert Block is the correct choice.

7. Enter the code in the Insert Code field.

   If you had chosen Wrap Selection, you'd enter the code to appear prior to the selection in the Insert Before field, and the code to appear after in the Insert After field.

8. Adjust the snippet, if desired.

   When creating CSS hack snippets, you'll need to indicate what could be different each time it's inserted. With this example, it's the selector, currently #container. To make it more generic (and obvious that it needs to be altered), I'll change the snippet like this:

   ```
   /* Start Commented Backslash Hack \*/
   * html SELECTOR {height: 1%;}
   /* Close Commented Backslash Hack */
   ```

9. Choose how you would like the snippet to be displayed in the preview area of the Snippets panel, rendered in Design view or as code. The only real choice for CSS hacks in general is Code, as shown in Figure 12-18.

10. Click OK when you're finished.

FIGURE 12-18: Be sure to indicate the variable elements in your CSS hack,
like the selector in the Holly Hack snippet.

To insert this snippet, first place your cursor where you'd like the code to appear. Then, you can either double-click the desired snippet in the Snippets panel or, with the snippet selected, click Insert. You can also drag snippets from the panel and drop them anywhere in the code.

Internet Explorer conditional comments are another likely candidate for the CSS Hacks snippet folder. I have my conditional comment snippets set up as a wrap-type snippet with this code in the Insert Before area:

```
<!--[if IE]>
<style type="text/css">
```

I use this code in the Insert After area:

```
</style>
<![endif]-->
```

Why do I set it up this way? I often copy and paste rules I need to change onto my page before I apply the snippet. For example, if I'm attempting to fix the Internet Explorer 3 pixel gap problem, I'll copy and paste the two declarations affected and adjust their properties as needed so I have the following code in the head area of my page:

```
#floatLeft {
    margin-right: -3px;
}
#content {
    margin-left: 0px;
}
```

In this case, I need to highlight the pasted declarations before I insert my snippet. Once highlighted, I can double-click my `If IE` conditional comment and the resulting code block looks like this:

```
<!--[if IE]>
<style type="text/css">
#floatLeft {
    margin-right: -3px;
}
#content {
    margin-left: 0px;
}
</style>
<![endif]-->
```

Another way of approaching this problem is to insert the snippet before adding the rules to be affected. In this situation, it's best to place your cursor where you want the snippet code to appear without highlighting any code. What happens when you bring in a wrap-type snippet without a selection? Both the before and after code sections are placed on the page, one after another, with the cursor right in the middle. All you need do is enter a carriage return and insert the needed rules.

Note Looking for quick way to create a snippet? Select a block of code, right-click (Control-click) and choose Create New Snippet from the context menu. How about a way to apply that template in a flash? Select Edit ➪ Keyboard Shortcuts and define a shortcut to any defined snippet. Just pick Snippets from the Command drop-down list, locate your snippet in the tree control, and choose a shortcut.

Creating CSS-Savvy Dreamweaver Templates

emplates are the real workhorse of Dreamweaver. To design a site without employing templates is to resign yourself to hours upon hours of repetitive drudgery. Why attempt to duplicate the same key elements for every page (including the header, navigation, and footer) when creating a new page based on a template instantly has the desired look-and-feel? Even more time-consuming is updating common areas across a site—unless you're using templates.

Style sheets are the perfect companion for templates. Change one property value on a style sheet linked to a template and not only do you instantly affect all the child pages (pages based on a template), but you also ensure that all future pages based on the template will have the same properties—and the same hacks. Attaching a CSS style sheet to a template is very straightforward with only one potential stumbling block (noted in the next section) to look out for. There are, however, numerous techniques for maximizing the potential held by the combination of templates and CSS. In this chapter, you learn how to work with templates for CSS consistency as well as adaptability. Templates and their child pages can be used in a wide variety of ways and you want to ensure that your CSS strategy can handle all the situations your workflow requires.

Dreamweaver's sister program, Contribute, is also CSS-savvy—in some ways more so than Dreamweaver itself. In the last section of this chapter, you'll find an exploration of the best ways to design CSS-based templates in Dreamweaver for use in Contribute.

 Note This chapter assumes you have working knowledge of building templates in Dreamweaver.

Setting Up Basic Templates for CSS

When you're developing templates in Dreamweaver, a little pre-planning goes a long way. In addition to all the up-front design work necessary, it's also helpful to keep in mind how the templates will be used. Following are the most common scenarios:

- *Single Developer/User*—The same person who creates the templates, uses them.

- *In-house Web Design Team*—One or more developers create templates that are put to use by other designers on staff.

- *Designer-Developed, Client-Applied*—Templates and initial child pages are created by designers and then posted to the site (including templates). They are handed off to the client, who can create additional child pages.

Note A fourth scenario in which Dreamweaver templates are created for use in Macromedia Contribute is covered later in this chapter.

How the templates are to be used determines how the CSS is applied. Each of the three outlined scenarios suggests a different approach. To understand these methods, you must be up to speed on how Dreamweaver templates work—especially in regard to the head area.

By default, everything in a Dreamweaver template is locked and unchangeable; in this state, each child page is a carbon copy of the template. Templates used in this way are pointless, and no designer I know works like this. The process of creating a useful template involves marking areas of the page as editable. Typically, these editable regions encompass main content areas or are targeted more specifically. Everything else (such as navigation) remains locked and reproduces identically on child pages.

When Dreamweaver creates a template, whether from an existing page or from scratch, an editable region is automatically inserted into the head area. The code for this area looks like this:

```
<!-- TemplateBeginEditable name="head" --><!-- TemplateEndEditable
-->
```

With templates, the code to attach external style sheets is, by default, always added outside of the head editable region and, thus, locked. Unfortunately, this does not mean that the styles in the style sheet are secure. It only means that the style sheet cannot be unattached from a child page. Moreover, anyone working with a child page can easily attach one or more additional style sheets—the link or @import code is inserted into the head editable region.

Note I was a little shocked when (while working on this chapter) I realized the flaw in Dreamweaver's template design with regard to CSS. As it stands now, there is no way to stop anyone with access to child pages on a site from altering the core CSS files attached to that page. The best alternative is to set the file to read-only, either by checking it in via Dreamweaver or by changing the file properties in another program such as Windows Explorer or Finder.

Another consideration is how Dreamweaver handles the placement of the external style sheet code. Where the code is inserted is differerent depending on when the style sheet is attached. If the template is created from an existing page that already has an external style sheet attached, the code appears above the head editable region in the newly created template, like this:

```
<style type="text/css">
<!--
  @import url(../css/rmap.css);
-->
</style>
<!-- TemplateBeginEditable name="head" --><!-- TemplateEndEditable
-->
```

This means that the properties in any CSS style sheets attached to child pages would override those attached to the template.

The reverse is true if the style sheet is attached to the template after the template has been created. In this situation, the link or @import code appears *below* the head editable region. This, of course, means that the style sheet inserted in the template will override any style sheet with the same properties added to a child page. Let's put all this understanding of how Dreamweaver operates to work. Here are some recommend approaches for the three previously described scenarios:

- *Single Developer/User*—When one person is in control of the creative process from start to finish, I find it best to attach all style sheets at the template level. This establishes a direct connection between style sheets and all ultimately resulting pages, and eliminates messy organizational situations such as two or more child pages derived from the same template with different style sheets.

- *In-house Web Design Team*—In this scenario, you have maximum creative input and need the most flexibility. To achieve this goal, ensure that the initial style sheet code that is attached to the template is *above* the head editable region. With this arrangement, the base styles are adhered to. However, if a designer must make an adjustment to accommodate a particular child page, any changes can be inserted into a new style sheet—which will appear in the head editable region and thus take precedence over any conflicting styles. I recommend that if you are in charge of a Web team using templates, you insist that no one working on child pages make changes to the core style sheets.

  As noted earlier, this particular code sequence happens naturally when you create a template from a page that already has the style sheet(s) attached. If necessary, you can also go into Code view and move the head editable region code (`<!-- Template BeginEditable name="head" --><!-- TemplateEndEditable -->`) below the link or @import code.

- *Designer Developed, Client Applied*—The key here is to balance stability of design with client need. You want to ensure that your pages render as designed—and as accepted by the client—but still allow the client to incorporate special cases without calling for a redesign. Under these circumstances, I recommend that the style sheet code attached to the template is *below* the head editable region. Because the designer-implemented style sheets are farther down the cascade, the CSS rules of inheritance give them priority. If the client tries to change an existing CSS style (for example, altering the body tag from white to black), the template-attached style sheets will prevent that from happening.

  Clients may still, however, add a new style sheet to incorporate necessary CSS classes that may not have been in the original design. Because these classes (or other selectors) are not part of the template-attached style sheet, they will render as expected.

Working with Nested Templates

If you're using nested templates, you're probably used to thinking ahead and planning your site and designs thoroughly. A nested template in Dreamweaver is basically a template of a template—or more specifically, a template of a child page derived from a template. As such, you can easily extend the strategies outlined in this section to include nested templates.

For example, suppose you're working on an intranet Web team and want to maintain a single overall look-and-feel of a given site, but allow different designs for various departments within that site. Attach the primary style sheet that is to affect all the site pages to the master template, above the head editable region. You're free to add any departmental style sheets to the proper nested template, also above the head editable region. This is possible because every time you save a template-derived page as a template and create a nested template, Dreamweaver inserts a new head editable region after the old one. As with standard templates, you can leave page-specific changes to be embedded or added as external style sheets in the head editable region of the child page.

Note You might think that removing the `head` editable region altogether from the template would solve the problem of unwanted style sheets, but you'd be wrong. If the `head` editable region is missing, Dreamweaver inserts `link` or `@import` code in the `title` editable region. Deleting the `title` editable region is really not an option; it makes the `title` attribute of the page editable, an essential element of child pages.

Embedding Design Time CSS Style Switching

In the previous section, you saw how to allow fellow members of your Web team or clients to add whatever external style sheets they like. But what if you want to operate under more controlled circumstances and provide a set number of specific choices? This is particularly important if you have painstakingly crafted CSS hacks for your style sheets. You may remember from Chapter 5 how a page was set up using JavaScript to allow the visitor to switch from one style sheet to another at run-time. In this section, you'll see how to set up a page to switch style sheets at design-time.

The template feature contains some of Dreamweaver's least-known (but more powerful) capabilities, including a complete template expression language. One aspect of the template expression language enables Dreamweaver to insert certain code if a particular condition is met or a defined parameter is set at design time. The Multiple-If template expression is perfect for setting up a template so that a variety of preselected CSS style sheets can be applied.

To demonstrate the potential of Multiple-If template expressions, let's construct the code necessary to choose between three different style sheets at design time. All of the following code is to be placed in the head area of the template outside of the head editable region. This placement locks the code against modification in all child pages. Whether you put it above or below the head editable region depends on your workflow as discussed in the previous section.

The first step is to insert the template parameter statement. In this example, the value expected for the template parameter should be a number. (A number parameter simplifies the error-checking process.) Here, the template parameter is called selectCSS:

```
<!-- TemplateParam name="selectCSS" type="number" value="1" -->
```

The default value is used to set a particular style sheet if the designer opts for another choice.

The Multiple-If template expression syntax has two main parts. The first part is the outer wrapping code that identifies the section as a Multiple-If expression:

```
<!-- TemplateBeginMultipleIf -->

<!-- TemplateEndMultipleIf -->
```

The second part consists of the Multiple-If clauses that evaluate an expression and, if the expression is true, insert the enclosed code in the document. A generic Multiple-If clause looks like this:

```
<!-- TemplateBeginIfClause cond="" -->
  <!-- Code to insert goes here />
<!-- TemplateEndIfClause -->
```

Dreamweaver's template expression language supports a full slate of unary (like the negating !) and binary (+, -, <, >, ==, and so on) operators for the value of the cond or condition attribute. Thus, to insert a link to a given style sheet if the selectCSS template parameter is set to 1, the Multiple-If clause would look like this:

```
<!-- TemplateBeginIfClause cond="selectCSS == 1" -->
  <link href="../css/stylesheet1.css" rel="stylesheet"
type="text/css" />
<!-- TemplateEndIfClause -->
```

The beauty of the Multiple-If syntax is that it allows for any number of conditional clauses. For this example, the goal is to allow the designer of a child page to choose from three different style sheets. So, three Multiple-If clauses are employed within the overall Multiple-If expression. In the following code, I've highlighted the condition to make the logic easier to follow:

```
<!-- TemplateBeginMultipleIf -->
  <!-- TemplateBeginIfClause cond="selectCSS == 1" -->
    <link href="../css/stylesheet1.css" rel="stylesheet"
type="text/css" />
  <!-- TemplateEndIfClause -->
  <!-- TemplateBeginIfClause cond="selectCSS == 2" -->
    <link href="../css/stylesheet2.css" rel="stylesheet"
type="text/css" />
  <!-- TemplateEndIfClause -->
  <!-- TemplateBeginIfClause cond="selectCSS == 3" -->
    <link href="../css/stylesheet3.css" rel="stylesheet"
type="text/css" />
  <!-- TemplateEndIfClause -->
<!-- TemplateEndMultipleIf -->
```

One last bit of code is necessary. To ensure that a value is within the acceptable range, a fourth Multiple-If clause is required for error-checking purposes. In this clause, if the `selectCSS` template parameter entered at design time is less than 1 or greater than 3, the default style sheet is applied:

```
<!-- TemplateBeginIfClause cond="selectCSS < 1 || selectCSS > 3" -
->
  <link href="../css/stylesheet1.css" rel="stylesheet"
type="text/css" />
<!-- TemplateEndIfClause -->
```

Note While I find Dreamweaver's template expression language extremely useful, it does have one irritating flaw. When you're working with the template, Dreamweaver does not apply the default value of the template parameter and evaluate the page accordingly as it should. In fact, the template is not evaluated at all. Consequently, in an example like this, you'll see all the style sheets rendered in the template's Design view. If you find this unworkable, use the Design-Time Style Sheet feature to hide unwanted templates.

How does the child page designer choose a particular style sheet? The Template Properties dialog box provides the required mechanism. In the example, for the designer to use `stylesheet3.css`, these steps would be necessary:

1. Open the child page. If the page has not been created yet, from the Assets panel, right-click (Control-click) the desired template and choose New from Template.

2. Select Modify ⇨ Template Properties.

3. When the Template Properties dialog box opens, choose the selectCSS parameter.

4. Enter **3** in the selectCSS text field, as shown in Figure 13-1.

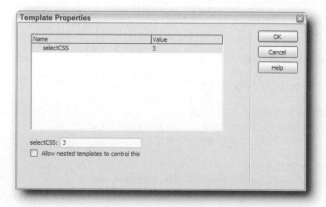

FIGURE 13-1: With the error-checking code in place, any value entered results in a style sheet being applied.

5. Unless you're working with a nested template, leave the "Allow nested templates to control this" option unchecked.

6. Click OK.

If you examine the code, you'll see that not only is the indicated style sheet inserted, but the code for the other, unused, style sheets are nowhere to be seen. Dreamweaver inserts only the code for the chosen style sheet.

Should your template design require a choice between one style sheet or another, an either/or approach is the way to go. To achieve this, the template parameter is defined with a Boolean type, like this:

```
<!-- TemplateParam name="mainDesign" type="boolean" value="true"
-->
```

The two Multiple-If clauses examine the state of the mainDesign template parameter as set in the Template Properties dialog box. If it is shown, the condition is true (mainDesign) and the main CSS style sheet is applied. If mainDesign is not shown, the condition is false(!mainDesign) and the alternative style sheet inserted.

```
<!-- TemplateBeginIf cond="mainDesign" -->
  <link href="../css/mainDesign.css" rel="stylesheet"
type="text/css" />
<!-- TemplateEndIf -->
<!-- TemplateBeginIf cond="!mainDesign" -->
  <link href="../css/altDesign.css" rel="stylesheet"
type="text/css" />
<!-- TemplateEndIf -->
```

Although you might find the learning curve for Dreamweaver's template expression language a bit steep, it's definitely worth mastering—especially if you need to control the style sheets available.

Adjusting Layout Styles via Template Parameters

Template parameters can do much more than switch between style sheets. With careful planning and a sprinkling of template expressions, you can set up a template to toggle between two or more different layout styles, much like switching between screen media and print media types. The primary difference is that the switch between layout styles is under designer (not user or automatic) control.

The key benefit of a template parameter-based control is template management. Rather than requiring multiple templates for the same site, you can have one template with a variety of layouts. This technique is a real time-saver when you must make changes to the template. Instead of updating several templates with the same modification (and processing the changes in the site), you only need to alter one. Moreover, template parameter-based layouts allow master designers to hand off carefully crafted templates to be implemented by junior designers or even those with no design skills whatsoever, like Contribute users.

Suppose that you have a basic three-column layout that occasionally must contract to two columns. The layout uses a graphic across the top and bottom to help form the column appearance. In this situation, you'd need to accomplish three main tasks to accommodate a two-column design:

- Remove the third column from the template.

- Change the images to compensate for the layout change.

- Increase the width of the main content column to allow the text to flow into the vacated third column area.

All these changes (and any others necessary) can easily be triggered through a single template parameter. Here's how you set it up:

1. Open the three-column template for editing. This assumes that this particular layout is the most commonly used and that the two-column design is the exception.

2. Select the content in the third column area within the container (typically a `div` tag). You may find it easiest to work in Code or Split view for this process.

3. Choose Templates: Editable Region from the Insert bar's Common category and enter a meaningful name for the region in the dialog box that appears.

   The idea here is to make the content within the `div` tag editable, but keep the `div` itself locked. By placing only the content within the editable region, you prevent the unwanted removal or alteration of the surrounding `div`.

4. Select the `div` tag encompassing the editable region and choose Templates: Optional Region. In the New Optional Region dialog box, enter a recognizable name for the area and ensure that the "Show by default" option is checked (see Figure 13-2). I chose `sideColumn` for the example editable region, which inserts this code into the `head` area:

   ```
   <!-- TemplateParam name="sideColumn" type="boolean"
   value="true" -->
   ```

   Ensure that you get the positioning of template regions correct. You can't have an optional region within an editable one, only the other way around.

Note Although Dreamweaver does offer an Editable Optional Region object that inserts the code for both areas properly, I don't recommend it. Although the tool lets you name the optional region and set the state to either shown or hidden, the editable region is automatically and generically named. Because the names of editable regions are one of the best ways to identify their use, I always end up renaming the automatic name (such as EditableRegion4) to something more useful.

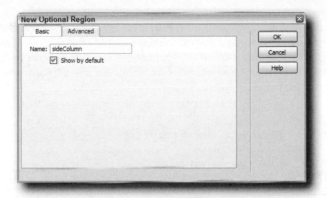

FIGURE 13-2: Determine the initial state of the optional region by selecting the "Show by default" option.

5. In the embedded style sheet, insert a template expression to modify the main content region's width value depending on the state of the sideColumn template parameter. To accomplish this in a single template expression, the conditional operator is used, like this:

```
#content {
    height: auto;
    width: @@(sideColumn==true?"500":"750")@@px;
    float: left;
    margin-left: 30px;
    margin-top: 15px;
}
```

Translated into English, this template expression reads, "If the template parameter sideColumn is displayed, make the value 500; otherwise, 750." Be sure to use the proper wrapping syntax of double at-signs around a parenthetical statement. Also note that the value the parameter is tested against (true) is not in quotation marks.

Note

As noted earlier in this chapter, Dreamweaver does not assign the default values to template parameters, so your display is likely to be a bit jumbled when you're working on the template itself. In the example design, the sample content from the main section overflows into the single column. This will not be the case when editing child pages.

The last task is to set up the images that frame the columns to change when the sideColumn property is modified.

6. Insert template expressions in each of the styles that define background images to illustrate the column widths. For this example, the file names are `top_2col.jpg` and `bottom_2col.jpg` for the two content columns variation, and `top_1col.jpg` and `bottom_1col.jpg` for the single content column. This naming convention allows me to target the template expression to just change the number in the file names. Again, the conditional operator is used:

```
#topBorder {
  background-image:
url(/images/top_@@(sideColumn==true?"2":"1")@@col.jpg);
background-repeat: no-repeat;
  margin-left: 190px;
}
#bottomBorder {
  background-image:
url(/images/bottom_@@(sideColumn==true?"2":"1")@@col.jpg);
background-repeat: no-repeat;
  margin-left: 190px;
}
```

7. Save the template and create a new page based on the template. The new page will initially display the side column, as shown in Figure 13-3.

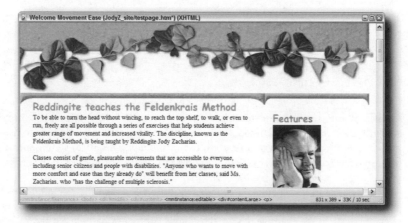

FIGURE 13-3: In the child page, the default setting is to include the side column, along with the graphics and appropriate style settings.

8. To test the template parameters, open the child page and select Modify ⇨ Template Properties. When the Template Properties dialog box opens, uncheck the "Show sideColumn" option.

After clicking OK, the displayed page in Dreamweaver is adjusted according to your template parameter and the column is hidden (see Figure 13-4).

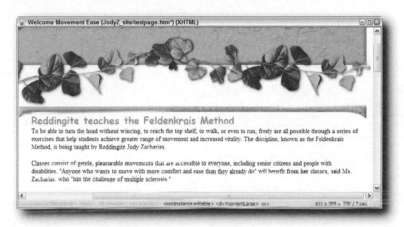

FIGURE 13-4: Changing one template parameter hides an optional region and resets three styles, including swapping two background images.

The technique just outlined works well for embedded styles. However, if you're using external style sheets, you'll need to take a different approach. Create a separate style sheet, one for each layout variation, and insert a template expression in the link code to switch sheets on demand. The following code assumes the two style sheets are in the same folder and named `main_2col.css` and `main_1col.css`:

```
<link href="../css/main_@@(sideColumn==true?'2':'1')@@col.css"
rel="stylesheet" type="text/css" />
```

Note that the quotation marks used inside the template expression are now single quotation marks rather than double. This change is necessary because the expression is contained within a quoted attribute value, `href`.

Constructing Contribute-Friendly CSS Designs

Macromedia Contribute is, in many cases, the ultimate client-acquisition tool. When a potential client comes to you and says, "We like your designs, but our content changes daily and I don't want to rely on you—or pay you—to do the updates. We want our secretaries and assistants to do that." What do you say? "Contribute." Contribute makes it easy for Dreamweaver designers to create the site's overall look-and-feel and for non-technical personnel to update static pages. Even more importantly from this book's perspective, the Dreamweaver-to-Contribute connection is very flexible when it comes to CSS and templates.

CSS Basics in Contribute

In general, CSS in Contribute 3 works as you would expect with few surprises. The pages render the same as in Dreamweaver MX 2004. When a new page is created from an available template in Contribute, any attached style sheets are automatically applied. Contribute gives the administrator a tremedous degree of control over the abilities of any declared role, especially when it comes to CSS. A Contribute administrator could, for example, grant those users assigned the roles of Publishers or Editors full access to CSS functionality on one hand, but restrict the options available to those in the Contributor role severely. All of the CSS preferences are handled through the Styles and Fonts category of the Edit Role Settings dialog box in Contribute (see Figure 13-5).

FIGURE 13-5: Via Contribute's Edit Role Settings dialog, you can limit the degree of CSS access available to any type of user.

Contribute users enabled to work with CSS see defined classes in a Style drop-down list when editing drafts. As you can see in Figure 13-5, the classes are depicted with the CSS font-family, size, color, alignment, and background-color properties, much as they are in Dreamweaver's Property inspector. The exception to this rule is undefined heading tags. In Figure 13-6, Headings 4 through 6 are not given a CSS declaration.

Note One technique I recommend for Dreamweaver designers creating sites to be used in Contribute is to give CSS classes obvious names. It's far easier for a novice user to understand how a class entitled `firstParagraph` is to be applied than one named `p1`.

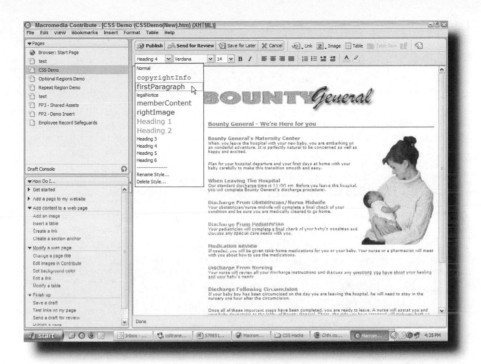

FIGURE 13-6: Contribute users pick from a visual style list to assign classes to text and other page elements.

Limiting Available Classes

From the Dreamweaver side, you may not want all of your classes to be available to Contribute users. You might, for example, employ a series of classes to style navigation buttons—something the Contribute user will never touch. To hide classes from Contribute users while keeping them active and rendered on the page, you'll need to take actions in both Dreamweaver and Contribute.

In Dreamweaver, create a CSS filter file that contains only the classes you want the Contribute user to see. The classes can be listed as a standard CSS declaration, complete with properties and values, as a single class name with the curly braces or as a series of comma-separated class names. All three of the following examples are valid:

```
.firstParagraph {
    margin-top: 0px;
}

.memberContent {}

.rightImage, .leftImage, .pullQuote {}
```

Once the filter file is completed, it must be posted to the Contribute site, which is typically the Dreamweaver remote site.

On the Contribute side, you or whomever is assigned to be the Contribute Administrator needs to opt to use the filter file for every role affected. This option is declared in the Edit Role Settings dialog box, again under the Styles and Fonts category. Select the "Show only CSS styles included in this CSS file" option and specify the previously transferred filter file. After the change is applied, the next time anyone in any of the affected roles edits a draft in Contribute, only the designated styles will be available, regardless if the pages are template-derived or standard.

Applying Template Features in Contribute

Although template use in Contribute is, for the most part, transparent to the user, there are two special cases I want to call to your attention. The first involves Design-Time Style Sheets and is actually an enhancement over what is currently available in Dreamweaver. When you use the Design-Time Style Sheets feature in Dreamweaver to hide or show style sheets, the settings are applied on a per-page basis, including templates. In other words, pages derived from templates (child pages) must have the Design-Time Style Sheets option reset.

Contribute goes Dreamweaver one better. Any Design-Time Style Sheets settings designated at the template level are carried through for all new pages created from that template in Contribute. This becomes especially important if you are using the Design-Time Style Sheets feature to overcome rendering shortcomings found in both Dreamweaver MX 2004 and Contribute 3. All you must remember is to put the template to the Contribute site; no additional steps must be taken in either Dreamweaver or Contribute.

Working with nested templates in Contribute, however, is a different story. To be able to create new Contribute pages from a nested template, not only does the nested template have to be uploaded to the site, but so does the master template. For example, suppose you have a nested template named `pediatrics_dept.dwt` that is based on a master template, `main.dwt`. Both of these files must be put to the Contribute site.

Unfortunately, this creates a bit of a problem. If a template is posted to a Contribute site, by default, it is available to all users of the site. Because you don't typically want users to base pages solely on the master template, you must hide the template from access.

Again, it is the job of the Contribute Administrator to specifically limit access to only those templates required by the end user. This option is set in the New Pages category of the Edit Role Settings dialog. With the "Use Dreamweaver templates" option checked, choose the "Only show users these templates" option. Then select the desired template or templates from the list of hidden templates and click Show (see Figure 13-7). Be sure to keep the master template on the Hidden Template side.

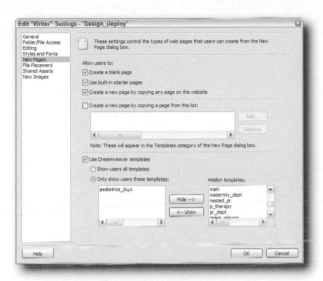

FIGURE 13-7: Both the master and nested template must be on the Contribute site, but you can easily hide the master template from the user.

The next time a user under the affected role attempts to create a new page from a template, only the selected templates will be listed.

Resources

An awesome amount of information about all matters related to CSS is available on the Web. The links that I've included here are a very small sampling of the wellspring of enthusiasm, knowledge, and flair to be found. If you're looking for a CSS education, you could do far worse than put aside a set number of hours every week to just explore these sites and the links spiralling off them.

Of course, the very nature of a web is its fragility. Some of these links are sure to be gone by the time this book hits the shelves, but most will remain. With a little persistance and inventive searching, you'll find these links a great jumping-off point for your own exploration.

General CSS Sites

Following are some links to general CSS sites:

- W3C CSS:

  http://w3c.org/Style/CSS/

- W3C CSS Validation Service:

  http://jigsaw.w3.org/css-validator

- CSS-Edge:

  http://www.meyerweb.com/eric/css/edge/

- Holy CSS Zeldman!:

  http://www.dezwozhere.com/links.html

- Mezzoblue CSS Crib Sheet:

  http://www.mezzoblue.com/css/cribsheet/

- QuirksMode CSS:

  http://www.quirksmode.org/css/contents.html

- Working with CSS—Introduction to CSS Layout:

  http://developer.apple.com/internet/css/intro
  csslayout.html

- MaKo 4 CSS:

  http://www.mako4css.com/

- CSS Creator: Useful CSS Links:

  http://www.csscreator.com/links/linkspage.php

- Position Is Everything:

  http://www.positioniseverything.net/index.php

- Digital Media Minute CSS:

  http://www.digitalmediaminute.com/?c=CSS

CSS Hack Information

Following are some links for CSS hack information:

- Css Hack—css-discuss:

  http://css-discuss.incutio.com/?page=CssHack

- Centricle—css filters (css hacks):

  http://centricle.com/ref/css/filters/

- Dithered.com:

  http://dithered.com/css_filters/css_only/

- Hide CSS from Browsers:

  http://w3development.de/css/hide_css_from_browsers/summary/

- Testing CSS-filters:

  http://www.gunlaug.no/homesite/main_8_1.html#itembottom

- Netscape 4 Issues—RichInStyle.com bug guide—Netscape 4:

  http://www.richinstyle.com/bugs/netscape4.html

- Internet Explorer Bugs and Fixes—How to Attack an IE/Win Bug (describing the Holly Hack and the relative fix):

  http://www.positioniseverything.net/articles/hollyhack.html.

- Internet Explorer Bugs V. 5 and Up:

  http://www.positioniseverything.net/explorer.html

- CSS—Conditional comments:

  http://www.quirksmode.org/css/condcom.html

- Conditional Comments in Microsoft Internet Explorer:

  http://webdesign.about.com/cs/htmltags/a/aacommentsie.htm

- Conditional Comments—Microsoft:

  http://msdn.microsoft.com/workshop/author/dhtml/overview/
  ccomment_ovw.asp

- Conditional Comments—Hack-free CSS for IE—Virtuelvis:

    http://www.virtuelvis.com/archives/158.html

- dean.edwards.name/IE7/:

    http://dean.edwards.name/IE7/

- HTC components in XP Service Pack 2 | Hoeben.net:

    http://www.hoeben.net/node/view/33

- Macintosh Bugs and Hacks—CSS Bugs in IE5 for Mac:

    http://www.macedition.com/cb/ie5macbugs/

- IE 5 Mac test pages—Hiding and Linking Styles:

    http://www.l-c-n.com/IE5tests/hiding/

- IE5/Mac Band Pass Filter:

    http://www.stopdesign.com/examples/ie5mac-bpf/

- Opera Filters—Albin.Net CSS—Owen Hack:

    http://www.albin.net/CSS/OwenHack.html

- Web Specifications Supported in Opera:

    http://www.opera.com/docs/specs/css/

- Safari Hacks—Safari 1.1 CSS hacks [dive into mark]:

    http://diveintomark.org/archives/2003/11/12/safari

- Liorean's Alternate Stylesheet Hack:

    http://liorean.web-graphics.com/css/althack/

- Debugging CSS—Common Coding Problems with HTML and CSS:

    http://www.communitymx.com/content/article.ctm?cid=67EEA

- Flash of Unstyled Content (FOUC):

    http://www.bluerobot.com/web/css/fouc.asp

CSS and JavaScript

Following are some links for CSS and JavaScript:

- CSS Vault—The Web's CSS Site:

    http://cssvault.com/cat_cssjavascript.php

- CSS Filters—JS Filter Summary (dithered.com):

    http://www.dithered.com/css_filters/js_summary.html

- JavaScript tutorial—Manipulating CSS using the W3C DOM:

  `http://www.howtocreate.co.uk/tutorials/index.php?tut=0&part=27`

- W3C DOM Compatibility—CSS:

  `http://www.quirksmode.org/dom/w3c_css.html`

- Rounded Corners with CSS and JavaScript:

  `http://www.sitepoint.com/article/rounded-corners-css-javascript/`

Server-Side CSS

Following are some links for server-side CSS:

- Creating Dynamic Cascading Style Sheets with ASP:

  `http://www.4guysfromrolla.com/webtech/tips/t071201-1.shtml`

- Use ASP in your .js, .vb, and .css Files:

  `http://www.devx.com/tips/Tip/14971`

- Compressing your CSS with PHP:

  `http://www.fiftyfoureleven.com/sandbox/compress-css-with-php/`

- PHP in CSS: Dynamic Background Color... Ack!:

  `http://www.webmasterworld.com/forum88/5025.htm`

CSS and Graphics

Following are some links for CSS and graphics:

- CSS Image Text Wrap Tutorial Part 2—the SandBag <DIV>:

  `http://www.bigbaer.com/css_tutorials/css.image.text.wrap.tutorial.htm`

- CSS Transparency for IE and Mozilla, Firebird and Firefox (-moz-opacity and filter: alpha):

  `http://www.domedia.org/oveklykken/css-transparency.php`

- CSS Scale Image Html Tutorial:

  `http://www.bigbaer.com/css_tutorials/css.scale.image.html.tutorial.htm`

- CSS2—background-attachment on any element:

  http://www.quirksmode.org/css/background.html

- Newt Edge:

  http://www.phoenity.com/newtedge/

- Information on Border Slants:

  http://infimum.dk/HTML/slantinfo.html

- Rubber Headers:

  http://www.pixy.cz/blogg/clanky/rubberheaders/

- The geekhell.net solutions page:

  http://www.geekhell.net/solutions/

- Mike Davidson—Introducing sIFR:

  http://www.mikeindustries.com/blog/archive/2004/08/sifr

- Image Replacement—css-discuss:

  http://css-discuss.incutio.com/?page=ImageReplacement

- Image Replacement—No Span:

  http://www.moronicbajebus.com/playground/cssplay/
  image-replacement/

- Cross-Browser Variable Opacity with PNG:

  http://www.alistapart.com/articles/pngopacity/

- PNG Behavior (WebFX):

  http://webfx.eae.net/dhtml/pngbehavior/pngbehavior.html

- Cross-Column Pull-Outs—A List Apart:

  http://www.alistapart.com/articles/crosscolumn/

CSS and Accessibility

Following are some links for CSS and accessibility:

- CSS, Accessibility, and Standards Links:

  http://www.dezwozhere.com/links.html

- Screenreader Visibility—css-discuss:

  http://css-discuss.incutio.com/?page=ScreenreaderVisibility

- Day 26: Using relative font sizes—Dive into Accessibility:

  http://diveintoaccessibility.org/day_26_using_relative_font_sizes.html

- Speech Stylesheets—css-discuss:

  http://css-discuss.incutio.com/?page=SpeechStylesheets

CSS Layouts

Following are some links for CSS layouts:

- Little Boxes:

  http://www.thenoodleincident.com/tutorials/box_lesson/boxes.html

- The Layout Reservoir—BlueRobot:

  http://www.bluerobot.com/web/layouts/

- Netscape 4, CSS layout, 3 columns with Header and Footer:

  http://www.fu2k.org/alex/css/layouts/3Col_NN4_RWS_C.mhtml

- CSS Layouts for Netscape 4—saila.com:

  http://www.saila.com/usage/layouts/nn4-layouts.shtml

- CSS Stuff—XHTML/CSS—3 column layouts—Netscape 4–compatible:

  http://www.fu2k.org/alex/css/

- 37signals css_layouts:

  http://www.37signals.com/css_layouts/

- Creating Liquid Layouts with Negative Margins—A List Apart:

  http://www.alistapart.com/articles/negativemargins/

- Flexible Layouts with CSS Positioning—A List Apart:

  http://www.alistapart.com/articles/flexiblelayouts/

- CSS positioning—some reflections:

  http://www.barry.pearson.name/articles/layout_tables/css_positioning.htm

- INP 170: CSS Positioned Layouts:

  http://courses.wccnet.edu/~jwithrow/schedule.php?f=170&p=css-positioning

- Browser support—page layout properties:

  http://www.westciv.com/style_master/academy/browser_support/page_layout.html

- Fixed Positioning for Internet Explorer on Windows:

  http://devnull.tagsoup.com/fixed/

- Fixed positioning—Anne's Weblog About Markup and Style:

  http://annevankesteren.nl/archives/2004/07/fixed-positioning

- Faux Columns—A List Apart:

  http://www.alistapart.com/articles/fauxcolumns/

- Table-less Layouts:

  http://www.tjkdesign.com/templates/

- Curing Float Drops and Wraps:

  http://nemesis1.f2o.org/aarchive?id=11

- Centering:

  http://www.wpdfd.com/editorial/wpd0103.htm#toptip

CSS in Navigation

Following are some links for CSS in navigation:

- Projectseven.com—Tutorials—CSS Uberlinks:

  http://www.projectseven.com/tutorials/css/uberlinks/

- Semantic (X)HTML Markup—Styling Lists:

  http://www.communitymx.com/abstract.cfm?cid=D6F9E

- Horizontal Nav:

  http://www.communitymx.com/abstract.cfm?cid=E6E3C80DBF1BF378

- CSS Tabbed Navigation:

  http://nontroppo.org/test/tab1.html

- CSS navigation menu:

  http://www.webcredible.co.uk/user-friendly-resources/css/css-navigation-menu.shtml

- Sons of Suckerfish—HTML Dog:

  http://www.htmldog.com/articles/suckerfish/

- Suckerfish Dropdowns—A List Apart:

  http://www.alistapart.com/articles/dropdowns/

- Simplicity:

  http://www.alexkeeny.com/simplicity/archives/entry-21/

- CSS Pop-Up Menus:

  http://www.moronicbajebus.com/playground/cssplay/pop-up-menus/

- CSS Vault—The Web's CSS Site:

  http://cssvault.com/cat_navigation.php

- Relatively Absolute—Cross-Browser CSS Tabs with Rollover:

  http://www.paulpgriffin.com/css/tabs/tabs.html

- Drop Down Llama Menu—CSS Play—Sea Mus N Squirrel:

  http://moronicbajebus.com/playground/cssplay/drop-down-llama-menu/

- Hierarchical dynamic menu with CSS:

  http://www.pixy.cz/blogg/clanky/csshiermenu/

- All CSS Flyout Navigation:

  http://www.positioniseverything.net/css-flyout.html

CSS Example Sites

Following are some links for CSS example sites:

- CSS Zen Garden:

  http://csszengarden.com/

- CSS hacks—Stylegala:

  http://www.stylegala.com/resources/css_hacks.htm

- CSS User Interface by Ivan Bueno:

  http://userwww.sfsu.edu/~ibueno/wireframe.html

- CSS Beauty:

  http://www.cssbeauty.com/

- Project Seven:

  http://www.projectseven.com/

CSS Hacks and Filters Charts

The CSS community enjoys a wealth of information. Unfortunately, the sheer amount of information can also be a detriment: finding the right fix often requires significant digging. One of the primary reasons I wrote this book was to make it easier to find specific hacks for specific browsers. The two tables in this appendix, "Hiding CSS from a Browser" and "Revealing CSS Hacks and Filters," are a direct approach to attempt to achieve that goal.

I structured these charts to be as useful and practical as possible. They are, by definition, limited in scope and by no means exhaustive. I concentrated only on the primary browsers: Internet Explorer, Mozilla/Firefox, Netscape, Opera, and Safari, because I find these are the ones required most frequently. The information in the tables was drawn from many sources, including my own testing. However, one source must be singled out: dithered.com. The charts compiled by Chris Nott at `http://dithered.com/css_filters/css_only/index.php` are indispensible and an amazing amount of work. Where his charts revealed a hack that I did not cover in the book, I shamelessly (and with great joy) included it for your use and credited it as such. I greatly appreciate his work.

Hiding CSS from a Browser

The hacks in Table B-1 are intended to be used when you need to hide CSS from a particular browser. Where possible, I indicated version ranges of browsers affected by a specific hack.

Table B-1 Hiding CSS Hacks and Filters

Browser	Hack/Filter	Example	Reference

Internet Explorer 6.x, Windows	Conditional Comment	```<!--[if !IE 6]>```
		 ```<style type="text/css">```
		 ```p { color: red; }```
		 ```</style>```
		 ```<![endif]-->```
			Chapter 4

Internet Explorer 5.5, Windows	Conditional Comment	```<!--[if !IE 5.5]>```
		 ```<style type="text/css">```
		 ```p { color: red;```
		 ```</style>```
		 ```<![endif]-->```
			Chapter 4

Internet Explorer 5, Windows and Mac	Comment After Selector Hack	```#header/* */ { text-align: left;}```	Chapter 3

Internet Explorer 5.x, Windows	Conditional Comment	```<!--[if !IE 5]>```
		 ```<style type="text/css">```
		 ```p { color: red; }```
		 ```</style>```
		 ```<![endif]-->```
			Chapter 4

Internet Explorer 5/6, Windows	Owen Hack (also hides CSS from Opera 6 and below)	```head:first-child+body #navSection {```
		 ``` background-image: url("navbar.gif");```
		 ```}```
			Chapter 3

	Conditional Comment	```<!--[if !IE]>```
		 ```<style type="text/css">```
		 ```p { color: red; }```
		 ```</style>```
		 ```<![endif]-->```
			Chapter 4

Internet Explorer 5 for Mac	@media Hack	```/* hide from Internet Explorer 5 for Mac */```
		 ```@media all {```
		 ``` #mainHeading { text-decoration: none; }```
		 ```}```
			Chapter 3

	Mac Band Pass Filter	```/**//*/```
		 ```@import "../styles/default.css";```
		 ```/**/```
			Chapter 3

Browser	Hack/Filter	Example	Reference
	Commented Backslash Hack	`/* Use backslash within comment \ to ignore next rule in IE5 Mac */`	Chapter 3
	Mac-modified Tan Hack	`*>html .endSection {he\ight: auto;}`	Chapter 3
Internet Explorer 4, Windows	@import Syntax	`@import "mystyle.css";`	Chapter 2

Internet Explorer 4/5, Windows	Selector + Empty Comment	`#testElement/**/ {`
		`  color: #00cc00;`
		`}`
			dithered. com

Opera 6.x	Modified Owen Hack	`html>body #navSection {`
		`  bac\kground-image: url("navbar.gif");`
		`}`
			Chapter 3

Opera 3/6.x	Owen Hack (also hides CSS from Internet Explorer 5/6 on Windows)	`head:first-child+body #navSection {`
		`background-image: url("navbar.gif");`
		`}`
			Chapter 3

Netscape 4.x, Windows	Netscape 4 Comment Hack (also called the Escaped Comment End Hack)	`/* Start hiding from NS4 */`
		`/*/*/`
		`.para1 { font-weight: bold }`
		`.para2 { font-weight: bold }`
		`/* Resume showing to NS4 */`
			Chapter 2

	Netscape 4 Element ID Hack	`div#content h1 { margin-bottom: 0px }`	Chapter 2
	Netscape 4 !important Hack	`border: 1px solid red !important;`	Chapter 2
Safari 1.0/1.1	Lang Pseudo-Class Hack	`p:lang(fr) { color: red; }`	Chapter 3

Revealing CSS to a Browser

Table B-2 is the opposite of Table B-1. The hacks here are used to pass CSS to a given browser and no other.

Table B-2 Revealing CSS Hacks and Filters

Browser	Hack/Filter	Example	Reference

Internet Explorer 6.x, Windows	Conditional Comment	`<!--[if IE 6]>`
		`<style type="text/css">`
		`p {      color: red; }`
		`</style>`
		`<![endif]-->`
			Chapter 4

Internet Explorer 5.5 +, Windows	Zoom Hack	`#container { zoom: 1; }`	Chapter 3

	Conditional Comment	`<!--[if IE gte 5.5]>`
		`<style type="text/css">`
		`p {      color: red; }`
		`</style>`
		`<![endif]-->`
			Chapter 4

Internet Explorer 5.5, Windows	IE 5.5/Windows Band Pass Filter	`@media tty {`
		`   i{content:"\";/*" "*/}}@m;`
		`@import 'styles.css'; /*";}`
		`   }/* */`
			dithered.com

Internet Explorer 5, Windows	Conditional Comment	`<!--[if IE 5.0]>`
		`<style type="text/css">`
		`p {      color: red; }`
		`</style>`
		`<![endif]-->`
			Chapter 4

	IE 5.0/Windows Band Pass Filter	`@media tty {`
		`   i{content:"\";/*" "*/}};`
		`@import 'styles.css'; {;}/*";}`
		`   }/* */`
			dithered.com

Internet Explorer 5.x, Windows	Conditional Comment	`<!--[if IE 5]>`
		`<style type="text/css">`
		`p {      color: red; }`
		`</style>`
		`<![endif]-->`
			Chapter 4

Browser	Hack/Filter	Example	Reference
Internet Explorer 5/6, Windows	Conditional Comment	```<!--[if IE]>` `<style type="text/css">` `p { color: red; }` `</style>` `<![endif]-->```	Chapter 4
Internet Explorer 5/6, Mac and Windows	Tan Hack (also known as the Star HTML Hack)	```* html .boxModel {` ` width: 230px;` ` w\idth: 200px;` `}```	Chapter 3
Internet Explorer 4, Windows	Dummy Selector	```null#testElement {` ` color: #00cc00;` `}```	dithered.com
Internet Explorer 4.x/6.x, Windows and 4.x/5.0, Macintosh	Underscore Hack	```#testElement {` ` _color: #00cc00;` `}```	dithered.com
Mozilla 1.x (up to 1.75)	Tantek Box Model Hack (typically used in conjunction with Be Nice to Opera 5 Hack)	```.boxModel {` ` width:230px;` ` voice-family: "\"}\"";` ` voice-family:inherit;` ` width:200px;` `}```	Chapter 3
Opera 7.x	Media Queries Hack	```html>body .boxModel {` ` width:200px }```	Chapter 3
Opera 5.x	Be Nice to Opera 5 Hack (also known as the Child Selector Hack)	```html>body .boxModel {` ` width:200px }```	Chapter 3
Opera 4/5, Windows; Opera 5, Mac	@media with Negated Media Type	```@media not all {` ` #testElement {` ` color: #00cc00;` ` }` `}```	dithered.com
Netscape 4.x, Windows	Fabrice's Inversion (also reveals CSS to Opera 5, Mac and Opera 4/5, Windows)	```#footer {` ` /*/*//*/ color:green; /* */` `}```	Chapter 2

Index

Continued